WATER IN BRITAIN

WATER IN BRITAIN

a study in applied hydrology and resource geography

KEITH SMITH BA, PhD

Senior Lecturer in Geography in the University of Strathclyde

MACMILLAN

First published 1972 by

THE MACMILLAN PRESS LTD

London and Basingstoke
Associated companies in New York, Toronto, Dublin, Melbourne, Johannesburg and Madras

SBN 333 13552 0

Text set in 10/12 pt. Monotype Times New Roman, printed by letterpress, and bound in Great Britain at The Pitman Press, Bath

Preface

Geographers have always been concerned with the changing relationships between the physical world and human activity, but it is only relatively recently that a really critical awareness of the earth's environment as a natural resource has emerged. Within the last ten years, however, there has been a rapidly growing interest in water resources which has been stimulated by events such as the inauguration of the International Hydrological Decade in 1965 and the passing of the 1963 Water Resources Act for England and Wales. Most university degree courses in geography now include some study of hydrology and its applications in terms of water supplies, and geographers have joined other specialists in researching into these fields. But, despite the abundant opportunities for co-operative efforts, there has been too little linkage between the physical and human spheres of the discipline.

The purpose of this book, therefore, is to present for the first time an integrated water resource geography of the British Isles. Throughout, an attempt is made to bring together the results of recent research in a number of fields in order to relate the physical occurrence and natural variability of water to the social environment and the increasing demands being made upon this most fundamental resource. Following a brief discussion of basic principles, the origins and growth of the current water situation are traced through time. Methods of measuring the resources are outlined next, and this leads on to a systematic analysis of the factors influencing water availability, including floods and droughts. The maldistribution, and often conflicting nature, of water need is then described for each of the major supply sectors, and attention is drawn to the significance of water quality in relation to utilisation. Finally, regional water problems are considered together with some possible solutions.

Other authors may well have adopted a different balance between the hydrological and the water development aspects, but I have tried to maintain what is, I hope, an acceptable emphasis. Similarly, whilst I have attempted to avoid the dangers of over-compression which inevitably arise in any comparatively short book, a number of systematic texts, not specifically referred to in the book itself, are listed as a guide to further reading in an appendix. It was originally intended to use SI units only, but English equivalents have been added both in the text and on illustrations as an aid to clarity. In all cases precedence has been given to the metric values.

It is hoped that this volume will provide a sound introduction to geographers who are seeking, either through systematic courses based on hydrology or regional studies of Britain, some information on the current water situation in this country. This book should also have relevance for students at various levels in associated fields such as civil engineering, economics, biology or regional planning. Hydrologists and other professional personnel in the water industry may find this a convenient background in which to place the realities of every-day practice, whilst the interested layman – should he exist – may discover some of the facts and implications which lie behind the newspaper headlines proclaiming a semi-permanent water crisis.

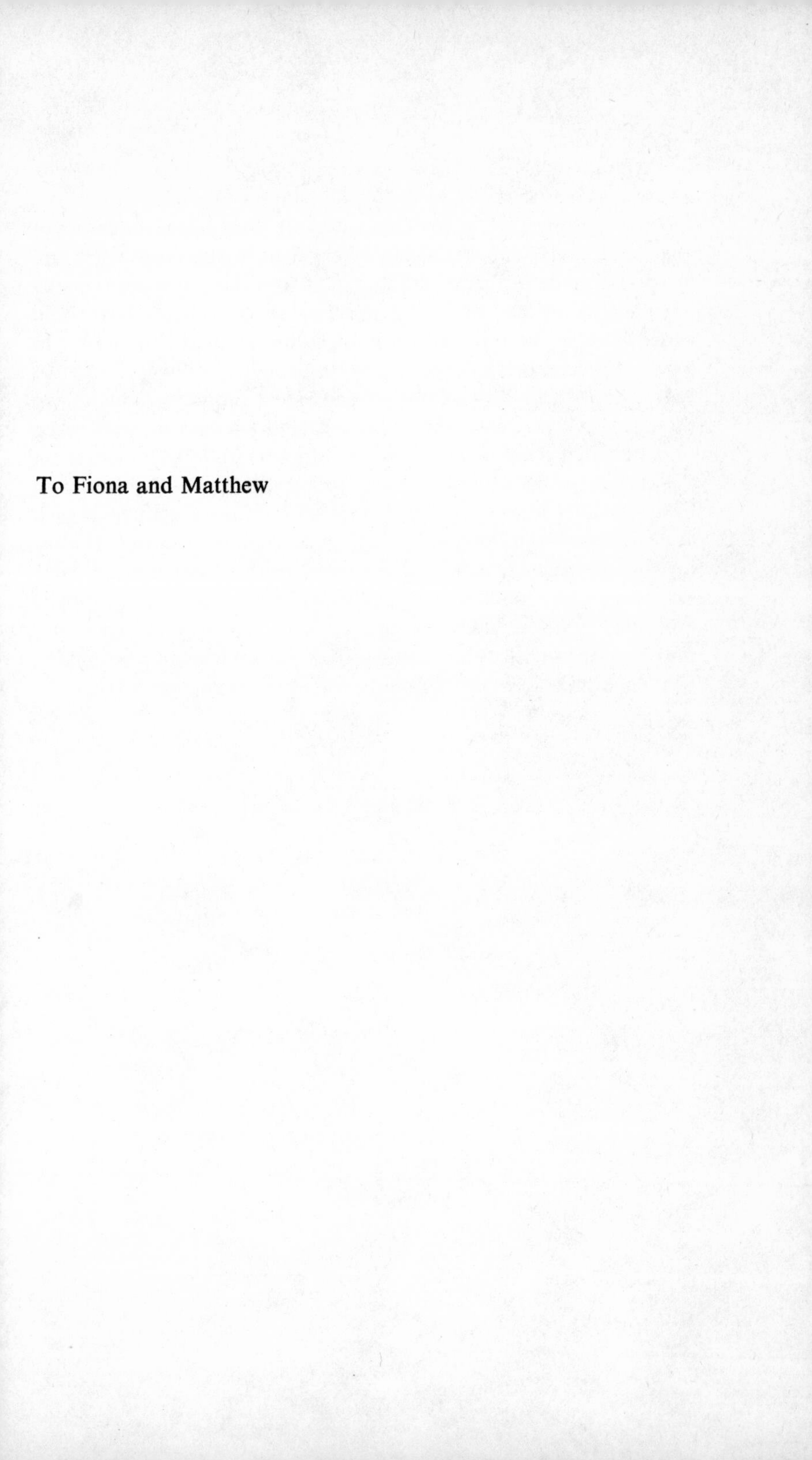

To Fiona and Matthew

Contents

Contents

List of Tables

Acknowledgements

My thanks are due to the many people who helped and advised me during the preparation of this book. I am especially grateful to the following for permission to reproduce the various illustrations stated below.

Editors of Periodicals: *Journal of the Institution of Water Engineers*, Figures 3.12, 4.9, 4.16, 5.4 and 9.1. *Institute of British Geographers, Transactions*, Figures 5.2 and 5.3. *Tijdschrift voor Economische en Sociale Geografie*, Figure 6.1.

Publishers: North-Holland Publishing Company, Amsterdam, Figure 4.4. Blackwells, Oxford, Figure 4.8. McGraw-Hill Publishing Co. Ltd., Figure 4.13. Institution of Civil Engineers, London, Figures 5.5, 5.6 and 7.2. Butterworths, London, Figure 8.1.

Official publications: The Controller, Her Majesty's Stationery Office (Crown Copyright Reserved) for Figures 3.1, 3.8, 4.1, 4.3, 4.12, 5.7, 7.1, 9.2, 9.3, 9.4 and 9.5. The Director, Institute of Geological Sciences for Figures 3.11 and 4.11. The Clerk to the Trent River Authority for Figure 8.2.

I must also record the practical assistance I received when writing this book at the University of Durham. In particular, I should like to thank Mr A. Corner of the Drawing Office, Department of Geography, University of Durham, who was responsible for drawing most of the illustrations. Finally, without the encouragement of my wife, this volume would never have been started.

KEITH SMITH

University of Strathclyde,
Glasgow.

1 The Global Context

With the exception of the air he breathes, water is the most abundant and important natural resource used by man (Walton 1970). The average human being has 65 per cent of his total body weight in the form of water. This percentage must be maintained within rigid limits for man is physiologically sensitive to variations as small as 1 or 2 per cent, whilst a deficiency of 15 per cent in water content is usually fatal (Leopold and Davis 1966). Man can exist for several weeks without food, but ten days is about the maximum survival period without water and it may be much less than this in certain parts of the world. Even when man has sufficient water to survive, its availability and quality have profound and continuing implications for his general health and well-being. As with other natural resources, the degree of water resources development contrasts greatly between the developed and the developing areas of the globe. In 1964 more than 900 million people were without a public water service of any kind, and only one person in every nine had a supply piped to his own premises (US Geological Survey 1967). In many parts women and children spent up to 50 per cent of their time carrying water from distant sources for domestic supplies and stock drinking. It has also been estimated that about two-thirds of the population of the developing world draws untreated water from polluted sources. Diseases which are either water-borne or water-related are endemic and affect some 500 million people each year. As many as 10 million, mostly infants, die annually as a direct result of these inadequate supplies.

Judged by these basic criteria, Britain is indeed fortunate. The modern science of water supply and public health engineering – as distinct from early efforts by the Romans and others – was pioneered in this country over a century ago. Accumulated experience has led to strict controls on sanitation and the wholesomeness of potable supplies so that less than one person in thirty is now without a reliable piped supply. Such provision has been made relatively easy by the natural asset of a humid climate. In comparison over 20 per cent of the land area of the globe may be classed as arid, with a further 15 per cent semi-arid, whilst it has been claimed by Walton (1970) that water deficiency is the chief limiting factor on human activity over more than one-third of the earth.

On the other hand, in common with most of the developed nations, Britain is facing more subtle problems created by the intensification of water use in modern industrial society. At the bare subsistence level a man requires only 2·3 litres (4 pints) of water per day for direct consumption, plus between 1360 and 11 365 l. per day (300 and 2500 gal/day) of fresh water which is used up in crop growth by plant transpiration. With rising social standards and an increasingly complex technology, new uses are found to exploit the versatility of water to the full. The ordinary w.c. flushing system takes 9–14 l. (2–3 gal) of water each time it is used, and individual domestic demand in Britain already averages more than 159 l. (35 gal) per day. There is no immediately foreseeable ceiling to this demand, and experience from the USA and elsewhere suggests that this per capita use may easily double. On a world scale irrigation is one of the largest uses of water. It takes about 227 kg (500 lb) of water to produce 0·45 kg (1 lb) of wheat, and up to maturation a corn crop can transpire enough water to cover its field to a depth of 279 mm (11 in.). It can take 272 770 l. (60 000 gal) of water to produce 1016 kg (1 ton) of steel, 20 $\times$ 10^6 l. (440 000 gal) to make 1016 kg (1 ton) of rayon and 91 l. (20 gal) of water to produce 4·5 l. (1 gal) of beer. The agricultural use of water by transpiration is *consumptive* with direct return to the atmosphere. Much of the water abstracted from lakes, rivers and underground, however, is subsequently returned to these sources for further use, but it is then effluent and often in a highly polluted state. To be removed itself, and to convey other wastes out to sea without loss of amenity or the creation of a health hazard, this water must be diluted by relatively clean water both underground and in river channels. Similarly the use of water courses for inland navigation requires the limitation of abstractive uses, whilst the growth of urban areas and the demand for outdoor recreation means that many fresh water surfaces now have an important leisure potential.

In other words, the water problems of the developed nations stem from *over-use* of water rather than *under-use*. With pressure on resources, the main aim must be to preserve and even improve the fundamental domestic supplies, whilst at the same time catering for the proliferation of other legitimate, but often conflicting, uses. Water resources have always had to fulfil a variety of functions, but the necessity for comprehensive management and multi-purpose use has never been greater. Water may now be used several times for many different purposes, and the resources have to be organised so that there is a minimum amount of conflict between the various requirements. For example, effluent disposal must not be allowed to contaminate drinking supplies irreparably or exterminate fisheries; water abstractions must be balanced against the needs of public health, navigation and water power; the need for land drainage must be reconciled with flood prevention. In Britain, as in other countries, we are only beginning to learn how this complex balance can be best achieved, and the relative difficulty of the task depends a great deal on the resources which are available.

The earth's capital stock of water is contained entirely in the earth-atmosphere system known as the *hydrosphere*. This is the globe's thin, outer skin, and extends from about 12 km (7·5 miles) up in the atmosphere to approximately 4000 m (13 000 ft) below ground-level. Within the system there is a gross water equivalent of 1330 million cubic kilometres (320 million cubic miles), which represents 7 per cent of the earth's total mass (Isaac 1965). The distribution and nature of occurrence of this water is in a constant state of flux and is controlled by the regional workings of the hydrological cycle which, in turn, is driven by solar energy. The hydrological cycle is illustrated diagrammatically in figure 1.1 where an attempt has been made to emphasise both the movement of moisture and the changes of state through which it passes as it circulates between the natural storage reservoirs in the hydrosphere.

Essentially the hydrological cycle may be seen as an *income* or *downstroke* which is dependent on the various forms of precipitation and an *outgo* or *upstroke* which results from evaporation. During this basic transfer process between the atmosphere and the earth, moisture may be temporarily stored as either a vapour, liquid or a solid. It is these storage units, indicated in figure 1.1, which have significance in terms of water resource development, although their relative contribution varies greatly both globally and regionally.

Thus, only a tiny fraction of the earth's water mass is held at any one time in a non-saline liquid state. Even much of this storage cannot be directly utilised by man, whilst some of the reservoir units are missing from certain parts of the world.

No less than 97·1 per cent of all water is saline (Nace 1960) and is stored in the *ocean basins* which cover almost three-quarters of the earth's surface. At the present time this water is almost totally unused, and probably the greatest single problem facing the water

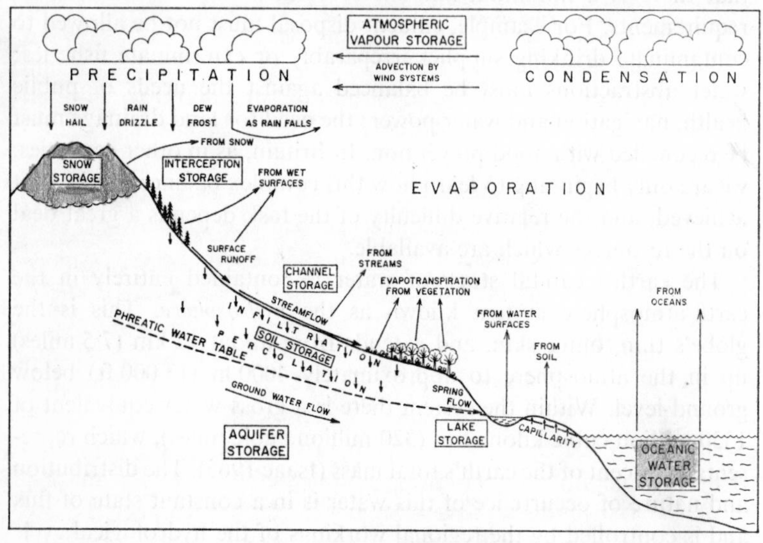

Figure 1.1 The hydrological cycle

technologist is to devise a cheap and efficient method of desalination capable of widespread application. Apart from actingas a colossal storage reservoir, the oceans provide over 80 per cent of the moisture which is evaporated into the atmosphere. Indeed, the oceans lose more water by evaporation than they gain by precipitation, and the deficit has to be balanced by streamflow from the continents over which precipitation exceeds evaporative losses as shown by Sellers (1965).

Under present climatic conditions, a further 2·15 per cent of water, comprising 74·7 per cent of all the world's fresh water supplies, is locked up as ice or snow in *glaciers* and *snowfields*. Like salt water, this frozen moisture is unavailable to man without the introduction of vast amounts of heat energy for conversion and it has been estimated that, depending on the time of year, snow accumulation covers between 14 and 24 per cent of the earth's surface. According to Barry (1969), two-thirds of this occurs on land. No permanent snow storage exists in Britain, whilst temporary snow storage occurs only rarely and always at a time of year when other supplies are plentiful. Nevertheless, the oceans and the icecaps together account for 99·35 per cent of the earth's entire water reserves.

By comparison, the *atmosphere* is only a minute storage unit, but serves as the immediate source of all fresh water supplies through precipitation. Over the globe the mean rainfall amounts to a depth equivalent of 991 mm (39 in.), with an average of 660 mm (26 in.) falling on the continents and 1118 mm (44 in.) over the oceans. Water vapour never comprises more than 4 per cent of the atmosphere by volume and the atmosphere can only retain 0·035 per cent of all fresh water resources. The release of this vapour as precipitation depends less on the moisture content of the air than on the presence of favourable rain-making processes in the atmosphere. Thus, even if all atmospheric moisture was released in a single storm, it would amount to a rainfall of no more than 25 mm (1 in.) depth over the world. Since much higher daily falls than this are experienced – up to 1270 mm (50 in.) on some Pacific islands – it follows that the main function of the atmosphere is that of an efficient horizontal transmitter of moisture. In temperate areas particularly most precipitation results from moisture advected over land by the prevailing wind systems and released in mid-latitude depressions. For example, it has been estimated by Benton *et al.* (1950) that less than 10 per cent of the precipitation over the Mississippi catchment, which covers almost half of the USA, is derived from local evaporation over the land. Table 1 shows the importance of the synoptic situation in tracing the origins of precipitation at three stations located on an east to west line across northern England. The warm front situation together with maritime polar airflows account for about half the total fall at each station whilst the contribution from local thunder activity is no more than 3 per cent.

When precipitation reaches the land areas of the earth it immediately begins its return journey to the atmosphere either through direct evaporation or through streamflow to the oceans. Some water follows a highly abbreviated route through the land-based portion of the cycle. *Interception storage*, for example, may be held on wetted surfaces for only a few minutes before subsequent re-evaporation. This water has no economic significance and *snow storage* is only directly useful in those countries where seasonal melting provides a source of water during otherwise dry summers, as in the western United States where about half of the total streamflow is derived from snowmelt. Although *soil storage* is not capable of direct appropriation as a source of supply, it is used by growing plants and

TABLE 1

PERCENTAGE OF ANNUAL PRECIPITATION (1956–60) ASSOCIATED WITH DIFFERENT SYNOPTIC TYPES

(After Shaw 1962)

	Synoptic Category								
Station	Warm Front	Warm Sector	Cold Front	Occlusion	Polar Low	MP air	CP air	Arctic air	Thunderstorm
Squires Gate	23	16	14	15	7	22	0·2	0·7	3
Greenfold Reservoir	21	15	14	15	8	24	0·5	0·4	2
Rotherham	26	9	11	20	14	15	1·5	1·1	3

crops thus providing most of man's food requirements. More than half of the moisture evaporated from the continents is used productively as evapotranspiration and this constitutes the greatest use of water for any single purpose, agricultural or otherwise. On the other hand, even in humid Britain, the soil is not in the optimum moisture condition for crop growth throughout the year and irrigation adds to this consumptive use.

We are then left with the three fresh water storage units which man utilises directly as water sources – aquifers, lakes and rivers. Of these, *aquifer storage* is by far the most important on a world scale. According to the work of Nace (1960) underground reserves account for about 25 per cent of all fresh water, or about 97 per cent of all water not locked up in the oceans or glaciers. The local availability of groundwater varies considerably according to geological conditions and is mainly stored in sedimentary rocks or alluvial deposits. Utilisation is also favoured by the relative constancy of supplies. Appreciable storage fluctuations normally occur on a seasonal time-scale, whilst some water may be held under virtually static conditions in deep aquifers for millenia and then exploited as a fossil reserve.

Surface storage is restricted to *lakes* and *river channels*. Owing to the natural regulation of storage, the former are often used as a water resource, as in the northern and western parts of Britain. Rivers are more commonly used. Although they comprise only 0·003 per cent of all the earth's fresh water, some rivers are extremely large and most of the world's surface flow is confined to a few drainage systems. Thus, the river Amazon at the tidal limit carries almost 20 per cent of the earth's total runoff (Nace 1969), whilst it has been estimated by Vallentine (1967) that the mean flow of the Yangtse Kiang could theoretically provide every person in the world with 682 l. (150 gal) of water each day. Rivers have the advantage of being widely available in Britain, but their relatively short length means that any water flowing in them is deposited in the sea within a matter of days. In their natural state rivers form the most variable water source. The dry weather flow at the end of a rainless period represents the only reliable yield, and the available water may fluctuate greatly over a period of hours therefore minimising the importance of channel storage.

The hydrological cycle provides an unending supply of fresh water for man's needs, but eventually it requires artificial modification in order to smooth out some of the inequalities of distribution in both space and time. In many parts of the world this transformation of a natural cycle to a largely man-made system has already reached impressive proportions, and, for example, it has been stated by Chorley and Kates (1969) that 10 per cent of the national wealth of the United States is invested in engineering structures designed to utilise one-quarter of the available surface water. In detail this human manipulation, often referred to as conservation, can take many forms, but it is basically dependent on just two techniques: (1) the creation of artificial storage; and (2) the conversion of fresh water from other states.

Water Storage. Storage is the key to the regulation and optimum use of all water resources. It is associated entirely with the land-based part of the hydrological cycle and with existing fresh water. The most obvious achievements in this field have followed from the use of dams and reservoirs to control the discharge of rivers but lake capacity may also be increased by similar means. More recently, with the growing awareness of the interdependence of surface and groundwater supplies, significant steps are likely to be taken in the manipulation of underground storage through the artificial recharge of aquifers and other means. All these methods have application in Britain.

The fundamental aim of water storage is to delay the disposal of surface water back to the oceans and a similar function is served by the artificial suppression of evaporation. So far this remains largely an experimental technique confined mainly to the USA and Australia where scientists have developed the use of chemical sprays to seal the surface of storage reservoirs and thus reduce evaporation losses. Much use has been made of cetyl alcohol, which has a suitable mono-molecular structure, but such layers are expensive to maintain and have only been applied in arid and semi-arid climates where open-water evaporation losses are very high. Such methods are unlikely to prove economic in Britain, although if estuarine barrages are eventually used for water storage, they will have a large surface area relative to depth and therefore suffer considerable losses from evaporation.

Water Conversion. If sufficient water cannot be stored on or in the earth's crust, the only other alternative is to hasten moisture movement through the non-utilisable phases of the hydrological cycle so that the delivery rate of fresh water is increased. This method is concerned with atmospheric and oceanic water, and involves the conversion of water from its natural state. It depends on either *desalination* or *artificial rain-making*.

Desalination is the least experimental of these two techniques and is likely to have the more universal application. It has formed an important source of water in some arid areas for many years, and is also used in the Channel Islands of Britain. For a country like Britain the problems involved in further development are economic rather than technical, but it is likely to become more important if only as a supplementary source.

On the other hand, rain-making or cloud seeding is still highly experimental. Conclusive benefits are difficult to prove, despite many experiments, and some authorities such as Maunder (1970) feel that too little is known of the indirect, and possibly disadvantageous, effects the various methods may have on the atmosphere. Even if rain-making becomes practical on a routine basis, it is unlikely to be of much help in Britain where water problems exist because of the broadly inverse distribution of precipitation and water demand rather than the overall inadequacy of the water income. More ambitious schemes for weather modification remain still further in the future.

Ultimately, water resources can only be evaluated in terms of the demands made upon them. The mean annual precipitation over Britain is 1079 mm (42·5 in.) or over 60 per cent more than the average fall on land areas of the globe. But, owing to the dense concentration of population and industry, especially in England, our available resources are less than in some semi-arid lands. Comparative data for European countries, quoted by Rowntree (1968), show that in terms of water available from rainfall per head of population only Malta is in a less favourable situation. In the European context, our reserves compare only with densely populated Belgium and the Mediterranean countries of Cyprus and Spain, whilst France has twice as much water available per person and Scandinavia twenty times as much.

There is, therefore, a genuine need for water to figure more prominently in our national consciousness. It is generally accepted that the demand for water in Britain will roughly double by the end of the century and a satisfactory solution to our water problems will only be achieved through a better understanding of our water reserves and the ways in which they may best be utilised.

2 Historical Background

It is only within the last two decades that the so-called 'water problem' of this country has received widespread attention, but, although current activity in hydrological research and water conservation is now running at a higher level than ever before, it would be wrong to consider such developments as being entirely recent. Indeed, it may well be argued that it is impossible to understand fully the existing state of knowledge and legislative background without some historical perspective on the evolution of hydrological thought and the development of a recognisable water conservation movement.

THE EMERGENCE OF BRITISH HYDROLOGY

The long evolution of hydrology as a recognisable scientific discipline has been traced back to Pre-Classical times by Biswas (1970). Before the Renaissance, and to some extent afterwards, the basic hydrological concepts were formulated by philosophers who produced elaborate but largely erroneous theories to explain the origins of moisture on the earth and the workings of the hydrological cycle. The Renaissance brought a new emphasis on experiment and direct observation in science, and, with progressive developments in instrumentation, the speculative approach began to be replaced by a more rational attitude in the sixteenth and seventeenth centuries.

Early developments

During the seventeenth century experimental work in France proved for the first time that precipitation alone was sufficient to act as the sole moisture source for all spring discharge and riverflow, and these important field observations were confirmed by experiments and calculations conducted by Edmund Halley, the English astronomer. Halley (1687) used laboratory techniques to simulate evaporation from the Mediterranean Sea, and was able to conclude that the quantity of water involved in oceanic evaporation was large enough to supply all forms of surface drainage. He then followed up this work (Halley 1691) with a realistic survey of water circulation over the earth, which included some comments indicating his awareness of the role of relief in producing orographic precipitation. It is this combination of vision and practical experimentation that gives Halley a considerable claim to the status of 'Father of British Hydrology'.

While Halley was theorising about the hydrological cycle, Richard Towneley was making the first extant rainfall measurements for this country between 1677 and 1703 (Towneley 1694), and, with a gauge some 12 m (40 ft) above ground-level, obtained an average annual fall of 1041 mm (41 in.) for the first ten years of record. Following Towneley's example in the Burnley area, other eighteenth century observers began to collect precipitation data, and soon some of the basic problems involved in the point measurement of rainfall became apparent. In 1769 William Heberden published the results of his gauging experiments in London (Heberden 1769), and from a year's observations, was able to show that the volume of rain caught by gauges exposed on the roof of Westminster Abbey and a nearby house was appreciably less than that recorded in an adjacent garden.

Towards the end of the eighteenth century the evaporation studies started by Halley were taken up again, only this time the evidence came from direct field observation. Between 1772 and 1775 measurements were taken by Dobson of open-water evaporation and precipitation at an open site overlooking Liverpool (Dobson 1777). Dobson rightly emphasised the importance of evaporation compared with precipitation alone in assessing the moisture balance, but, since his evaporating vessel was small by modern standards and exposed above ground-level, it gave an excessively high mean value of 934 mm (36·78 in.) over the four years. Nevertheless, Dobson showed his measurements to be more realistic than many of the evaporation estimates made by his contemporaries, whilst his paper also indicated a clear understanding of the significance of air temperature and wind speed in promoting evaporation.

In 1802 evaporation theory took a large step forward with the publication of two papers by John Dalton. In the first of these contributions (Dalton 1802*a*) he discussed the role of evaporation in the natural process of water circulation, and most of his paper was devoted to a complex attempt to calculate the mean water balance over England and Wales. In collaboration with Thomas Hoyle during 1795–8 he measured the evaporation from a cylindrical soil-filled tank which was remarkably similar in design to certain lysimeters introduced over one hundred and fifty years later. At first the soil surface was kept bare, but a grass cover was allowed to develop later, thus replicating evaporation and percolation processes from natural surfaces. Rodda (1963) has commented on some ambiguous aspects of these experiments and shown that, as a result of over-exposure, the resultant values were too high, but Dalton's paper remains an important landmark in the development of field techniques in hydrology.

Dalton's second contribution is more widely known. In this paper (Dalton 1802*b*) he presented his famous evaporation law, stating that the evaporation from a water surface is directly proportional to the vapour pressure deficit, assuming that the other factors remain constant. Dalton was, therefore, the first person to produce an evaporation formula based on meteorological data, and the vapour pressure relationship has been embodied in most subsequent formulae which adopt the vapour transport approach to evaporation theory.

The Nineteenth Century

The great upheaval in nineteenth century life caused by the Industrial Revolution resulted in a quickening of the pace of many scientific disciplines, and hydrology was no exception. For the first time the great practical value of hydrology was realised. This was particularly so in the field of surface-water hydrology with the exploitation of upland catchments to supply the water requirements of the rapidly expanding industrial communities in northern England, and the main work in the period was in applied hydrology.

In 1854 a Meteorological Department was established by the Board of Trade. It was here that G. J. Symons acquired his consuming interest in both rainfall and evaporation measurement, and his work has influenced the development of British hydrology down to the present day. Symons was concerned about the lack of guidance and oversight given to the collection of rainfall records, and in 1863 he resigned from the Meteorological Department to found the

British Rainfall Organisation which he directed personally until 1900. The British Rainfall Organisation relied almost entirely on enthusiastic amateurs, for both financial support and precipitation data, and its chief function was to act as a co-ordinating and advisory agency for these observers. In the collection and elementary processing of rainfall statistics the British Rainfall Organisation was outstandingly

Figure 2.1 The site of raingauge experiments at Strathfield Turgiss Rectory. After *British Rainfall* 1868.

effective and, starting with 168 returns in 1850, the annual publication, *British Rainfall*, contained records from some 3500 stations by the close of the century.

Symons exercised strict control over the quality of his rainfall data, and it is largely through his efforts in organising gauging trials that uniformity in raingauging practice began to be achieved in the nineteenth century. One of the most important of these experimental sites, which was used subsequently for evaporation measurements, was at Strathfield Turgiss Rectory near Reading shown in figure 2.1. Rainfall records were started there in 1867, and as a result of these experiments the orthodox copper gauge with a 127 mm (5 in.) diameter funnel became accepted as a convenient standard, although many observers continued with a 203 mm (8 in.) diameter gauge well into the present century.

A satisfactory standardisation of raingauge exposure took even longer, despite the fact that most of the nineteenth century experimentation was designed to assess the amount of catch deficit with increasing gauge height above ground originally described by Heberden. Ever since Towneley's early rainfall observations there had been a tendency to place gauges on the over-exposed roofs or corners of buildings, and for many years it was thought that precipitation did actually decrease with height. This idea was not finally disproved until fairly reliable measurements were obtained for areas in the Lake District in the 1840s by Miller (1849). These pioneer upland observations showed a consistent increase in rainfall up to 610 m (2000 ft) but over-exposure of the highest gauges, which were often located on mountain summits, led Miller to conclude that beyond about 600 m the volume of precipitation declined owing to the inability of the atmosphere to hold large amounts of vapour. It is strange that he fell into this error, for he appreciated the difficulty of snow gauging, and correctly attributed a greater winter deficiency in catch in his high-level gauges to defects of exposure during snowfall.

Although several earlier workers had suggested that wind effects were responsible for the progressive decrease in catch above ground-level, Jevons (1861) was the first person to prove conclusively that this was so by reproducing experimentally the disturbed windfield across the funnel of a gauge. Symons' collaborators confirmed this work by quantifying the reduced efficiency of the raingauge at various heights, and it was eventually decided that a gauge with horizontal rim installed at 0·3 m (1 ft) above the ground surface provided the most satisfactory compromise between the wind eddies caused by height and the insplashing of rain created by ground-level installation.

Symons' initial concern with the lack of conformity in raingauging procedure soon extended to the more complex problems of open-water evaporation measurement. By the mid-nineteenth century a bewildering variety of evaporimeters was in use. In 1869, in collaboration with Roger Field, Symons persuaded the indefatigable Rev. Griffith of Strathfield Turgiss Rectory to undertake field trials of no less than twenty of the most common instruments. Symons already believed in the importance of having a large evaporimeter containing a sufficient volume of water to reproduce evaporation processes from a large water body by reducing to a minimum the excessive evaporation caused by overheating of the water, and an iron tank built to his specifications was installed at Strathfield Turgiss as a standard. This tank holding 1818 l. (400 gal) of water was easily the largest instrument in the experiment, and regular measurements of surface water temperatures in all the evaporimeters revealed that the Symons tank had the closest thermal relationship with values obtained from an adjacent river. When most of the other evaporimeters disintegrated with frost or showed abnormally high values compared with his tank, Symons became rightly convinced of the superiority of his gauge. A small stilling chamber was added to the design in 1871 to reduce the observation error due to wave turbulence, and records were maintained at Strathfield Turgiss until 1885 when the tank was removed to Symons' garden in Camden Square where it continued in use for a further seventy years, thus providing the longest series of evaporation observations in the country. No similar tank was installed until 1892 when Southampton Waterworks established one at the Otterbourne Pumping Station but in 1900 there were seven such instruments in operation, mostly in southern England, and eventually Symons' evaporation tank, like his raingauge, became accepted by the Meteorological Office as the standard British instrument.

During the later nineteenth century there was increasing co-operation between the British Rainfall Organisation and the water supply authorities, and it was through this contact that *British Rainfall* made another contribution to hydrological development in this country. For years Symons had appreciated that measurements of open-water evaporation, however carefully obtained, were of little use for assessing the amount of actual evaporation taking place from natural surfaces, and in 1867 he proposed (Symons 1889) a system of nine separate lysimeters, which, by artificial control of the water content, could be used to determine evaporation rates from grassed and arable soils of different types, plus peat and open water. This ambitious system never came to fruition, but the idea of percolation or drainage gauges was subsequently taken up by water engineers interested in discovering how much natural recharge was taking place in their aquifers.

Quite early in the nineteenth century attempts had been made to follow Dalton's work on evaporation from and percolation through natural surfaces, and in 1836, for example, an experiment on percolation through soil and chalk was started at Nash Mills, Hertfordshire, and continued for many years. As time progressed, further instruments were set up, notably the famous percolation gauges established at Rothamsted in 1870 where great attention was paid to the problem of filling the gauges with the least possible disturbance of the natural soil profile. All these early experiments were conducted in the south of England, and by 1900 many sites were in operation. Symons and others began to analyse rainfall and percolation values in relation to the measured evaporation from open-water tanks, but the relatively short period of record and the lack of understanding of soil moisture storage led to few satisfactory correlations.

During the nineteenth century the basic principles affecting groundwater became understood, although progress was largely dependent on the newly developing science of geology. The Geological Survey of Great Britain was founded in 1835 but the first official Memoir on Water Supply was not published until 1899, and, as in other fields, some of the early initiative was taken by individuals. For example, William Smith, the 'Father of English Geology', was in 1802 the first person to apply stratigraphic principles directly to groundwater exploitation, whilst in 1827 he became involved in the provision of a groundwater supply for Scarborough as demonstrated by Sheppard (1917). From about this time onwards, however, much of the emergent hydrogeological activity was concentrated on the chalk aquifers of southern England.

With the development of new sources of upland water to supply towns, hydrology became increasingly dominated by civil engineers such as Thomas Hawksley and J. F. La Trobe Bateman. The latter's long career in engineering consultancy was closely identified with gravitational supply schemes for large towns in northern England, and, although he started with reservoirs on the River Bann in Ireland in 1835, his major works were for Manchester and Glasgow. Bateman's chief interest lay in rainfall and runoff relations, and the storage capacity provided by these new reservoirs allowed some of the first accurate measurements of flood discharge to be taken. He saw long-period rainfall and runoff observations as the most practical method of achieving data on mean annual evaporation, and in 1846 he published a paper (Bateman 1846) showing his understanding of the importance of geology and antecedent moisture conditions in producing runoff, as well as the effect of road construction and land drainage in increasing the magnitude of flood peaks.

The rapid growth of engineering hydrology led to the publication in 1850 of Beardmore's *Manual of Hydrology*, which was the first such text to appear in English (Beardmore 1850). This volume was designed to meet the reference needs of the practising civil engineer, and a large proportion of the book is devoted to hydraulic and tidal tables, although two sections are given over to riverflow, rainfall and evaporation. It contains a remarkable digest of hydrological data, not only for Britain, but for Europe and Asia too.

As the nineteenth century progressed engineers made increasing contributions to hydrology, particularly with regard to the theory of flow in open channels. Thus, developments in fluid mechanics, such as Manning's equation for uniform flow in open channels (Manning 1891), and the work of Osborne Reynolds, who investigated viscosity and the nature of laminar and turbulent flow, laid the foundations for later progress in streamflow measurement. Unfortunately, however, the yield of virtually all the early water supply schemes was calculated on the basis of rainfall information alone. Actual measurements of runoff were not undertaken until the reservoirs had been constructed and a record of discharges became a legal requirement for the assessment of compensation water.

Another civil engineer to exert a lasting influence was A. R. Binnie. He made an analysis (Binnie 1892) of long-period precipitation data for Britain and elsewhere which showed that the reliability of a calculated average increased with the length of data record available, and Binnie concluded that records extending over thirty to forty years would produce an average value which would not deviate from the 'true mean' by more than 2 per cent. Binnie's work coincided with that of the Austrian geographer, E. Brückner, on the 35-year cycle of weather events, and between them they influenced data processing for many decades. It is from this time that records began to be averaged over 35-year periods, and the resulting values were all too frequently accepted as rigid standards without realising that, owing to climatic fluctuations, such averages are not stable.

The Period 1900 to 1950

The late nineteenth century was a period when increasing use was made of empirical solutions in hydrology as the demand for water continued to outstrip physical theory and direct measurement. This trend continued into the present century. Despite the lead which Britain had achieved earlier in hydrological matters, in particular that of raingauging, the first half of the twentieth century was to prove a period of relative stagnation which could possibly have been avoided with the guidance and co-ordination of hydrological activity by a central organisation. Certainly it was during these decades that many other developed countries of the world established national hydrometric authorities. In many cases a distinction was maintained between the organisation of meteorological and hydrological measurements, but in Sweden and the Soviet Union, for example, central authorities combined both hydrological and meteorological services.

One of the major deficiencies of British hydrology has always been the lack of attention given to streamflow measurement. This resulted directly from the early emphasis on raingauging and the once widely held view that most aspects of river behaviour could be predicted from a knowledge of rainfall characteristics alone. Nevertheless, a few rivers were measured fairly early on a routine basis. For example, daily flows for the Thames at Teddington are available since 1883, whilst records for the Derbyshire Derwent and the Elan and Claerwen valleys in Wales date from 1905 and 1908 respectively. The first strong advocate of systematic rainfall and runoff gauging on a catchment basis was W. N. Maclean. Maclean began river gauging in the Scottish Highlands in 1912 because he found it impossible to estimate the hydrological basis of proposed hydro-electric power schemes without discharge measurements, and eventually he formed a private organisation, known as River-Flow Records, which published flow data for the Ness Basin and the Aberdeenshire Dee. Apart from Maclean's work, little attention was given to rivers in the first decades of this century, although the Research Committee of the Royal Geographical Society did sponsor some research into rainfall and runoff of the Exe and Medway rivers before the First World War (Strahan 1909).

In the field of precipitation records the British Rainfall Organisation (BRO) continued to take the lead, even after being absorbed into the Meteorological Office in 1919. Before incorporation into the Meteorological Office, the BRO had foreseen some of the hydrological implications of precipitation data, and had begun to publish isohyet maps and group rainfall stations on a catchment basis rather than within administrative counties. Experiments into the exposure and performance of raingauges were maintained, and a series of tests started in the late 1920s by Hudleston (1933) led to the general screening of exposed upland gauges by a turf wall surround.

Isolated work on groundwater characteristics continued, although most of it was confined to the chalk areas of south-east England. A leader in this field was D. H. Thomson, who made important analyses of rest-water levels recorded on the South Downs from 1893 (Thomson 1921 and 1938), and was able to show that the water-table fluctuations could be directly related to the balance between recharge of the aquifer through percolation and the discharge from springs and other drainage. Thomson also drew attention to the exponential fall of the water-table during dry spells, and it is interesting to note that this discovery mirrored work undertaken elsewhere on the dry-weather depletion curve of rivers.

Some progress was also made in the realm of soil moisture relationships. In the dry summer of 1921 Keen (1931) measured the declining position of the water-table in deep cylinders filled with different types of bare soil and found that the range of capillary movement of water from the water-table to the ground surface depended largely on the nature of the soil profile. Soil moisture studies also benefited from the introduction of the term pF by Schofield (1935) to express logarithmically the capillary potential of a soil.

Although such research developments did take place in Britain, it gradually became clear that there was no comprehensive attitude to hydrological activity, and that little, if any, of this work was organised on a catchment basis. Water engineers and others had for years been advocating the centralisation of hydrological measurements, particularly streamflow, but there was little official response to this lobby. In 1920 the Water Power Resources Committee recommended the formation of a Water Commission which would be concerned with assessing the nation's water resources, but it was not until further pressure was brought to bear, mainly by the British Association for the Advancement of Science Committee formed in response to discussions at York in 1932, and the anxiety provoked by the dry summer of 1934, that the Government finally appointed a committee to advise on the establishment of a national inland water survey. Eventually, the Inland Water Survey was set up in 1935 by the

Ministry of Health, and publication of Year Books detailing rainfall and runoff began immediately. In the first volume for the water-year 1935–6 there were only twenty-seven gauging stations in operation, seven of which had been established by Maclean, and after only two issues further progress was halted by the outbreak of war.

The Water Act of 1945 authorised the setting up of a Central Advisory Water Committee (CAWC) to advise the Ministry of Health on conservation and the use of water resources. But the main emphasis was on the utilisation and supply of water, and, although the collection of groundwater data by the Geological Survey was encouraged, the Inland Water Survey was eventually converted into a sub-committee of the CAWC. In 1948 the River Boards Act was passed, Section 9 of which required the new Boards to submit proposed hydrometric schemes to the Minister, who could then approve the schemes and provide grant aid for the establishment of rainfall and runoff gauging networks. Some River Boards were quick to take this opportunity, but for most the hydrological implications of the 1948 Act became submerged under other River Board functions. The post-war interest in water resource assessment soon died away, and in 1952 the sittings of the Central Advisory Water Committee and the work of the Inland Water Survey were both suspended.

Developments since 1950

Although the early 1950s was a period of general administrative inactivity, important progress had been made in hydrological theory a few years before. Thus, Thornthwaite (1948) in the United States and Penman (1948) working at Rothamsted both produced, quite independently in the same year, new formulae for the estimation of potential evaporation from natural surfaces. In addition both these workers were interested in the role of soil moisture in the water balance, and shortly afterwards Penman (1950) published an important paper employing these principles in the Stour drainage basin, thus becoming the first person to apply water balance techniques successfully to a British catchment.

In 1955 the Central Advisory Water Committee resumed its work, and the functions of the Inland Water Survey were transferred to the newly created Surface Water Survey Centre, which was charged with responsibility for advising River Boards on the design and operation of river gauging stations. The Centre also had the duty of collating routine measurements made by the River Boards, and the publication of records was restarted with the appearance of a new series of Surface Water Year Books in 1955. The Central Advisory Water Committee (1959*a*) drew attention to the lack of basic information relating to water resource planning and urged that hydrological surveys should be undertaken to provide data on water availability and consumption. A start was made in the areas with the most urgent problems, and the first surveys were completed by the Ministry of Housing and Local Government for the Great Ouse and Severn basins in 1960 and for the Essex rivers and the Stour in 1961.

At this time there was growing criticism of the excessive fragmentation of interests in British hydrology, and these views were endorsed by a CAWC sub-committee which reported on the availability of information on water resources (Central Advisory Water Committee 1959*b*). The Government responded to the need for reorganisation of activities by creating a Department of Scientific and Industrial Research Committee on Hydrological Research, but the first positive move came from the water supply industry which sponsored the formation of the Water Research Association. Aided by the Metropolitan Water Board, this organisation moved into its first premises in 1955, and began to undertake research work relating to the practical needs of the public supply authorities. At first it was concerned mainly with water treatment and financed entirely by the supply industry, but in 1959 it became eligible for a DSIR grant and in 1961 moved to new headquarters at Medmenham, Bucks. This move coincided with a recognition and expansion of the Association's activities including the formation of a Hydrology Division, which almost immediately commenced work on a small experimental catchment in the Chilterns.

In 1962 the Government acted on a recommendation of the DSIR Committee on Hydrological Research and sanctioned the establishment of the Hydrological Research Unit at a site at Wallingford, Berkshire, already partially occupied by the Hydraulics Research Station. The terms of reference of the Unit included research into all phases of the hydrological cycle, but special emphasis was laid on the possible effect of land-use changes on hydrological behaviour. On 1 June 1965, the Natural Environment Research Council was created with responsibility for promoting research in several fields including hydrology, and the Hydrological Research Unit, renamed the Institute of Hydrology from 1 April 1968, then fell under its jurisdiction.

The developments in hydrological research were complemented in 1963 by the passing of the Water Resources Act which provided a new organisational framework for the assessment of water resources in England and Wales. This Act was concerned with the whole field of water conservation and replaced the existing River Boards with twenty-nine River Authorities as well as creating a central advisory body in the Water Resources Board. Priority was given to hydrological measurements in relation to water resources planning, and the River Authorities were required to submit comprehensive hydrometric schemes for the measurement of rainfall, runoff and evaporation within their areas. Such schemes were to be examined by the Water Resources Board, particularly by the Hydrometry Division of the Board, which was to represent an expanded version of the Surface Water Survey Centre.

As a result of these organisational changes, hydrology now has a much more integrated national structure. Broadly speaking, the Natural Environment Research Council, acting through its Hydrology Committee and the Institute of Hydrology, serves as the main focus for research activity, whilst the Water Resources Board and the River Authorities are largely responsible for routine hydrological work in connection with the assessment and management of water resources. In practice, however, these basic functions can become somewhat blurred, and it has proved necessary for the Water Resources Board to initiate research projects within certain River Authority areas in order to provide basic hydrological information.

Despite these recent attempts to streamline and co-ordinate hydrological effort and research, the detailed responsibility for various aspects of hydrology still rests with a proliferation of different organisations. Thus, the Meteorological Office, which is part of the Air Force Department of the Ministry of Defence, has prime concern for hydrometeorology. This includes the organisation and maintenance of precipitation networks as well as evaporation data based on pan observations or on calculations from formulae. Stream gauging practice is mainly in the hands of the Hydrometry Division of the Water Resources Board, but the theory of riverflow and its measurement is studied by the Hydraulics Research Station, whilst the Institute of Geological Sciences deals with the assessment of groundwater. It is true, of course, that many of these functions are amalgamated at the local level by the River Authorities and on a national scale by the Water Resources Board, but the essential unity of hydrological processes has still to be recognised on an administrative basis. Some attempt is now being made to provide a common storehouse of hydrological information through the publication of a standardised series of Year Books which will be published in three parts dealing with rainfall, surface water and groundwater respectively. This will replace the previous largely independent appearances of *British Rainfall* and the *Surface Water Year Book* and will provide, for the first time, for the regular publication of routine data on underground water.

THE MOVEMENT TOWARDS WATER CONSERVATION

The Nineteenth Century Legacy

Before the Industrial Revolution there was little real pressure on Britain's water resources. Settlement and industry remained on a relatively small scale, and adequate supplies of pure water were obtained from the immediate vicinity of the towns, this arrangement in turn being possible because of the low output of domestic and industrial effluent and the subsequent general absence of water pollution. At this time, the major need for water was domestic, and most supplies were obtained from communal wells and springs, although in some places, such as London, fairly early attempts were made to conduit surface supplies from rivers. Apart from the use of processing water and isolated instances of water power development at industrial sites such as corn and fulling mills, there was very little need of water for manufacturing purposes.

In this situation an individual's riparian rights at Common Law offered sufficient protection and control of resources. Although no one could own surface water, each person having land abutting a watercourse had, subject to any prescriptive rights which may have been established, equal rights with his neighbours to the natural flow of water past his land. Any riparian owner could also utilise this flow as long as it was subsequently passed downstream unimpaired in either quantity or quality. Clearly, the actual usage of water under this arrangement depended on the interest and tolerance of riparian proprietors downstream, and, although limited abstraction and pollution did occur with the tacit approval of others, an overall balance of use was normally preserved along each river course.

The Industrial Revolution brought about a complete change. The growth of towns and manufacturing industry on an unprecedented scale created new, concentrated centres of demand, and water consumption rapidly increased. Potable water was urgently needed for the fast-growing urban populations, and was obtained from increasingly distant parts as the old sources of supply were either exhausted or rendered unusable through pollution. With the expansion of water supplies came the equally necessary provision of water for sewage disposal, which was largely responsible for the contamination of original supply sources. In addition to domestic requirements, the developing factory system produced a great intensification of traditional water use in industry, and also created completely new demands for water. For example, although rivers had always been used to some extent for inland navigation, the canal movement of the eighteenth century was an entirely new phenomenon. Canals were quickly followed by the rise of industrial water power, and the small storage reservoirs built to serve the canals and water-mills represent the initial regulation of surface supplies on an appreciable scale.

The advent of the railways and steam-power brought a relatively rapid decline in both these uses, but soon industrial requirements included water for boiler feeding and cooling in addition to the needs for processing a new and growing range of manufactures. The increasing use of industrial water caused an associated upsurge in trade effluent which, together with domestic water, was usually discharged directly to the nearest watercourse below the town, and pollution became accepted as an inevitable by-product of urbanisation and industrialisation in the manufacturing areas of the North and Midlands. The quality of river water declined rapidly, and Klein (1962) has reported that a memorandum to the 1868 River Pollution Commission on the state of the Yorkshire Calder was written not in ink but with 'river water taken this day from the point of junction between the River Calder and the town sewer'.

Eventually, the gross deterioration in water quality and the general loss of amenity resulted in some official action. An early attempt to conserve fisheries was made by the Fishery Acts of 1861 and 1865, which reflected the beginnings of angling as a popular national pastime, but the most comprehensive approach to pollution control was undertaken by the Rivers Pollution Prevention Commission which lasted in a variety of forms from 1865 to 1874 and, through a series of reports and recommendations, was responsible for the Rivers Pollution Prevention Act of 1876. Together with the Public Health Act of 1872, this legislation contained some apparently important remedies, including the abolition of prescriptive rights to pollute and the banning of solid waste from rivers, but safeguards were incorporated for the benefit of industrial interests, whilst the enforcement of the legislation was left to existing local authorities and organisations. This was a fundamental mistake, common to other early legislation, since the vested interests in pollution were allocated the dominant role in cleaning up the rivers. Local authority sewers were the major single cause of pollution. In the absence of generally recognised standards for water quality or accepted methods of waste treatment, local authorities were understandably reluctant to undertake expensive pollution control measures, particularly since it was argued that any subsequent benefits would be enjoyed only by their downstream neighbours with no guarantee of equivalent improvements upstream. Since the local authorities were themselves major polluters, they found it impossible to prosecute the manufacturers. Local authorities and local industry were closely related, and the latter frequently stressed the mutual disadvantages of any recession in trade and prosperity which might ensue from the imposition of uneconomic controls on current industrial practices. Therefore, despite growing protests, river quality continued to decline.

The re-structuring of local government in 1888 placed the enforcement of the Rivers Pollution Act on the new County Councils as well as on smaller authorities, but the control details were again left to local discretion. No real progress was made until the early 1890s when four river authorities were established in some of the more heavily polluted districts of the North, to complement the Thames Conservancy Board and the Lee Conservancy Board which had been formed earlier in the nineteenth century. These authorities, such as the West Riding Rivers Board, were both financially and administratively independent, and were charged with the control of pollution over wide areas. By efficient inspection and law enforcement these organisations did much to persuade local authorities and manufacturers to adopt improved waste disposal methods and gradually some of the worst abuses were suppressed.

Nevertheless, the growth of water pollution during the nineteenth century led inevitably to the contamination of public water supply sources, and it was not long before the expanding urban communities, especially in the North of England, were obliged to seek large new sources of potable water from the adjacent uplands. Once again, however, there was little general guidance, and whenever a town wished to secure a new water supply statutory powers had to be obtained through a special Act of Parliament. The promoters of the Bill, together with any objectors, appeared before the Local Legislation Committee of both Houses of Parliament who could then approve, reject or amend in any way the Bill before them. This machinery was expensive and time-consuming and gradually standardised procedures were adopted, although strictly speaking, the Parliamentary Committees were empowered to treat each scheme on its own merits. This meant that no oversight could be given to the regional allocation of water sources, particularly since the Committees had no continuity of existence. Cruickshank (1965) has shown that similar competition for upland resources existed in the areas surrounding the Central Valley of Scotland, but the widespread development of gathering grounds did not occur until the passing of the Burgh Police (Scotland) Act of 1892.

A considerable proportion of any Bill's time in Parliament was occupied by the assessment of compensation water, which was legally required when large water supply schemes interfered with the normal riparian rights of parties downstream by impounding and abstracting water in the upper reaches of a river. In a few cases a direct financial settlement was agreed, but for the most part Parliament imposed a statutory obligation on the supply undertaking to release a guaranteed minimum flow below their works for the benefit of users downstream. Many of the early impounding schemes took place in the head-waters of Pennine valleys in both Lancashire and Yorkshire. These valleys had already undergone industrialisation during the phase of water power, and, although steam was becoming increasingly important in the nineteenth century, the mill owners on these streams formed powerful local bodies. At this time their interests in riverflow were the only ones which really mattered, and every proposed water supply scheme had to be notified to all industrialists using the river for a distance of 32 km (20 miles) below an intended abstraction point. Indeed, so dominant was the water power interest that many of the first compensation awards specified that the compensation discharge should be released intermittently to coincide with the working hours at the mills. The principle of intermittent flow, which appears to have arisen in England in the mid-eighteenth century and was generally unknown in Scotland, was detrimental to the river system as a whole. At times the dry weather flow of rivers became inadequate for other purposes such as effluent dilution, although this was not legally recognised until the Rivers Pollution Prevention Act of 1876. Apart from sacrificing the well-being of the river to one sectional interest, it was eventually realised that it was impossible to phase intermittent compensation discharges with working hours right down the river, and in some cases, as illustrated by Paterson (1896), the releases passed the mills in the middle of the night. Finally, the advocates of continuous flow argued their case successfully in 1890, and the Standing Orders of both Houses of Parliament were changed to ensure that all future awards should be based on continuous flow.

Although the issue of continuous flow was important at the time these schemes were being planned, the most lasting feature arising from the strength of the manufacturing lobby has undoubtedly been the generous total amount of compensation water which they were able to obtain. In order to reduce the time spent on disputes between water authorities and the mill owners regarding the allocation of compensation water, the Parliamentary Committees evolved a broad rule whereby the water authority offered a compensation flow which was equivalent to a fixed proportion, usually one-third, of the total estimated yield of the reservoir project. This procedure had the merits of simplicity and ease of application, but its widespread use led to a serious under-utilisation of resources, particularly on rivers with little industrial development (Risbridger 1963).

By the end of the nineteenth century the 'scramble' for upland gathering grounds was largely over, but considerable controversy still existed about the best method of allocating sources of supply. Some argued that local resources should always be fully exploited before distant sources were appropriated, but there were obvious deficiencies in a strict drainage basin allocation since no reliable correlation existed between supply and demand in individual catchment areas. A wider approach had been recommended as early as 1869 by the Duke of Richmond's Royal Commission on Water

Supply which did suggest the initial development of local sources, but also made the points that where a long distance conduit was constructed an attempt should be made to supply areas through which it passed, and that applications to Parliament for Water Bills should be considered in a regional context. In 1878–9 several suggestions were made by Toplis *et al.* (1878–9) for dividing England and Wales into watershed districts, which would be responsible not only for potable water supplies but for overall conservation including waste disposal and pollution prevention. Following this, the Rivers Pollution Prevention Commission recommended that all rivers should be placed under the supervision of a central authority, whilst in 1870 the Rt. Hon. Lord Robert Montague, a member of the Royal Sanitary Commission of 1869–71, advocated a system of river regulation for multiple benefits based on reservoirs which '. . . must be at high levels in order to scour the river, to supply water to the towns, and for use in irrigating the land, and therefore they cannot be in the hands of any other authority but a Watershed Board' (Water Power Resources Committee 1920). This concept of broad conservation in the interests of the whole community was echoed in 1901 by the Royal Commission on Sewage Disposal and by the Royal Commission on Salmon Fisheries in 1902, but successive Governments declined to take any action.

Developments 1900–1950

The early years of the present century saw a continued increase in pressure on the nation's water resources. In 1920 the Board of Trade Committee on Water Power Resources stressed that, in the continued absence of a systematic approach to water conservation, '. . . there is real danger that at no distant date some of our communities in England and Wales may not be able to provide themselves with proper and adequate water supplies . . .' Some impetus was given to the conservation movement by the rising popularity of angling and the creation of Fishery Boards in certain areas, but still the emphasis remained on separate sectional interests. The water supply industry did agree to some rationalisation and, after consultation with the Minister of Health, several Regional Advisory Water Committees were established from 1924 to co-ordinate possible joint action between water authorities before Parliament was approached for large new supply schemes. However, despite Government encouragement, only nine such committees were formed, and, since they lacked any legal authority, they were dependent on voluntary co-operation within the industry.

In 1927 pollution prevention took an important step forward with the foundation of the Water Pollution Research Board, but increased Government interest before the Second World War was largely generated by the drought of 1934 which revealed just how precarious supplies were in certain areas. This resulted in the rapid implementation of legislation to improve piped water supplied outside the urban areas and to provide for more re-distribution of water between authorities in times of shortage. At this time there was also growing dissatisfaction with the narrow role of the Regional Advisory Water Committees, composed as they were of representatives of the public supply industry and Ministry officials, and in March 1937 a non-statutory Central Advisory Water Committee was formed with members from the water supply industry, local authorities, catchment and fishery boards, industry and other bodies concerned with water resources. The creation of the Central Advisory Water Committee marked a new phase in attitudes towards water resources based on a wider and more realistic approach, and the committee produced a number of influential reports. In a Third Report dated 1943 the possibility of co-ordinating the various interests in water within broad, catchment-based organisations was raised once more, and this document led directly to the 1944 Government White Paper, entitled 'A National Water Policy', which formed the foundation for the 1945 Water Act.

The Water Act of 1945 gave responsibility to the Minister of Health for the conservation and proper use of water resources in England and Wales, including public supplies, and was the first real attempt at water resource legislation in this country. The Minister was empowered to promote the further rationalisation of the water supply industry and to appoint Joint Advisory Water Committees to make regional resource surveys for any area, whilst the Minister had authority to make Water Orders to provide new sources of supply available to combinations of undertakings in Joint Water Boards. The 1945 Act also recognised the general lack of statistical information relating to water use, and water abstractors were required to keep records of water taken from both surface and ground sources, whilst controls were established on the sinking of new wells and boreholes. The Act made it obligatory for the Minister to appoint a statutory Central Advisory Water Committee with representation and powers similar to the previous non-statutory organisation, except that the new body was to advise any Minister who might be involved in the conservation and use of water resources.

The recommendations of the previous Central Advisory Water Committee concerning catchment-based conservation authorities were not implemented until 1948 when the River Boards Act was passed. This Act created from 1950 a system of thirty-two River Boards which were based on drainage basin boundaries and covered the whole of England and Wales with the exception of the Thames Conservancy and Lee Conservancy areas and the administrative county of London. These organisations absorbed the rather limited land drainage functions previously vested in the Catchment Boards set up in 1930, and assumed regional responsibility for pollution prevention and the preservation of fisheries. Thus, a variety of bodies responsible for administering existing pollution and fisheries legislation were replaced by authorities with much wider functions operating over specially created administrative areas. Considerable emphasis was placed on the assessment and conservation of water resources at the local level, and the River Boards were charged with obtaining information on rainfall and runoff in their areas together with data on abstractions from and discharges into their streams and rivers. Similar provisions were made for Scotland by the setting up of several River Purification Boards, although these were responsible for only the more densely populated parts of Scotland and their functions were restricted more to pollution control.

Recent Developments and the Current Situation

With the creation of the River Boards in 1950 it was felt in many quarters that a suitable and lasting framework had been provided for the conservation of water resources in Britain, and, where deficiencies were recognised, attempts were soon made to make them good. Thus, the pollution functions of the River Boards were clarified and strengthened in 1951 by the Rivers (Prevention of Pollution) Act. This legislation followed the recommendations contained in the report of the Central Advisory Water Committee Rivers Pollution Prevention Sub-Committee published in 1949, and the Act required the consent of the appropriate River Board for all the new trade or sewage effluent discharges, whilst the Board had powers to impose conditions relating to the volume and quality of such discharges.

As the 1950s progressed, however, it gradually became clear that a greater degree of organisation and control was necessary. For example, although the 1945 Water Act conferred responsibility for conservation on the Ministry of Health, there was little effective machinery to allow for its implementation, and the Minister's real powers were confined to certain aquifers which had been declared conservation areas and to the rationalisation policy for the water supply industry. Like the River Boards themselves, the Minister had no direct powers to construct hydraulic works or storage reservoirs for conservation. In fact, most of the energies of the River Boards were taken up by their pollution prevention functions, and further pollution legislation in 1961 extended their consent procedures for effluent disposal to pre-1951 discharges. Another problem lay in the fact that the public water supply industry remained outside the jurisdiction of the River Boards, and water undertakings continued the largely independent appropriation of new supply sources. The River Boards were also hampered by the absence of an effective central organisation capable of co-ordinating their activities to ensure conservation on a larger regional scale than the individual administrative areas.

In 1955 the Government asked the Central Advisory Water Committee to enquire into the extent to which demands for water were rising. The Sub-Committee on the Growing Demand for Water published its First Report in 1959 (Central Advisory Water Committee 1959) and, in view of the rapid increases indicated, the Committee's terms of reference were extended to consider the case for establishing control over all surface-water abstractions. In a Second Report (Central Advisory Water Committee 1960) the Sub-Committee expressed the need for further control over surface abstractions, especially with regard to the marked upsurge in demand for spray irrigation water, but the Committee also suggested that positive conservation measures should be implemented rather than attempting control through wholly negative restrictions on usage. The abnormally dry summer of 1959 and the floods of the following year gave added urgency to these proposals, and in 1962 the

Sub-Committee produced its Final Report on the Growing Demand for Water, often known as the Proudman Report (Central Advisory Water Committee 1962).

The Proudman Report re-emphasised the problems associated with the multiple interests in the nation's water resources, and concluded that it should no longer be left to independent organisations to develop these resources according to their separate and sometimes conflicting requirements. A positive policy of water conservation was urged which would bring about '. . . the preservation, control and development of water resources (both surface and ground) by storage, including natural ground storage, prevention of pollution or other means, so as to ensure that adequate and reliable supplies of water are made available for all purposes in the most suitable and economic way whilst safeguarding legitimate interests'. To achieve these ends the Report suggested the creation of comprehensive new River Authorities to replace the existing River Boards and administer water management at the local level with a separate control authority designed to promote conservation and the proper use of the country's water reserves. The Sub-Committee further recommended that River Authorities should give consent and issue licences for all surface and groundwater abstractions in their area, and the money derived from licence fees should be used to finance conservation works. These proposals were accepted, with only a few modifications, in the Government White Paper of the same year (H.M. Government 1962), and in 1963 statutory effect was given to the Sub-Committee's work with the passing of the Water Resources Act.

The Water Resources Act provided for the establishment of twenty-nine River Authorities covering the whole of England and Wales except for the London area, as shown in figure 2.2. North of the border, different legislation was responsible for the creation of the River Purification Boards which perform a roughly equivalent role in the more populated parts of Scotland. In addition to absorbing the River Board functions relating to land drainage, river pollution, fisheries and navigation, the new Authorities were given extra powers for the overall control and planning of water resources. This control was achieved through the licensing system, which includes all abstractions other than those made by individuals for domestic use and by farmers for purposes other than irrigation. Although this does mean that the cost of private abstraction will increase, the

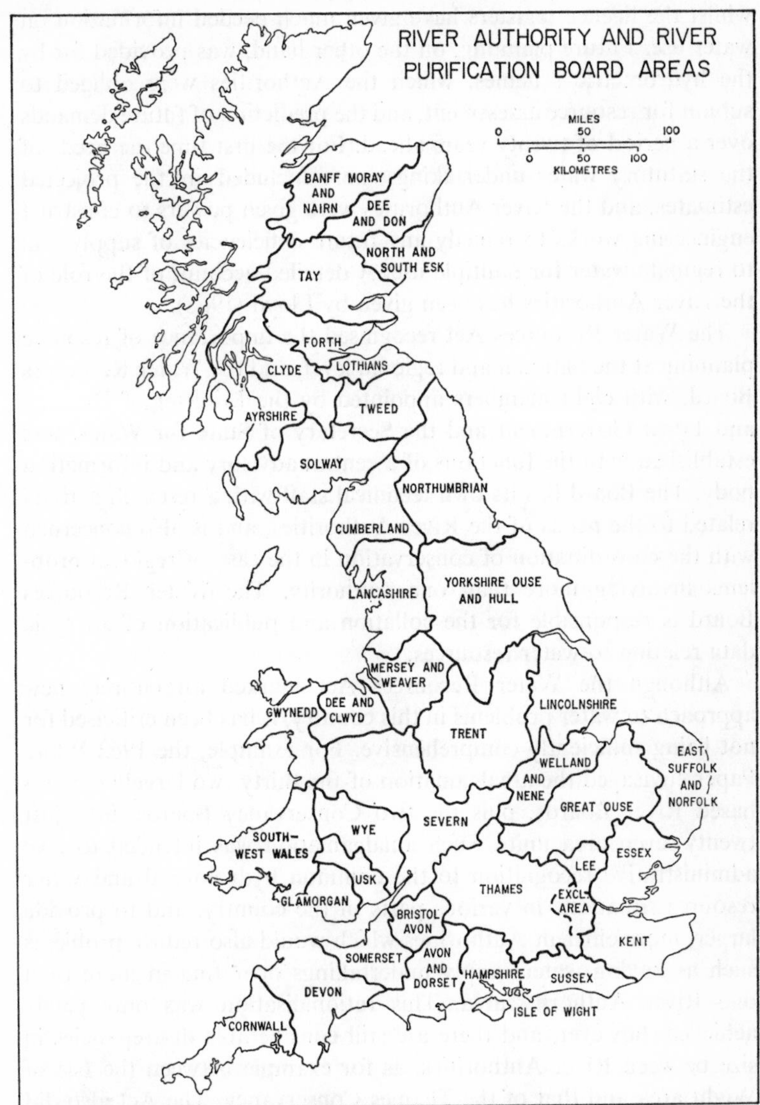

Figure 2.2 River Authority and River Purification Board areas.

abstractor now has an assured supply from the River Authority whilst the licence registers have given much needed information on water use. Future planning, on the other hand, was provided for by the hydrometric schemes, which the Authorities were obliged to submit for resource assessment, and the prediction of future demands over a period of twenty years ahead. For the first time the needs of the statutory water undertakings were included in the projected estimates, and the River Authorities were given powers to construct engineering works to remedy any future deficiencies of supply and to regulate water for multiple use. A detailed account of the role of the River Authorities has been given by Lloyd (1968).

The Water Resources Act recognised the importance of resource planning at the national and regional level, and the Water Resources Board, with eight members appointed by the Minister of Housing and Local Government and the Secretary of State for Wales, was established with the functions of a central advisory and information body. The Board has its own technical staff with a research activity related to the needs of the River Authorities, and is also concerned with the co-ordination of conservation in the case of regional problems involving more than one Authority. The Water Resources Board is responsible for the collation and publication of all basic data relating to water resources.

Although the Water Resources Act marked an entirely new approach to water problems in this country, it has been criticised for not being sufficiently comprehensive. For example, the 1962 White Paper envisaged the amalgamation of the thirty-two largely county-based River Boards, plus the two Conservancy Boards, into just twenty-seven area units. Such amalgamation was intended to give administrative recognition to the common hydrological and water resource situations in various parts of the country, and to provide larger, more efficient Authorities which would also reduce problems such as having water supply undertakings operating in more than one River Authority area. This rationalisation was only partly achieved, however, and there are still considerable discrepancies in size between River Authorities, as for example between the Isle of Wight area and that of the Thames Conservancy. The Act also did relatively little to solve the problem of diverse interests in hydrology, whilst neither Scotland nor Northern Ireland has had directly equivalent legislation. It can be argued that the water resource problem is less severe in these areas and that co-operation does exist, as between the Scottish Office and the Water Resources Board with regard to the collection and publication of hydrological information, but there is still a case for extending the legislative framework over the whole of the United Kingdom.

3 Hydrological Networks and Data

All water resource studies must start from an assessment of the available supplies, and the value of such an assessment depends ultimately on the accuracy and relevance of standard hydrological measurements. It is the aim of this chapter, therefore, to outline the methods by which basic hydrological data are obtained and processed in this country. The major theme will be to consider some of the problems associated with existing methods from the viewpoint of water resource evaluation, and show how recent developments may bring improvements in the near future.

General Considerations

Since hydrology is an observational field science, its data cannot approach the accuracy attainable under controlled laboratory conditions, and, despite attempts to standardise recording equipment, many values cannot be related to an absolute standard in the way that, for example, distance or temperature measurements can be calibrated against an accepted rigid scale. Thus, in addition to the *accidental* or *random* group of observational errors always present, there is often an element of *systematic* or *instrumental* error built into the measurement. Random errors arise from such inevitable cause as temporary failure of either a human observer or an instrument to record a given situation as accurately as usual. Although this can produce serious complications, the error can frequently be detected and reduced to acceptable limits by duplicating instruments and increasing the number of observations in both space and time. Systematic errors, on the other hand, result from the difficulty of designing and installing instruments which will perform to an absolute standard under field conditions so that the parameter being measured is not consistently over or under-estimated. Such an error is inherent in the design of the instrument, and is impossible to remove by adding to the density of the recording network.

The problem of random and systematic errors applies to many measurements made at recording stations, but an equally fundamental problem in hydrological measurement is the extrapolation of such point data over a meaningful area such as a drainage basin. Area values of precipitation or the regional shape of the groundwater table are of much more use to the hydrologist than scattered measurements from individual raingauges or observation wells, since such point records first require translation by one or more of the various methods available. The only exception is that of streamflow measurement since, given the assumption that the watershed of the catchment area above the gauging station is coincident with the topographic watershed, the discharge recorded represents the total runoff from the contributory area rather than a sample measurement as in the other cases. For this reason streamflow data may be easily and accurately transformed into area values.

If most hydrological measurement is a sampling process, it will also be apparent that the hydrologist is dealing with only a very small sample of the total variable over a catchment area. For example, the collecting area of a standard raingauge is less than 130 cm^2 (20 sq in.) although the results may well be taken as representative of precipitation over many square kilometres. Furthermore, hydrological samples are neither regular nor random in distribution, but are biased generally towards preferred locations which have been subjectively selected to meet personal and practical requirements. So long as hydrological instruments need to be read or maintained frequently by observers, so the data sample will continue to be biased towards accessible areas of the settled lowlands. This is particularly true of the rainfall network, which depends largely on the daily gauges. With the exception of water supply gathering grounds, most of these gauges are at relatively low altitudes, and there is a broadly inverse relationship between the density of gauges and the volume of precipitation to be measured.

Whilst satisfactory sampling in a spatial context is a basic problem in hydrological measurement, a major difficulty associated with the analysis of records is that of inadequate samples in time. Most measurements relate to fixed calendar units such as days or months which only occasionally coincide directly with natural hydrological processes. This problem operates over a variety of time-scales and Bleasdale (1961), for example, has shown that in the dry year of 1959 the effect of calculating the rainfall deficiency for the twelve calendar months from October 1958 to September 1959, instead of considering the actual daily extent of the dry spell from 16 October 1958 to 15 October 1959, was to under-estimate the deviation from the mean by 8 per cent in some areas. It is also accepted now that secular changes of climate occur on a variety of scales. Thus, there is no physical reason why two successive 35-year periods, which have been conventionally employed in the past for the calculation of average values, should show uniform conditions, whilst frequency analysis and extreme events, such as floods and droughts, can only be interpreted for the period to which they relate. This indicates the real difficulty of forecasting future events from past records, and shows the problem of placing hydrological records in a suitable time framework.

These sampling problems have always been a limitation in hydrological measurement, and it is not over-emphasising the point to state that future progress in hydrology is largely dependent upon improved instrumentation and data. Within recent years, however, important developments have taken place in the field of electronics, whilst the advent of automatic recording systems and high speed computers suggests that these advances will find special applications in hydrology.

After several years of experimental field trials, it seems probable that fully automatic data-logging systems will soon become sufficiently reliable for routine measurement in most branches of hydrology including rainfall, runoff, groundwater and the various meteorological parameters required for the estimation of evaporation. Details of one such system have been given by Strangeways and McCullogh (1965). Although differing in details, the systems allow for the measurement of a number of these variables at regular pre-selected time intervals and the storage of the observations on magnetic tape, or in some cases on a punched plastic tape. The recording systems have a self-contained power supply, and can normally be left unattended for several months with the usual sampling interval of 15 minutes. Subsequently the magnetic tape can be translated to produce either a digital print-out of the individual values or a punched paper tape which can be fed directly into a computer for rapid analysis.

Once proved reliable, this method of data recording is likely to revolutionise data collection in hydrology. The main advantages are that, for the first time, data will become available for more remote areas, and gaps in the national networks can be plugged. More detailed sampling in time will result in a better appreciation of short-period events such as floods and the relation of measurements more directly to natural hydrological periods. In addition, the ready computerisation of the data means that analysis will be more complete than ever before and that more information will be extracted from a larger body of records. Taking the example of rainfall once again, it has been estimated by Bleasdale *et al.* (1963) that in the pre-computer period probably less than 5 to 10 per cent of the potential value has been extracted from the last 100 years of daily rainfall records for the United Kingdom because of the large investment of time required for the manual collection and elementary processing of the data. The final advantage of such logging systems is that they can be remotely interrogated at any time, if connected up to the telephone network, so that current conditions or recently recorded events can be quickly assimilated from a wide area. This could produce several benefits, but the most obvious application lies in more sophisticated flood warning schemes.

Precipitation Measurement

Most precipitation measurements in Britain are made with the Meteorological Office Mk 2 gauge which has a 127 mm (5 in.) diameter rim installed horizontally 305 mm (12 in.) above ground-level (Meteorological Office 1956). The majority of these gauges are read daily at 09.00 hours GMT to provide a total volume of precipitation for the preceding 24 hours of 'rainfall day', but in more remote areas larger capacity gauges may be read only once per week or calendar month. However, Maidens (1965) has reported that an entirely new range of fibreglass raingauges has been approved for use by the Meteorological Office.

Although apparently a simple operation, the accurate point measurement of precipitation with a standard gauge is fraught with difficulty. Most of the errors are systematic in origin and arise from the exposure of the gauge above ground-level and the effect of this on wind-driven precipitation. The gauge acts as an obstruction to the flow of air near the ground surface, thus causing turbulence and eddying around the aperture of the gauge. As demonstrated by Robinson and Rodda (1969) and shown in figure 3.1, the leading edge of the gauge produces accelerated air currents across the top of the gauge, so that precipitation is carried over the top of the gauge and is deposited to leeward rather than in the collecting funnel. The gauge, therefore, systematically underestimates the precipitation

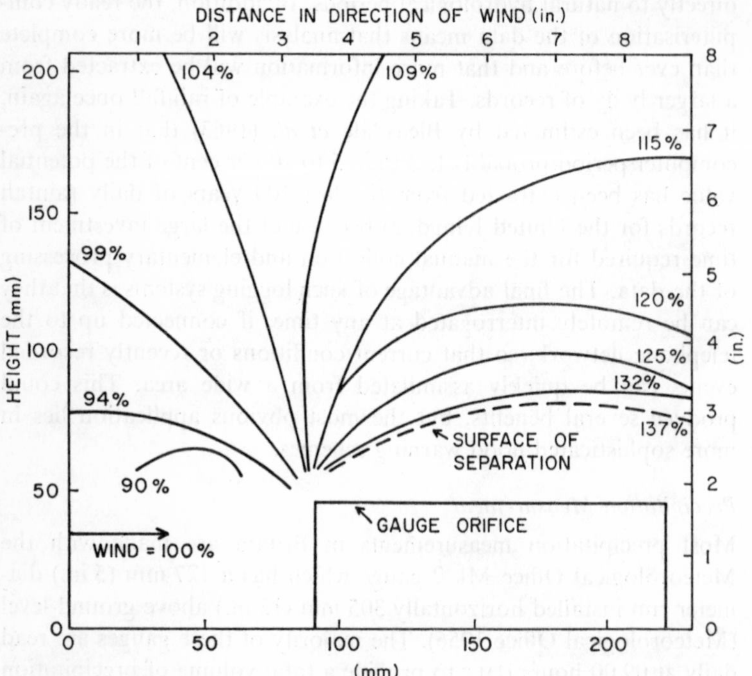

Figure 3.1 The structure of the windfield above a standard raingauge as revealed by wind-tunnel experiments. At a wind velocity of 3.5 m/s (11.6 ft/sec), air currents over the gauge are accelerated by up to 37 per cent. After Robinson and Rodda (1969).

reaching the ground surface in the vicinity, the actual deficit increasing with wind speed. The deficiency is also high during rainfall with a small median droplet size and during snowfall because small raindrops and snow-flakes have lower terminal (falling) velocities and are carried away from the gauge more easily.

As indicated in chapter 2, this problem has been appreciated for many years, and the usual solution in Britain has been to reduce the

Figure 3.2 A ground-level raingauge with polystyrene grid surround.

wind turbulence, particularly in upland areas, by the construction of a turf wall surround. Even with regular maintenance, wind effects are not completely eliminated by the turf wall, and there has been a recent emphasis on the installation of ground-level gauges in order to calibrate adjacent conventional instruments. Various solutions have been adopted to eliminate excessive precipitation catches due to in-splashing, but the most common one has been the establishment of an open polystyrene grid surrounding the gauge at ground-level as shown in figure 3.2. Experimental evidence from this type of gauge collected by Rodda (1970) indicated that, at a typical site in lowland England, the conventional gauge under-estimates annual precipitation by 3 to 7 per cent, with a small deficiency of 2 per cent in the summer months rising to 10 per cent in winter owing to the seasonal variation in mean wind speeds. No reliable generalisations can be made for the uplands, where the problem is more variable and severe due to higher wind speeds and greater snowfalls, but many gauges show a three-fold increase in deficiency over the lowland stations. In terms of actual amounts of precipitation this can mean a considerable error, since it is a larger percentage of a much higher rainfall. Thus, whilst such catch deficiencies make it impossible to measure mean annual precipitation in the lowest, driest parts of the country to within an accuracy of 25·4 mm (1 in.), in the highest and wettest areas existing gauges could be under-estimating annual totals by up to 500 mm (20 in.). Although an initial under-estimation of available resources may well be preferable to over-estimation, there are clear incentives for a better understanding of this problem.

Another source of systematic error lies in the establishment of gauges with rims horizontal irrespective of the surrounding area receiving rainfall, especially in hilly districts where windward slopes tend to intercept more rainfall per unit of projected area than a horizontal surface, with the reverse being true of a leeward slope. Although this problem is normally ignored in Britain, it can be minimised by the installation of gauges at ground-level with their rims and surrounds parallel to the average slope of the immediate vicinity. On the other hand, a much denser network of gauges would be required to sample adequately the great variety of slope orientation, and the method is not likely to be used for routine measurement.

At present there are rather more than 6000 standard gauges in Great Britain, and it is expected that this total will rise to 8000 within a few years (Meteorological Office 1968). Even the current total represents a relatively dense network, with about one gauge for every 39 km^2 (15 sq miles) on average, and in 1960 the overall national density was second in the world only to Israel according to data presented by Gilman (1964).

In this country the standard method for the estimation of areal rainfall is that of isohyet mapping. Although a subjective technique, the gauging network is sufficiently dense to permit accurate results when the method is employed by experienced cartographers, and for routine work, such as the calculation of areal values for inclusion in the *Surface Water Year Book*, it is not generally considered worthwhile to use some of the more complicated geometrical or statistical methods. In many instances, however, the Meteorological Office does use a modified form of isohyetal analysis known as the 'isomeric method'. Although the unweighted arithmetic average of the precipitation from a number of gauges cannot be directly representative of an area's catchment value, except in the rare cases where there is either a very even distribution of gauges or a low range of altitude and precipitation, it is possible to express individual gauge values over any time interval as a percentage of the long-period mean annual precipitation at that station. These percentages, or *isomeric values*, may then be averaged over the drainage basin, and the mean percentage so derived can be applied to the long-period mean for the whole area, thus providing an areal value of precipitation depth for the catchment concerned. Apart from ease of application, the method can be employed in areas with widely varying rainfall totals since, although individual gauges may show sharp differences in actual catch, the predominantly frontal origin of precipitation over Britain means that, over periods of a few days or longer, there is a fairly consistent distribution of precipitation which leads to similarity in the isomeric values. This similarity enables an initial quality control check to be made on the data, since an anomalous record will stand out in the isomeric form, and, provided that a generally even scatter of gauges exists, the method will work for areas of limited data.

Daily rainfall values provide little information on rainfall intensity. The need for more frequent time-sampling has been met by the continuous recorders, of which according to the Water Resources Board (1971) there were 670 in operation during 1970. The traditional recording gauge is the Dines tilting-siphon instrument invented in

1920. This gauge employs a combined float and siphon action so that the progressive rise of the float with increasing rainfall is transferred by a pen arm to a paper chart, which is fixed to a revolving drum driven by a daily clock. When the float chamber is full, it is emptied automatically by a siphon. Another type of recording gauge operates on the tipping-bucket principle, whereby two counter-balanced receivers tip successively with a see-saw action under the weight of a known volume of rainfall entering the gauge. In some ways this system is less satisfactory than the tilting siphon in that, unless a very small bucket capacity is selected, a fully continuous record cannot be obtained since the gauge only indicates rainfall through a stepped trace with each 'step' corresponding to a tipping event. Thus, the first tip during a particular storm cannot be taken as the start of precipitation as much will depend on the amount of water, if any, remaining in the bucket from the previous fall. This gauge is least effective during light rain and in summer when evaporation of water from the buckets between rainfalls may lead to some under-estimation.

Until recently both the Dines and tipping-bucket gauges recorded either on small daily charts, which meant that they required daily servicing, or on weekly charts which so compressed the time-scale that multiple storms could not be easily isolated for study. However, the increasing demand for intensity measurements in more remote areas has led to the development of strip-chart mechanisms, operated by weekly or monthly clocks, which provide a greatly expanded time-scale with up to 152 mm (6 in.) per hour of chart travel for the weekly gauges and 25·4 mm (1 in.) per hour for the monthly mechanisms.

Other recent improvements in raingauging have included the introduction of an automatic gauge which provides daily totals over periods up to a month in length. In this system 32 polythene bottles are housed below the gauge inlet, and at 09.00 hours each day a clock-actuated mechanism transfers the inlet pipe from one collecting bottle to the next. Such a method does not, of course, provide information on intensities, and, together with the chart recording mentioned above, it is being superseded by automatic data-logging. In raingauging the automatic data-logging principle has been most widely applied to the tipping bucket gauge, although attempts have been made to use it with float gauges. It may be that such gauges will be fairly reliable during spells of cold weather, although, in the absence of mains electricity, no suitable method of frost protection has yet been devised for any gauge.

The difficulty of keeping raingauges operational throughout the winter leads on to one of the major limitations of precipitation measurement, which is that of snow-gauging. Despite the application of a great deal of inventive effort in many countries, there is still no completely satisfactory snow-gauge, and in this country values are obtained as water equivalent from melted snow caught in the funnel of the standard gauge. This causes a significant under-estimation of snowfall, not only because of the exposure factors which beset rain measurement, but also because snow blows out of the gauge funnel, especially if the funnel becomes blocked by snow bridging across the gauge aperture. After heavy falls in the uplands gauges are frequently buried, since there is no tradition, as in other countries, of establishing shielded snow-gauges above the probable maximum snow depth.

Snow lying on the surface of a catchment may represent an important storage phase of the hydrological cycle, and in these cases one of the hydrologist's chief concerns is the accurate measurement of the water equivalent of the snow pack and the maximum melt rate which is likely to occur to produce a snow-melt flood. The use of empirical ratios such as 10:1 or 12:1 between accumulated snow depth and the equivalent depth of water has been shown to be only a rough guide, and there is a need for a greater research effort into snow hydrology in Britain, particularly in northern England and Scotland.

EVAPOTRANSPIRATION MEASUREMENT

In water resource studies evapotranspiration is often termed 'water loss', since it represents the difference over a catchment area between precipitation and the residual runoff and is therefore that portion of precipitation which is unavailable for development in water schemes. It is perhaps because of the complexities of the evaporation process that the measurement of these 'losses' has lagged behind that of most other hydrological variables, and in Britain the only 'standard' instrument available for evaporation measurement is the Symons open-water tank which was developed over 100 years ago. Similarly, although the Water Resources Act 1963 placed a statutory obligation on the River Authorities to measure evaporation within their areas, this requirement was somewhat premature and has not been fully implemented in the regional hydrometric schemes.

The practical problems arise from the dual nature of evapotranspiration which, as the term implies, is made up of two different processes. Transpiration is basically a biological process, partly dependent on plant physiology and soil conditions, whilst direct evaporation from water, soil or other surfaces is subject to purely physical influences. In general, however, both processes are largely interrelated and can be considered collectively, although formidable obstacles still limit satisfactory measurement. The main reason is that, for most of the year, the actual rate of evapotranspiration varies so much, according to the variety of natural surfaces and the availability of soil moisture to different vegetation types, that it is impracticable to attempt representative field sampling. Because of this, most methods of estimating actual evapotranspiration depend either on inadequate sampling or on calculations which rely too heavily on other indirect measurements. The simplest method of determining evaporation from an open-water surface is to measure the loss which occurs in a small body of water exposed to the weather elements. The standard tank is 1·8 m (6 ft) square and 0·6 m (2 ft) deep, and is installed slightly above the ground surface with an overhanging rim to minimise outsplash due to wind effects. Apart from exposure problems, which may result in the splashing of water into or out of the tank, a further limitation is that the measurements cannot be compared directly with the loss from a large body of water since the different thermal characteristics of lakes or reservoirs have to be considered, and this necessitates the application of a transfer coefficient. On the other hand, evaporation work carried out on a reservoir in the Thames valley by Lapworth (1965) suggests that, because the British tank is sunk into the ground it suffers less from over-exposure than many other instruments, such as the American Class A pan which is raised above the ground on timbers, and therefore the annual correction coefficient may be near unity. In any case, such tank coefficients are only valid for annual periods. This is because heat storage plays an important part in influencing evaporation from a deep water body such as a reservoir on a seasonal scale, and correlations between tank and reservoir over such periods could only take place if water temperatures were available for both water bodies.

At the present time, there are probably about twenty-five tanks in operation over the country with variable lengths of record. During the International Geophysical Year the Meteorological Office installed ten Class A pans at existing sites for the purpose of comparative testing. Although the major emphasis has been on the summer records, since both types of instrument suffer from freezing in the winter, it has been found by Holland (1967) that the Class A pans show evaporation losses which are normally about three times higher than the Symons tanks.

The combined effects of evaporation and transpiration are seen in the actual evapotranspiration taking place from natural surfaces, and this can be measured by unirrigated lysimeters, which are also known as percolation or drain gauges. These usually consist of watertight, soil-filled tanks about 0·91 m (3 ft) square and of similar depth with a drainage outlet in the base leading to a collecting vessel. Precipitation is measured in an adjacent raingauge, and evapotranspiration is computed by subtracting the measured drainage from the precipitation, with both observations usually taking place daily.

Several factors make such instruments unsatisfactory, but the main limitation is that a direct estimate of actual evapotranspiration based on the difference between precipitation and drainage is only valid for the natural hydrological time units between two falls of rain producing drainage, since estimates for other time intervals must take into account changes in soil moisture conditions. For short periods of time, such as a month, the results will have little significance, but over several years the equation will become increasingly meaningful as the amount of water involved in storage change becomes small in relation to the other two variables. Clearly such gauges have little use apart from giving some indication of long-term conditions.

In recent years attempts have been made to overcome the problem of soil moisture variations by utilising weighing lysimeters. These instruments do not have a drainage outlet, so that changes in weight of the system over any period can be related to the soil moisture content of the container. Thus, differences in weight equivalent between incoming precipitation and the pre-calibrated vegetated and soil-filled lysimeter can be directly related to evapotranspiration processes from the container surface. A difficulty with such systems is that the weight fluctuations are partly dependent on temperature changes. Although the method is still experimental, it is being used increasingly, especially in horticulture where an extremely sensitive device has been developed by Hand (1968) using the principle of electrical strain gauges.

The sampling problems associated with lysimeters may be overcome by employing similar residual methods on a catchment scale, and, for a drainage basin, the relationship between 'total losses' and the other hydrological elements over any period may be expressed by the following equation:

$$L = P - Q \pm U \pm S$$

where L = total evapotranspiration losses, P = precipitation, Q = runoff, U = watershed leakage and S = storage change, all as uniform depth over the catchment area.

The most serious criticism of this method is that it ultimately depends on the accuracy of the rainfall and runoff measurements, plus the usual assumption that the catchment in question is watertight. As with the percolation gauge, storage change can only be ignored over long periods which normally means calendar or water-years in this context. Furthermore, the individuality of lag characteristics of catchments, which is largely a function of geology, makes it difficult to define a minimum period over which groundwater storage change becomes insignificant. This method is, therefore, again only suitable for the assessment of mean annual conditions, and it is as a result of dissatisfaction with such residual techniques that the concept of *potential evapotranspiration* was advanced by Thornthwaite (1948).

Potential evapotranspiration (PE) has been defined in several ways, but it is based on the assumption that abundant soil moisture is always available for the needs of a reasonably uniform vegetation which completely covers the catchment or other area involved. Under such conditions the rate of evapotranspiration will be limited only by the evaporation opportunity offered by the weather elements, and biological complications which influence actual rates, such as variations in rooting depth, leaf area, etc., are considerably minimised. Therefore, since it is much easier to measure the evaporative power of the air than the actual losses from a natural surface, the concept of PE has been adopted enthusiastically.

There are a variety of ways of measuring PE, but the most common method is through formulae which are based on weather factors. The successful estimation of PE depends on a suitable combination of both the energy balance and the aerodynamic approaches to the problem, for whilst the former provides a measure of the solar energy which is available for heating and evaporation, the second is concerned with the efficiency with which atmospheric turbulence removes the water vapour produced, thus preventing the air near the ground from becoming saturated. Penman (1948) was the first researcher to combine these two aspects into a single formula based on four standard weather observations, namely mean air temperature, mean air humidity, mean wind speed and the duration of bright sunshine.

Although criticisms have been levelled at some of the empirical assumptions contained in the formula, the results from Penman's method are not only more realistic within the British environment than those from other methods, but they also compare well in terms of overall accuracy obtainable for several other hydrological parameters. The formula can be applied over periods of a day, or a few days upwards, and can meet most hydrological needs. For these reasons indirect calculations of PE by Penman's method have become one of the most standard forms of hydrological measurement in Britain and observations are currently obtained from 140 weather stations over the country (Water Resources Board 1971).The calculations now undertaken on a routine basis by the Agriculture and Hydrometeorology Branch of the Meteorological Office are used for a variety of purposes. Thus, at the end of every summer month the National Agricultural Advisory Service issues PE values to help farmers with irrigation schedules, whilst River Authorities frequently employ 7-day PE estimations as a guide to antecedent soil moisture conditions in case heavy rain should fall.

It is possible to measure PE directly by lysimetry, usually with two soil tanks, as shown in figure 3.3, in order to provide some cross-check on the values. As with other systems the two vegetated field tanks of the evapotranspirometer are exposed to the natural precipitation, which is measured nearby, whilst in dry weather this is supplemented by a known quantity of sprinkled irrigation water. The difference between the daily income (rainfall plus irrigation) and the drainage received in the collecting cans represents the PE, provided once again that allowance can be made for soil moisture changes. This correction is necessary even with irrigation since, because of the time-lag involved in water draining through the soil, the tanks are not maintained continuously at field capacity or indeed any other fixed level of soil water storage. For daily observations a correction is normally made by using a smoothing curve to link the days with equal storage conditions, but in upland areas the high frequency of heavy rainfall hinders the application of this technique and it may be impossible to recognise such points of equal storage over periods of a month or perhaps longer.

In addition to the problems caused by frequent rainfall, variations in storage can occur during winter when excessive lag effects are

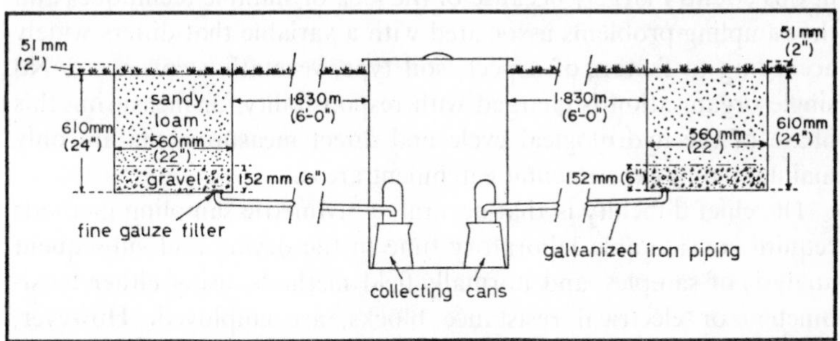

Figure 3.3 An evapotranspirometer for PE measurement.

present, owing either to the apparatus freezing up or to snowfall, whilst drifting snow often causes discrepancies between the amounts of precipitation caught in the raingauge and the quantities percolating through the soil tanks when the thaw arrives. During the summer months errors of an entirely different origin can be present in dry spells when the rate of PE exceeds rainfall and actual evapotranspiration so that the artificially watered soil tanks become 'over-exposed' in relation to the drier surfaces in the vicinity. In this situation the tanks record excessive values owing to the advection of the relatively dry air from the surrounding environment.

It is generally accepted that, provided uniform vegetation and moisture conditions are maintained between the tanks and their surroundings, the irrigated lysimeters or evapotranspirometers will provide an accurate measurement of PE. The use of evapotranspirometers has spread in Britain since the mid-1950s, mainly as a result of the activities of the Nature Conservancy. Published data first appeared in *British Rainfall* for 1958, and by 1961 there was a total of twenty-two stations, of which thirteen were maintained by the

Conservancy. The initiative of the Conservancy has produced an atypical distribution of instruments compared with most other hydrological measurements since no less than five of these stations are at 305 m (1000 ft) above sea level or higher.

SOIL MOISTURE MEASUREMENT

The direct measurement of soil moisture has been generally neglected in this country largely because of the lack of suitable techniques and the sampling problems associated with a variable that differs widely according to factors of aspect, soil type, vegetation cover, etc. No single organisation is charged with responsibility for measuring this phase of the hydrological cycle and direct measurements are only maintained in experimental catchment areas.

The chief difficulty is that accurate gravimetric sampling methods require considerable laboratory time in the drying and subsequent analysis of samples, and normally field methods, using either tensiometers or electrical resistance blocks, are employed. However, tensiometers do not perform satisfactorily in fairly dry soils whilst, although resistance blocks of gypsum or nylon work over a wide range of soil water content, their performance is affected by soil temperature and by the salt content of the soil. Recently the advent of the neutron probe method, which allows speedy measurement together with the lack of disturbance of the field site, should result in better observations, although its high basic cost has to be considered.

As a result of these problems, routine soil moisture measurements are not carried out by the Meteorological Office and other organisations, but estimates are made using the indirect water balance method whereby a comparison of Penman PE values and rainfall over periods of a few days can show the shortfall of summer rainfall and the accumulation of a soil moisture deficit. The basis of this method is more appropriately considered in chapter 4.

STREAMFLOW MEASUREMENT

It could well be argued that measured streamflow is the most important record available in applied hydrology, for it is the runoff phase of the hydrological cycle which offers the greatest scope for storage and conservation, and it is on the accuracy of streamflow data that the success of most water schemes depends. Streamflow has a further importance in that the variations in river discharge constitute a total integration of the hydrological events immediately preceding them in time as well as space. Thus, the volume of water passing through the outfall of a drainage basin constitutes the final residual element in the water budget and represents, for a given period of time, the water surplus after precipitation has satisfied the various evaporative and storage demands of the catchment. It is fortunate, therefore, that because streamflow is unique in constituting the only areal measurement in hydrology, it is possible to record river flow more accurately than any other phase in the hydrological cycle.

The rate of flow in open channels may be measured in a great variety of ways, and the most appropriate method is the one that most nearly matches the particular limitations of the gauging site, the regime of the river involved, the purpose of the station and the capital in hand. Some methods are particularly suitable for intermittent observations at second-order stations, but the techniques discussed here will be limited to those in common use at permanent gauging sites where a continuous record over the entire range of flows is required. On the other hand, it will be appreciated that on some rivers it is not possible to measure the variations in flow by a single method without serious loss of accuracy under either flood or dry weather flows, and in such cases a 'combined station' is often established.

About 40 per cent of all flow measuring stations currently operating in Britain are of the velocity-area type, with the largest concentration occurring in Scotland. This method enjoys a wide application since it can be employed over a large range of flows, is relatively cheap to establish and causes no interference to the natural flow of the river or to the passage of navigation or migratory fish. The method is basically simple, and depends on a determination of the cross-sectional area of the stream, which can be obtained by a variety of surveying methods, together with velocity measurements made at fixed points across the stream channel from which the mean speed of flow can be calculated. When the mean velocity is multiplied by the cross-sectional area, the total discharge at the time of measurement is obtained.

Although the method is theoretically very sound, a number of

3

practical difficulties exist and have been discussed by Boulton (1967*a*). For example, velocity measurements are usually made by means of a current meter, where the speed of revolution of either a propeller or a system of revolving cups is made proportional to the velocity of the stream. At high flows, however, it may be difficult to obtain representative readings across the full width of the stream, and if the current meter is suspended from above, as from a cableway or a boat, it is virtually impossible to overcome the downstream deflection from the vertical which occurs in a fast flowing river. Normal current meters also fail to perform properly at velocities below 0·15 m/s (0·5 ft/sec) which are frequently reached in some British rivers. Despite the recent introduction of new surveying techniques, such as echo-sounding, there still remains a practical problem of accurately measuring the cross-section of the river channel and precisely positioning the current meter when readings have to be taken across a wide river.

It will also be apparent that the velocity-area method is only capable of producing discharge measurements for the time when observations are actually being made, and to obtain a continuous record of flows it is necessary to relate the calculated surveyed values to the stage or height of the river above some arbitrary datum. Thus, by establishing a continuous water-level recorder on an adjacent section of the river it is possible to plot individual values of measured discharge against the river stage at the time of measurement and then interpolate a smooth curve linking the scattered points to produce a stage-discharge relationship for the site in question. A good stage-discharge or rating curve should extend over the entire range of flows experienced at the station, but while there may be ample opportunities to draw up a reliable relationship for the frequently occurring low and average flows, the rating curve will almost certainly have to be extrapolated outside its measured limits for flood discharges. This is not only because flood peaks occur rarely and are short-lived, but, even if an observer should be in the vicinity by chance, the condition of the river may well make it too dangerous to attempt a current meter observation.

A further disadvantage of the permanent velocity-area station is that, unless the gauging section lies in bedrock, it is impossible to guarantee the stability of the river channel over a period of years. Sediment movement, weed growth and a variety of morphological

Figure 3.4 A compound rectangular thin-plate weir on the Clow Beck at Croft, near Darlington, North Yorkshire. Drainage area 78·2 km² (30·2 sq miles) and altitude of station 29·4 m (96·5 ft) OD

Figure 3.5 A trapezoidal flume on the headwaters of the river Severn near Llanidloes, central Wales. This Institute of Hydrology station measures the flow from a forested experimental catchment of about 10·4 km² (4 sq miles).

Figure 3.6 A compound Crump weir on the lower river Tees at Broken Scar, County Durham. Drainage area 818 km^2 (316 sq miles) and altitude of station 37 m (122 ft) OD

Figure 3.7 A flat-vee weir on the Harwood Beck in upper Teesdale, County Durham. Drainage area 40·1 km^2 (15·5 sq miles) and altitude of station 378 m (1240 ft) OD

changes in the geometry of the channel section can upset the initial calibration of the rating curve. Thus, although a velocity-area station needs a relatively small capital expenditure, there is a continuing future commitment of manpower for checking the rating curve and maintaining the site.

Many of the above problems can be overcome by the use of artificial gauging structures, built to pre-determined specifications and located within the stream channel to provide a fixed control of known and stable geometry. The flow of the river is then canalised through this control and made to fall on the downstream side so that, once again, a measurement of river stage upstream can be directly related to the discharge of water passing over the structure. The great practical advantage of gauging structures is that, not only do they provide the most accurate continuous measurements of streamflow, but they may be pre-calibrated either by formulae embracing known hydraulic principles or by the use of scale models in the laboratory, although it is normally desirable to check the theoretical rating curve in the field.

There are many types of gauging structures in operation. In the early days of flow measurement in this country it was considered worthwhile to calibrate existing structures by current meter as an economy measure, and in some areas records were obtained from old mill weirs and reservoir spillways. Although broad-crested weirs are still often used for flow measurement on large rivers, there are now many more purpose-built structures. At the other end of the discharge scale, small streams are often gauged by thin-plate weirs, which may be either rectangular as shown in figure 3.4 or with a v-notch to contain the lowest flows. Flumes are becoming increasingly popular for small- or medium-sized streams, especially in the lowlands where a low stream-bed gradient would cause inundation of the surrounding land if the streamflow were to be ponded up behind a weir. A particular advantage of the trapezoidal flume, illustrated in figure 3.5, is that the narrowing of the throat section provides a high order of accuracy at low flows, but flumes are not practical on many of the wide shallow rivers characteristic of this country, and much use has been made of the Crump weir since it was invented in 1952.

The Crump weir is a versatile structure which has been used successfully on a wide range of rivers. The first one was installed on the River Tees in 1957 and is shown in figure 3.6, whilst there are now about seventy of these structures over the country. The Crump structure is essentially a horizontal weir which operates satisfactorily under high heads of water, and therefore can be used to measure the flow of large rivers. On the other hand, the crest can be divided into different levels, known as 'compounding', which allows a more accurate measurement of low flows. However, such compounding requires the construction of divide walls, which are somewhat unsightly and tend to collect floating debris during high flood flows, and a flat-vee weir has recently been developed from the original Crump profile in order to provide even greater sensitivity at low flows without the necessity of compounding. This type of structure, which is illustrated in figure 3.7, has been installed on several rivers in the last few years, either as a structure for the entire range of flows or as a low flow control at velocity-area stations.

Apart from the obstruction to the stream channel, the chief disadvantage of all control structures is that of cost, and there is no doubt that the majority of stations are of this type because of the absence of really large rivers in the United Kingdom. It has been claimed by Wilson (1965) that structures are only economic for catchments up to about 52 km^2 (20 sq miles) in area, although it is difficult to make such generalisations without reference to the nature of the available gauging sites and the range of flows to be catered for. Certainly the real need for more accurate low flow information is likely to lead to further expansion of gauging structures despite the ever-present dilemma of spending a fixed capital sum on either one highly accurate, and therefore expensive station, or perhaps two or three stations with a more limited performance. In theory the degree of accuracy at a gauging station can be as high as is required, although practical considerations frequently place some limit on this. Nevertheless, theoretical calibration for structures can now be achieved to within 2 per cent, whilst it is believed that an accuracy to within 8 per cent can be obtained on a single gauging which reduces to 1 per cent on total discharge (Wilson 1965).

In recent years, the dilution methods of river-gauging have become increasingly popular. These methods normally rely on the injection of a chemical tracer of known concentration into a river followed by measurements of the dilution that occurs at a suitable downstream sampling site. The tracer can be introduced either suddenly or at a constant rate, and the accuracy of the technique depends on a thorough mechanical mixing of the substance with the river water. Since the most efficient lateral mixing takes place in rocky, upland streams, it will be clear that these methods have applications at remote sites where it may be difficult to obtain records by other means. In the most favourable circumstances, dilution gauging probably provides the cheapest and most accurate instantaneous measurements of flow which can be achieved on small and medium-sized rivers. As a result, it has become widely used for the field calibration of structures.

It will be apparent from what has already been said that all continuous measurements of riverflow depend on an accurate determination of the head of water, and this is normally measured with a float recorder operating in a stilling well. Traditionally, recording has been achieved by a pen trace on a revolving drum. Although the advent of the punched tape recorder has released the hydrologist from much tedious chart analysis, it is still considered necessary to retain chart recorders, not only to provide a dual system of recording but also to give an immediate visual record of flow variations which may reveal some defect in the gauging system which otherwise could remain undetected for weeks until the tape is processed.

Mention has already been made of the late start made with the flow gauging network in Britain and in 1970 there were still only 560 stations in operation. Many of the existing stations have been established since the formation of the River Boards in 1950, and there is a lack of stations with a record sufficiently long for an accurate estimation of peak flood flows. Thus, even in 1965, prior to the inception of the hydrometric schemes in England and Wales, there were fewer than 400 stations in operation. It has been forecast by Sharp (1970) that this number will more than double to 800 or 900 by 1974 when the present hydrometric programme should be substantially complete, but it seems unlikely that the ultimate total for both permanent and special purpose stations will exceed 1500. Most of the stations will be equipped with punched-tape recorders and more than 80 per cent of the capital cost of the hydrometric schemes has been allocated to flow gauging with the remainder distributed between rainfall, evaporation and water quality instrumentation.

The logical development of a gauging network would firstly involve the measurement of the major rivers just above the tidal limit with the subsequent progression of gauges up the main stream and its tributaries until the further duplication of records provided no more useful information. However, in the earlier absence of a central body responsible for streamflow measurement, the network has developed haphazardly, and, largely because of the technical difficulty and expense of gauging major rivers, there has been a tendency, as shown in figure 3.8, to concentrate on sub-catchments within the main drainage basins of the country. In fact it has been shown by Boulton (1967*b*) that the observations for the river Thames at Teddington and the river Tees at Broken Scar are the only examples of stations measuring practically the whole flow from principal drainage basins in the country, and there is a real need for new stations on our larger rivers. There is also a concentration of gauging stations in the lowlands, and, although steps are being taken to rectify this imbalance, there are still hydraulic problems resulting from steep bed gradients and sediment accumulation which detract from accuracy at high level stations. These problems have been discussed by Harrison (1965) and Harrison and Owen (1967).

GROUNDWATER MEASUREMENT

True groundwater, as opposed to sub-surface moisture stored in the soil, is held within the saturated interstices of water-bearing rocks known as aquifers, and groundwater measurement attempts to assess the storage characteristics of such underground reservoirs. As in the case of evaporation, there are several methods suitable for the measurement of underground water resources, and the selection of one or more of these approaches depends mainly on the mode of occurrence of the water itself. Thus, although the general availability of groundwater is controlled by the prevailing climatic conditions, which determine the amount of water surplus existing at the surface and therefore the amount which is subsequently available to recharge aquifers by deep percolation, the detailed location and occurrence of groundwater depends on geological and topographical factors. In particular, these factors give rise to three different types of aquifer.

In an *unconfined* aquifer the upper level of the stored water is represented by the phreatic water-table as shown in figure 3.9, and this water-level rises and falls in response to net recharge or discharge of the aquifer. In fairly uniform strata, without marked lithological

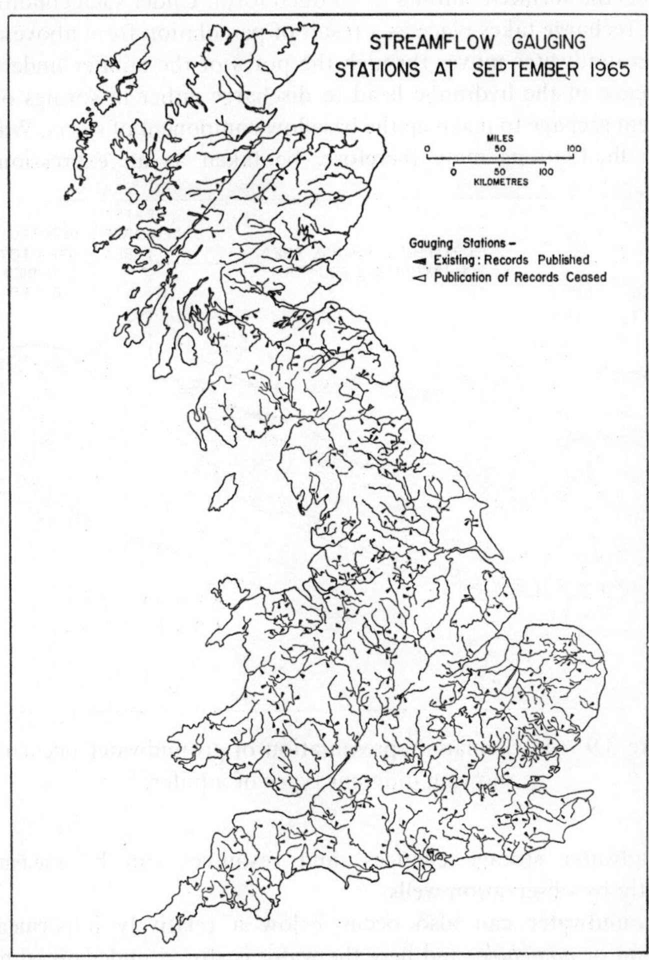

Figure 3.8 The distribution of streamflow gauging stations in September 1965, before the inception of the River Authority hydrometric schemes. After *Surface Water Year Book of Great Britain* (Supplement) 1965.

or structural complications, the water-table will assume a form which reflects the surface contours in subdued form. Under such conditions most recharge takes place as a result of percolation from above, and the groundwater moves through the pores of the aquifer under the influence of the hydraulic head to discharge either in springs or as effluent seepage to make up the baseflow component of rivers. Water-table fluctuations may, therefore, be taken as an expression of

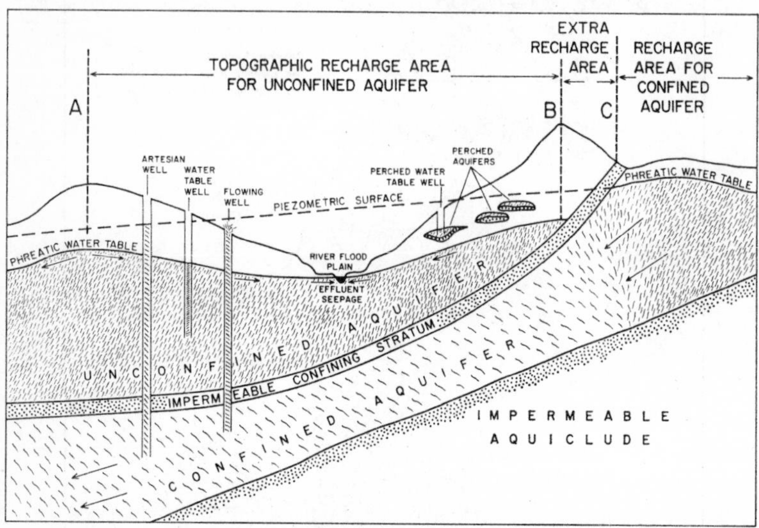

Figure 3.9 A schematic representation of groundwater occurrence showing different types of aquifer.

groundwater storage changes, and resources can be measured directly by observation wells.

Groundwater can also occur below a relatively impermeable stratum or *aquiclude*, and here the water is stored under pressure in a *confined* or *artesian* aquifer. In this case the impermeable overlying rock rules out the possibility of much direct recharge from above, and the natural recharge area for a confined aquifer may be many miles away where the water-bearing rocks come to the surface as depicted in figure 3.9. The water-table in the recharge area represents the hydrostatic pressure level to which, in theory, the confined water would rise if released. If the confining stratum is pierced by a well or borehole the water will rise to an elevation represented by the *piezometric surface*, which is the projected level of water in the recharge area. In such an artesian well the water-level may rise considerably higher than the phreatic water-table, and, if the piezometric surface lies above ground-level at that point, the well will flow continuously. Fluctuations of piezometric level cannot be used as a direct index of underground storage change, and, confined aquifers often serve mainly as transmission links between major recharge and discharge areas. Where fluctuations do occur they are usually in

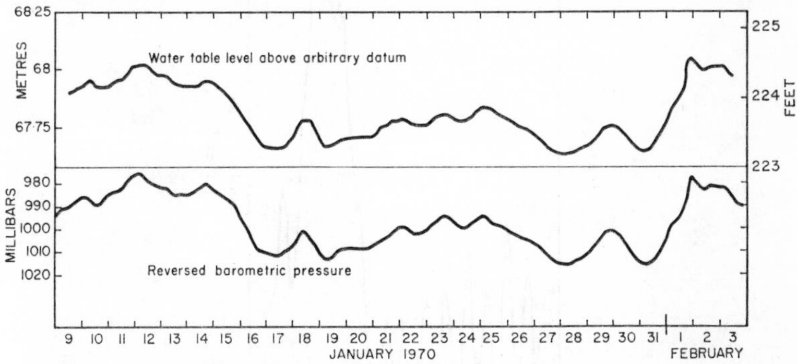

Figure 3.10 The relationship between reversed barometric pressure and water-table fluctuations in a confined aquifer near Berwick-on-Tweed during part of January and February 1970. (Based on data supplied by the Northumbrian River Authority.)

response to changes in the pressure loading at the ground surface which are then absorbed by the aquifer. To a limited extent such pressure changes will be mirrored in the phreatic water-table, but in a confined aquifer, where the water is stored under hydrostatic pressure greater than that exerted by the atmosphere, conditions are much more elastic and fluctuations of piezometric level are due almost entirely to such external factors. Variations in atmospheric pressure are one of the most common explanations for changes in piezometric level, and this inverse relationship between barometric pressure and piezometric level is shown in figure 3.10 for a sandstone aquifer which is confined by younger shales and drift deposits.

The third type of groundwater storage is caused by a *perched* aquifer which usually occurs when fragments or lenses of impermeable strata are found above the phreatic water-table and support shallow localised water bodies. Theoretically, true water-table conditions apply in such aquifers and observation wells should record direct changes in water storage, but the total storage capacity of such

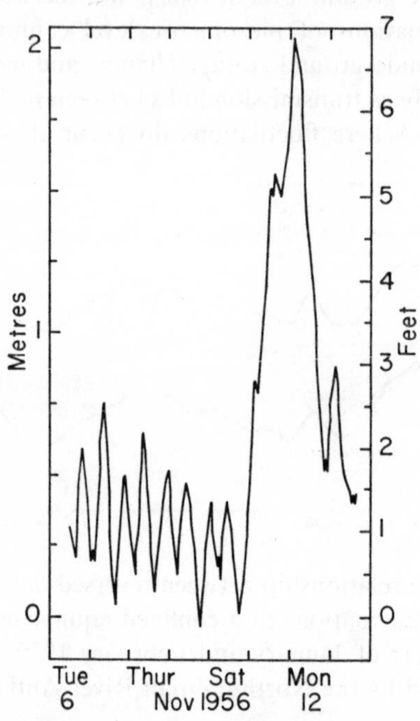

Figure 3.11 A weekly hydrograph for a chalk borehole near Grimsby showing the effects of tidal loading and industrial abstraction on a confined aquifer. After Gray (1964). Crown Copyright Reserved.

aquifers is generally so small that water-table fluctuations may have little relevance for the main unconfined aquifer below.

It will be clear that a record of observed rest water-levels in wells can be difficult to interpret, especially for confined aquifers. Other complications result from the fact that there are few wells in Britain which have been sunk purely for observational purposes, and most wells are either used for supply purposes themselves or are within an area where the water-table may be artificially depressed by pumping nearby. Figure 3.11 shows an autographic weekly hydrograph for a borehole in the Lincolnshire chalk near Grimsby which illustrates some of the problems in interpreting a well hydrograph. At this point the chalk is confined, and the regular oscillations which dominate the record from the start of the period are caused by the pressure effect of tides (Gray 1964*a*). Superimposed on these diurnal fluctuations is an overall decline in water-level associated with industrial abstractions during the working week, and the largest fluctuation in the period is caused by the rapid recovery of rest water-level which occurs over the weekend.

Past responsibility for groundwater observations has been divided between water supply interests and the Water Department of the Geological Survey, and, until recently, there was no attempt to establish a planned network of observation wells. Surprisingly, no specific mention of rest water-levels was made by the Water Resources Act in connection with the hydrometric schemes, but encouragement has been given to the River Authorities in this respect by the Water Resources Board which has assumed responsibility for the systematic monitoring of groundwater on a national scale.

An account of the groundwater network over the United Kingdom was presented by Ineson (1966). This showed that returns from about 600 observation wells were being received by the Water Resources Board, although this total could double by 1975. In most cases, measurements are obtained manually at fixed time intervals of one month or less, but in 1966 autographic records from float-operated instruments similar to those used for river level were maintained at 113 known sites in England. Gray (1964*b*) has described some of the equipment used for monitoring groundwater levels.

The vast majority of groundwater measurements are made in south-east England, and the distribution of observation wells is biased towards the chalk, which has about three-quarters of the total records. Thus, in 1966, whilst sixty-one automatic water-level recorders were located over the chalk outcrop with a further twenty-three placed where the chalk is concealed by younger deposits, there were only four such instruments sited over the Triassic sandstones which comprise the next most important aquifer. Another feature of the groundwater observation network is that since most of the wells were originally sunk for supply purposes, they mainly occupy valley sites and there is a consequent relative lack of information for the higher, wetter areas where most of the recharge takes place.

Indirect point measurements of groundwater can be made either by measuring spring flow or by observing the drainage through percolation gauges. Most variations in the flow of gravity springs,

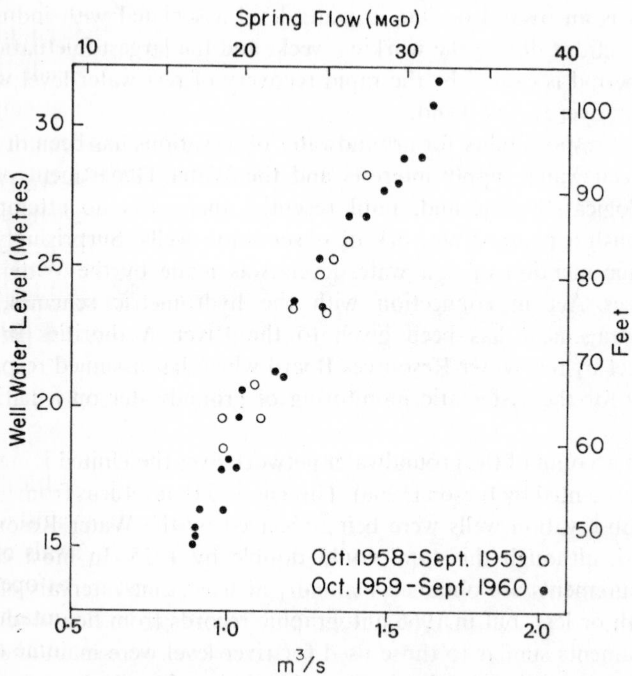

Figure 3.12 The correlation between rest water-levels and the discharge from springs for an unconfined aquifer in the Hampshire chalk. After Ineson and Downing (1964).

as opposed to artesian flows, occur in response to storage changes in the aquifer which the spring is draining, and figure 3.12 indicates the linear relationship between rest water-levels in the Hampshire chalk and the discharge from springs in the same catchment for a two-year period. On the other hand, this method is limited by the distribution of natural springs and there may also be a considerable time-lag between water-table change and the spring flow response, especially if the recharge and discharge points are some distance apart. For this reason percolation gauges have been used. In this method surplus water draining through the soil-filled gauge is assumed to continue draining down through the ground until it reaches and recharges the water-table. This method appears reasonably reliable for highly permeable areas, but there is some evidence to suggest that it can lead to an over-estimate of recharge in areas where a greater proportion of precipitation enters more directly into streamflow (Smith 1966).

A method designed to overcome the general problems associated with point samples of groundwater conditions is that of the water balance where information on precipitation and evaporation can be used to compute areal recharge and discharge for an aquifer. The basic principles of this method are considered in chapter 4, but mention must be made of a special problem relating to groundwater assessment created by the lack of coincidence which sometimes occurs between a surface catchment and the under-lying aquifer. By reference to figure 3.9, it can be seen that while the area between the surface summits at A and B represents the contributory catchment for surface drainage, the total groundwater divide stretches between A and C since some precipitation falling between B and C will infiltrate at the surface catchment. Similar underground leakage between catchments will take place as water is transmitted down the dip of the confined aquifer, and will, therefore, be lost to the recharge area. In such circumstances it is frequently difficult to decide for which surface area a water balance calculation should be made, and, for example, the contributory groundwater catchment of the river Itchen in Hampshire has been estimated by Ineson and Downing (1964) to be 22 per cent larger than the gauged surface drainage basin.

4 An Outline of British Hydrology

The broad upper limit of water resource availability is determined by the balance which is struck in any area between the incoming precipitation and the demands which are made upon it by evaporation and transpiration from natural surfaces. An appreciation of these elements in both space and time is, therefore, necessary before we consider the nature of the utilisable water in rivers and aquifers later in the chapter.

PRECIPITATION, EVAPORATION AND THE WATER BALANCE

Precipitation

Precipitation is probably the most variable hydrological element and shows considerable fluctuations on various scales of both time and distance. In terms of mean annual values it varies from about 500 mm (20 in.) around the estuarine coast of the Thames up to almost 5000 mm (200 in.) on exposed slopes in parts of north-west Scotland, the Lake District and Snowdonia. Although these extreme totals are confined to relatively small areas, as indicated in figure 4.1, they emphasise the important effect of local conditions, particularly relief, on regional values. Altitude is undoubtedly the major control and an 'index of raininess', calculated as the product of mean annual values and the number of days on which rain falls, reveals an increase over sea level totals by 8 per cent for every 30 m (100 ft) of elevation (Lamb 1964). This general increase varies, however, according to the orientation of slopes and their distance from the western seaboard, and figure 4.2 illustrates the considerable scatter which exists between elevation and mean annual precipitation in the Gwynedd and Dee and Clwyd River Authority areas in North Wales. Especially steep increases of precipitation with altitude may be related to slopes exposed to the prevailing winds from the Atlantic, and Lacy (1951) has shown that the volume of rain received from the south-west exceeds that coming from the north, which is the driest direction, in the ratio of 4:1. This fact, together with the displacement of our major upland massifs towards the west coast, results in much larger precipitation totals to the west and north, and the highest recorded precipitation received during a calendar year rests with Sprinkling Tarn in Cumberland where 6530 mm (257 in.) fell in 1954.

Mean annual rainfall is, however, something of a fiction. In order to have a finite period of manageable length, precipitation records are usually averaged over periods of 35 years in length, and in this country we now have two such Standard Periods from 1881 to 1915 and 1916 to 1950. Over the country as a whole the second period was some 4 per cent wetter than the first, whilst in parts of Scotland the increase was as much as 14 per cent (Bleasdale *et al.* 1963). This clearly raises a problem with regard to the standardisation of data and the extent to which uncertainty must always be present in estimates of water resources due to the natural variability of so-called 'average' rainfall.

In any one year the rainfall may vary from over 150 per cent of the mean to less than 60 per cent of this value, although in more than 50 per cent of all years the fluctuation will be within ±10 per cent. The variation of annual precipitation about the mean has an almost Normal statistical distribution, but the occasional very wet years are balanced by a slightly greater number of years with below average totals. In Britain, with the necessity for some over-seasonal water storage from winter to summer, it is customary for the water supply industry to calculate the capacity of impounding reservoirs to cope with the three driest consecutive years, and it is generally assumed that annual rainfall over this period will not average less than 80 per cent of the long-term mean (Glasspoole 1924).

Another important feature of rainfall variability is its lack of uniformity over the country and there is a marked tendency for variability to decrease towards the north and west. This feature is thought to reflect the diminished role of 'continentality' in these areas, and the percentage coefficient of variation of annual rainfall changes from as low as 8 per cent in Northern Ireland to over 18 per cent in parts of central and southern England. From the viewpoint of water resources, this means that rainfall is least reliable in the low

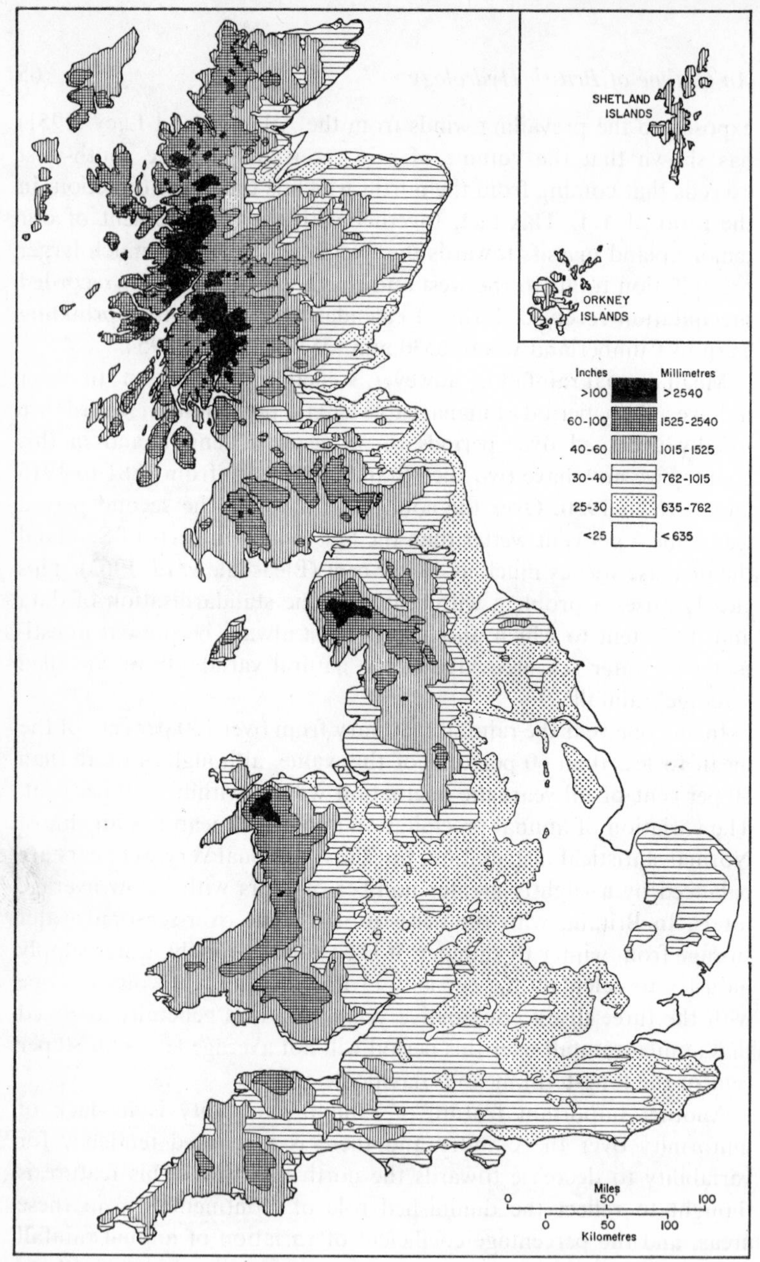

Figure 4.1 Mean annual precipitation over Britain, 1916–1950. Based on Ordnance Survey 1/625 000 rainfall map, prepared in 1967 by Ministry of Housing and Local Government. Crown Copyright Reserved.

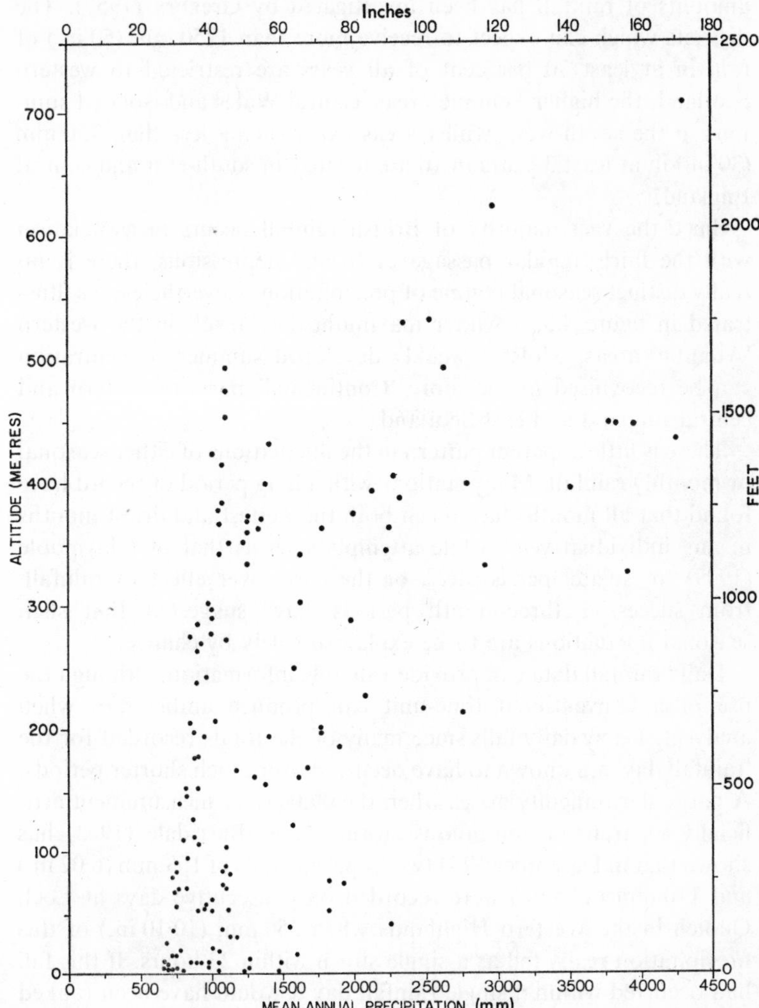

Figure 4.2 The relationship between altitude and mean annual precipitation over the Gwynedd and Dee and Clwyd River Authority areas in North Wales.

rainfall areas, and the probability of different areas receiving given amounts of rainfall has been investigated by Gregory (1957). The districts which can expect to receive more than 1250 mm (50 in.) of rain in at least 70 per cent of all years are restricted to western Scotland, the higher Pennine areas, central Wales and isolated summits in the south-west, whilst areas experiencing less than 750 mm (30 in.) in at least 3 years in 10 are located in south-east and central England.

Since the vast majority of British rainfall occurs in association with the fairly regular passage of frontal depressions, there is no really distinct seasonal regime of precipitation. Nevertheless, as illustrated in figure 4.3, a winter maximum does result in the western 'Atlantic' areas, whilst a weakly developed summer concentration can be recognised in the more 'Continental' parts of eastern and central England and east Scotland.

There is little apparent pattern in the fluctuations of either seasonal or monthly rainfall. Many stations with a long period of record have found that all months have been both the wettest and driest months in any individual year, while attempts such as that of Glasspoole (1949) to isolate 'persistence', or the carry-over effect of rainfall, from successive three-month periods have suggested that such seasonal fluctuations are to be explained solely by chance.

Daily rainfall data can provide valuable information, although the use of a conventional time-unit can produce ambiguities when analysing heavy daily falls since many of the totals recorded for the 'rainfall day' are known to have occurred over much shorter periods. A particular difficulty arises when the 09.00 GMT measurement artificially separates a continuous storm. Thus, Bleasdale (1963) has shown that in December 1954 two 'separate' falls of 153 mm (6·02 in.) and 110 mm (4·35 in.) were recorded on consecutive days at Loch Quoich in the Western Highlands when 256 mm (10·10 in.) of this precipitation really fell as a single storm within 23 hours. If this fall had occurred within a single rainfall day it would have been ranked second only to the daily record for the UK of 280 mm (11·00 in.) which was recorded at Martinstown, Dorset on 18 July 1955.

Bleasdale (1963) has also demonstrated that there are very few places in Britain where a daily fall of at least 102 mm (4 in.) has not been recorded over the past 100 years, and it is unlikely that any area is totally immune from such an event. In the period 1863 to 1960 over

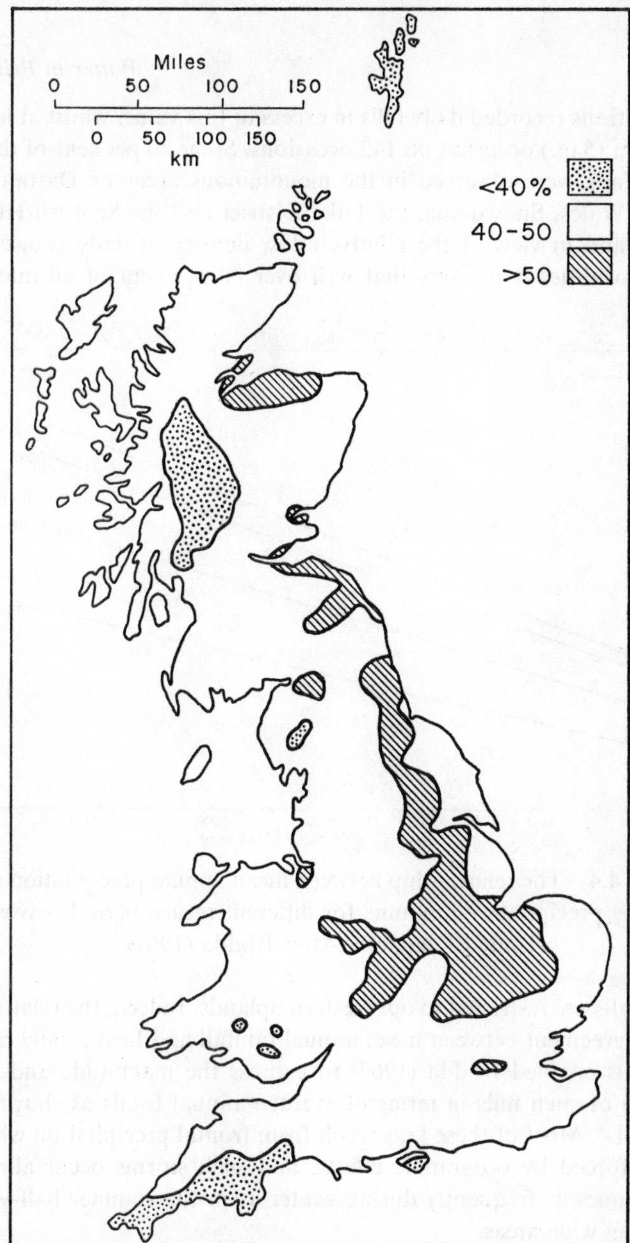

Figure 4.3 The proportion of the mean annual precipitation 1916–1950 which occurred during the summer half-year. Based on Ordnance Survey 1/625 000 rainfall map, prepared in 1967 by Ministry of Housing and Local Government. Crown Copyright Reserved.

450 stations recorded daily falls in excess of this value, whilst at least 127 mm (5 in.) occurred on 142 occasions. Some 70 per cent of these latter falls were observed in the mountainous areas of Dartmoor, South Wales, Snowdonia, the Lake District and the Scottish Highlands, and in view of the relatively low density of daily gauges in these localities it is likely that well over 80 per cent of all intense

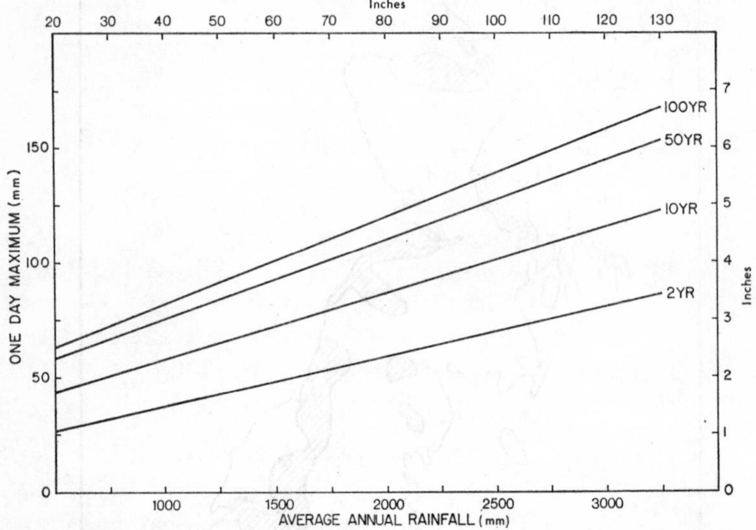

Figure 4.4 The relationship between mean annual precipitation and one-day precipitation amounts for different return periods over the United Kingdom. After Rodda (1967).

daily falls are restricted to our western uplands. Indeed, the relatively close agreement between mean annual rainfall and heavy daily rainfalls has enabled Rodda (1967) to express the magnitude and frequency of such falls in terms of average annual totals as shown in figure 4.4. Most of these falls result from frontal precipitation which is reinforced by orographic effects, and such storms occur almost three times as frequently during winter as in the summer half-year affecting wide areas.

By comparison the remaining heavy falls show a decided summer concentration. They are largely confined to the low rainfall zone along the east coast of Britain, and are usually associated with thunderstorm activity. On the other hand, the highest daily falls on record of 229 mm (9 in.) or more have all occurred in either Somerset or Dorset, and show the marked tendency which exists for summer cloudbursts in south-west England.

Snow plays a regular seasonal role in British hydrology only in the Scottish Highlands where a snow cover lasts for an average of more than 100 days in the year. In restricted upper parts of this area there is a gradual accumulation of snow through the winter months which is finally released in a few snow-melt floods during spring, but in most other parts of Britain this pattern becomes at least partially obscured by alternate snowfalls and melt periods resulting from the rapidly changing weather conditions which are typical of winter. The frequency of snow is controlled even more than that of rainfall by altitude, although the influence of latitude goes some way towards explaining the importance of snow hydrology in the Grampians. Similarly, extensive areas of the Southern Uplands and the Northern Pennines have snow lying for more than 30 days each year compared with the equivalent altitudes in Wales which have much lower values. In the lowlands the frequency of snowfall usually exceeds the number of days with snow lying, but, as a result of lower temperatures and larger initial accumulations, the reverse applies in the uplands.

Evaporation

It will be apparent from what has already been stated in chapter 3 that the amounts of evaporation recorded over the country will vary according to which method of estimation is employed. In the absence of any adequate tank or lysimeter networks, nationwide cover exists only for calculations derived from meteorological formulae, although there has been an attempt to map PE values obtained from evapotranspirometers by Green (1970). As shown in figure 4.5, mean annual values of potential evapotranspiration based on Penman's method indicate an overall range from 356 mm (14 in.) in the Shetland Isles to more than 584 mm (23 in.) in the Scillies. It can be seen that the broad latitudinal decrease from north to south is occasionally interrupted by relief, although the thin scatter of upland stations makes the map somewhat provisional in the higher areas.

In contrast to precipitation, there is a very definite seasonal concentration of PE. Penman values in particular show rapid increases in spring, and over 80 per cent of the annual amount is recorded in the

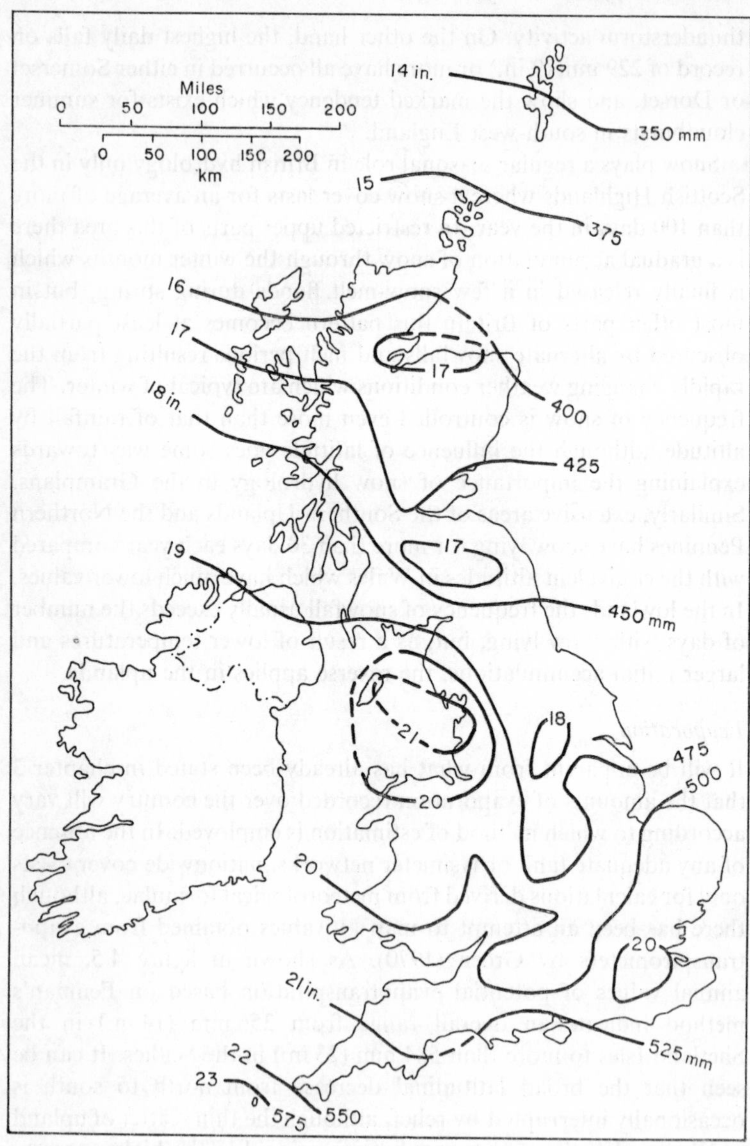

Figure 4.5 Mean annual potential evapotranspiration. (Compiled from data in *Irrigation*, Bulletin No. 138 of Ministry of Agriculture, Fisheries and Food, H.M.S.O., 1962.)

summer months of June, July and August. PE is one of the most reliable hydrological elements, and this steadiness compensates to some extent for the uncertainties involved in measurement. There are few published data relating to the long-term variation of evaporation, but a study of monthly values over a 26-year period by Smith (1964) showed a maximum annual deviation of 20 per cent from the Penman mean.

Until recently there have been few attempts to assess the degree of reliability of the other methods of evaporation estimation, but a comprehensive survey by Holland (1967) indicates that there is a discrepancy of about 102 mm (4 in.) between the mean annual regional values of open water evaporation recorded by two groups of Meteorological Office tanks. There is some evidence to suggest that these tanks are measuring virtually the same atmospheric conditions as represented by PE, and there is a good agreement between the 'high value' stations and local Penman estimates. As one might expect, direct open water measurements show more variation than the Penman method since a body of water fully exposed to the atmosphere will be more sensitive than estimates based on selected meteorological parameters, and the maximum range of variation of the tank values is probably double that of the Penman formula.

Even more discrepancies are apparent in the regional estimates of actual evaporation obtained by residual methods using either lysimeters or river basins, and in the case of tanks or percolation gauges the question of exposure appears critical. It may well be that some of the errors are due to an under-estimation of precipitation at certain sites which, in turn, will lead to an under-estimation of evaporation.

The Water Balance

An appreciation of the water balance is fundamental to water resource studies, and the budget method is being used increasingly to help solve problems in applied hydrology such as the estimation of changes in groundwater storage, the detailed scheduling of irrigation need and as an index in runoff forecasting. The basic principles date back to 1948 when the American climatologist C. W. Thornthwaite devised his method of calculating PE from temperature data and then employed the interplay between precipitation and PE as a guide to the relative 'wetness' or 'dryness' of a place (Thornthwaite 1948).

The simplest way to keep a water budget would be to calculate the arithmetical difference, either positive or negative, between precipitation and PE for certain periods, such as a month, throughout the year. This would be quite successful for the winter months when the cumulative excess of precipitation over PE represents the seasonal water surplus, but in the months when PE is greater than rainfall the 'water deficiency' is not necessarily the overall amount by which precipitation falls short of PE. This is because growing plants are able to draw on a limited amount of soil water which is stored within the root range of the vegetation. The amount of soil water available to the plant is variable. It depends on such factors as soil texture and the depth and efficiency of the plant rooting systems, but Thornthwaite overcame this by adopting the simplifying assumption that a total of 102 mm (4 in.) of soil water could be withdrawn by plants. Thornthwaite also assumed that the whole of this water could be withdrawn at the potential rate of evapotranspiration, so that PE could continue uninterrupted until the 102 mm of soil storage had been exhausted, at which point PE would be replaced by a lower rate of actual evaporation which would be restricted to the amounts of incoming rainfall. Under such a system a true water deficit would only exist when all soil moisture storage had been utilised, whilst any such utilisation would require replacement later in the year before excess precipitation could produce a seasonal water surplus.

Thornthwaite's method is illustrated in table 2 and figure 4.6 for Harrogate in West Yorkshire which has been selected because its water budget is similar to the mean conditions for England and Wales. Soils are at field capacity at the beginning of the calendar year, and rainfall continues to exceed PE until May, when a soil moisture deficit starts to build up as PE then exceeds rainfall through to September inclusive. Until early August the soil water storage is drawn upon to maintain evapotranspiration at the potential rate, but in August and September this storage becomes exhausted and the actual evapotranspiration rate sets in. With the onset of rainfall exceeding PE in October the existing soil moisture deficit is progressively eliminated but does not finally disappear until early December when a water surplus occurs.

The assumptions contained in Thornthwaite's model regarding soil moisture have been queried by other workers, especially those who believe that, as the soil moisture deficit is built up, there is a decreasing availability of water as plants find it more and more difficult to extract water from the drying soil. Penman (1949) advanced a modified concept based on an average *root constant* for certain vegetation types. Penman's root constant represents the mean depth to which rooting systems penetrate and also the depth to which water can be abstracted from the soil at the potential rate, whilst below the root constant water becomes less easily available as actual evapotranspiration falls below the potential rate. On the basis of experiments with

TABLE 2

WATER BALANCE AT HARROGATE ACCORDING TO THE THORNTHWAITE AND PENMAN METHODS (MM)

Thornthwaite	J	F	M	A	M	J		A	S	O	N	D	Year
PE.	8	10	25	42	70	95	110	97	68	42	21	12	600
Rainfall	80	62	49	53	62	51	72	74	63	75	79	71	791
Storage change	0	0	0	0	−8	−44	−38	−12	0	+33	+58	+11	
Storage	102	102	102	102	94	50	12	0	0	33	91	102	
Soil moisture deficiency	0	0	0	0	8	52	90	102	102	69	11	0	
Water deficiency	0	0	0	0	0	0	0	12	5	0	0	0	
Water surplus	72	52	24	11	0	0	0	0	0	0	0	49	208

Penman	J	F	M	A	M	J	J	A	S	O	N	D	Year
PE	4	8	29	46	72	86	84	70	41	18	4	3	465
Rainfall	80	62	49	53	62	51	72	74	63	75	79	71	791
Storage change	0	0	0	0	−10	−35	−12	+4	+22	+31	0	0	
Storage	76	76	76	76	66	31	19	23	45	76	0	0	
Soil moisture deficiency	0	0	0	0	10	45	57	53	31	0	0	0	
Water deficiency	0	0	0	0	0	0	0	0	0	0	0	0	0
Water surplus	76	54	20	7	0	0	0	0	0	26	75	68	326

soil drying curves, Penman argued that, in practice, about another 25 mm (1 in.) of water can be abstracted fairly easily below the root constant, but beyond this point there is increasing divergence between actual and potential evaporation.

Since it has been claimed by Penman that a root constant of 76 mm (3 in.) is representative of shallow rooted vegetation such as grass, the Penman water budget will be similar to Thornthwaite's during the early build up of a soil moisture deficit but differs in that a deficit can be extended beyond 102 mm (4 in.). This is a more realistic

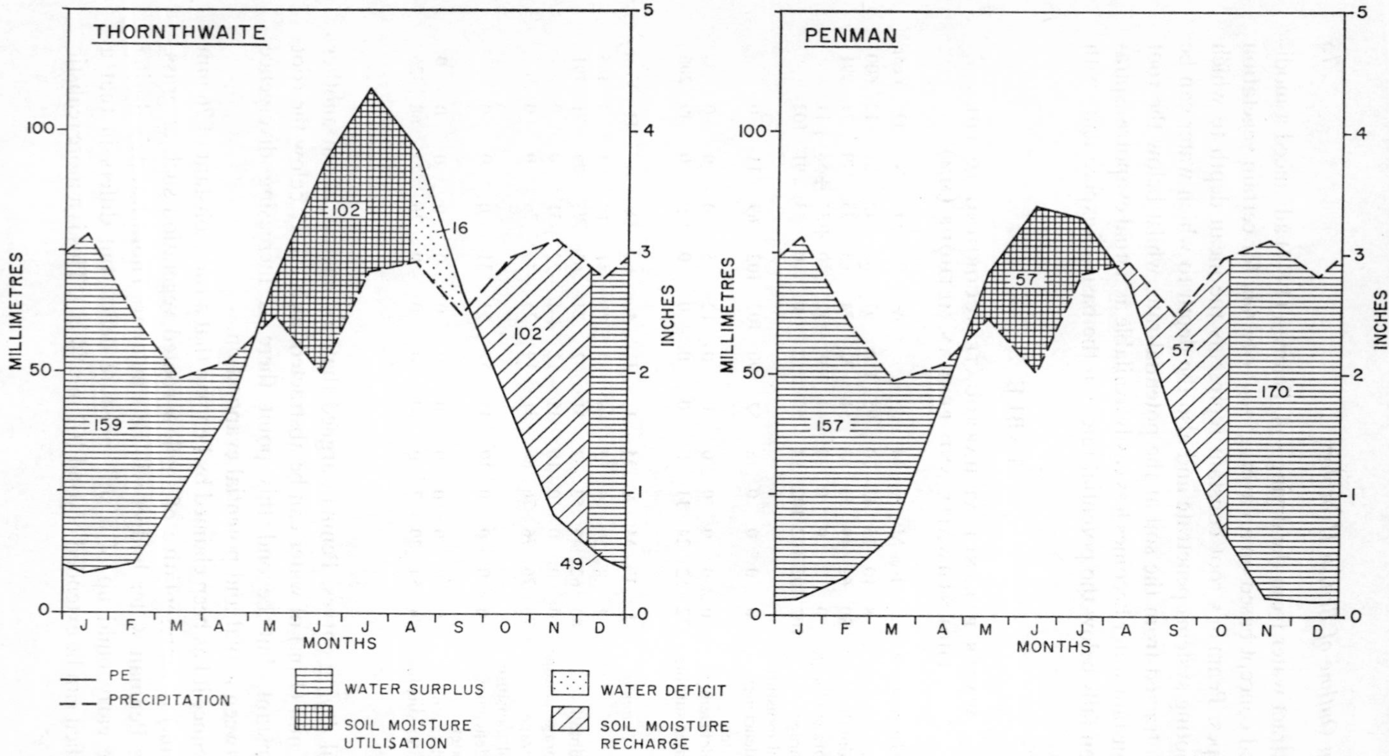

Figure 4.6 Mean monthly water budget (mm) for Harrogate, West Yorkshire, computed according to the Thornthwaite and Penman methods

concept which is made even more appropriate because Penman's PE values are lower than Thornthwaite's and much closer to evaporation conditions in the British Isles. Thus, taking the Harrogate example once again, it can be seen from table 2 and figure 4.6 that Penman's method produces a maximum soil moisture deficit of only 57 mm (2·26 in.) and a true water deficiency does not arise, largely because the calculated PE values are over 127 mm (5 in.) less than the Thornthwaite estimates over the course of the year.

Despite the success which has been achieved with Penman's method, there are certain limitations which can be recognised. Firstly, there is the natural variation in root constants which Penman (1950) tried to cater for by averaging over river basins and assuming that 50 per cent of the area is grass (root constant 76 mm), 30 per cent long-rooted vegetation (root constant 203 mm) and 20 per cent of the area riparian and therefore able to draw continuously on ample supplies of shallow groundwater. Clearly this generalisation will not hold good in all cases, and there can be few catchments in this country which have the extensive flood plain conditions necessary for the riparian requirement.

An entirely separate problem is caused by working out the water budget for monthly periods, because nowhere in Britain does PE not exceed rainfall for at least a few days in summer. This means that a monthly water surplus may result from heavy rainfall concentrated on a few wet days and therefore any monthly deficits are likely to under-estimate the real deficiency by artificially smoothing the rainfall over the calendar period.

There are considerable variations from the mean water budget in individual months or years since a change to relatively warm, dry weather means low rainfall and high PE demands whilst unsettled weather produces the reverse effect, but even average conditions show great contrasts over the country. For example, Margate in north-east Kent is one of the driest places in Britain where, as shown by figure 4.7, PE exceeds rainfall from March to August inclusive and a soil water deficit of 118 mm (4·63 in.) is not eliminated until December. At the other end of the scale, Loch Quoich in the Western Highlands has an excess of precipitation in all months and a water surplus all year round.

These relationships have been mapped by Green (1964), but figure 4.8 is somewhat simplified since it assumes no limit to soil moisture

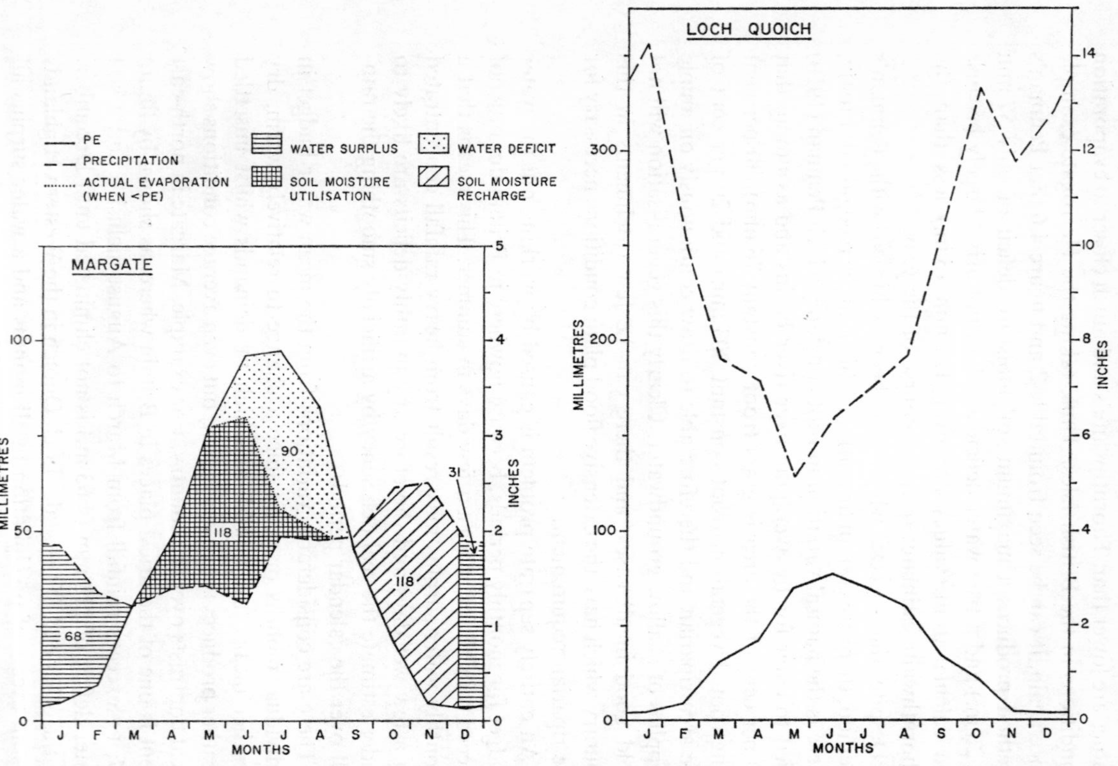

Figure 4.7 Mean monthly water budget (mm) for Margate and Loch Quoich according to the Penman method

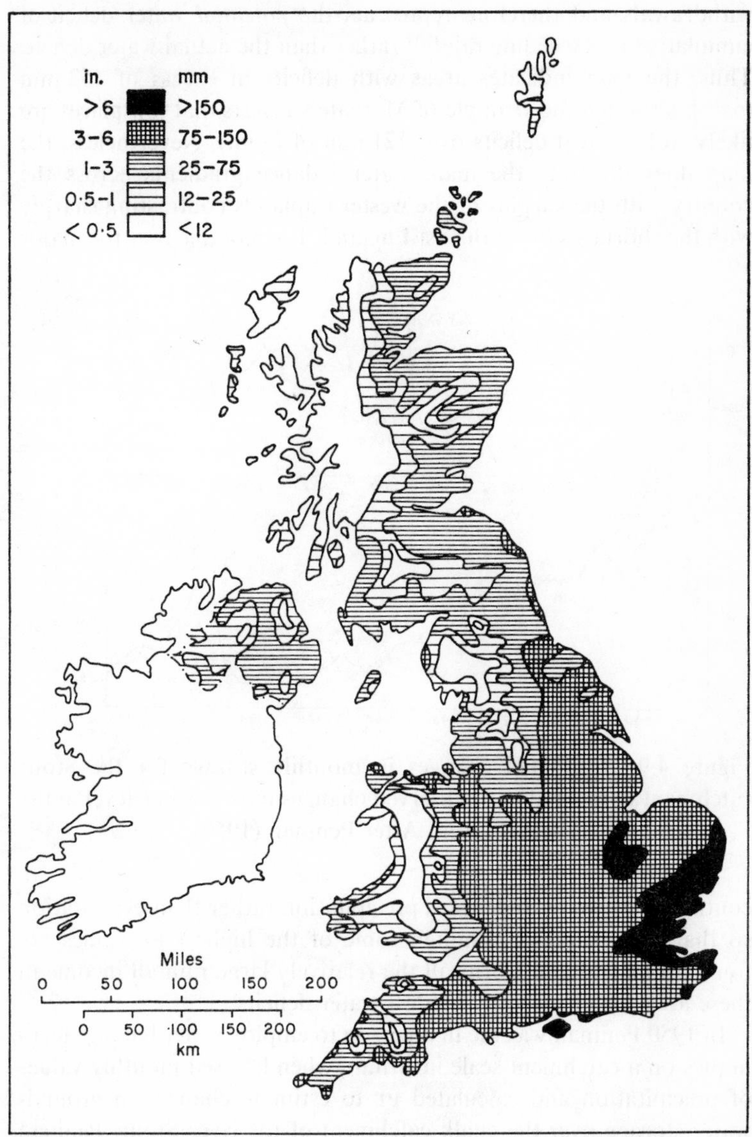

Figure 4.8 Mean annual potential soil moisture deficit over the British Isles. After Green (1964).

withdrawals and therefore represents the *potential* water deficit of cumulative PE exceeding rainfall rather than the actual water deficit. Thus, the map indicates areas with deficits in excess of 152 mm (6 in.), although the example of Margate suggests that few places are likely to have real deficits over 121 mm (4·75 in.). Nevertheless, the map does illustrate the main water balance gradients across the country with the surplus of the western uplands contrasting sharply with the shortages in south-east England. It is notable that the major

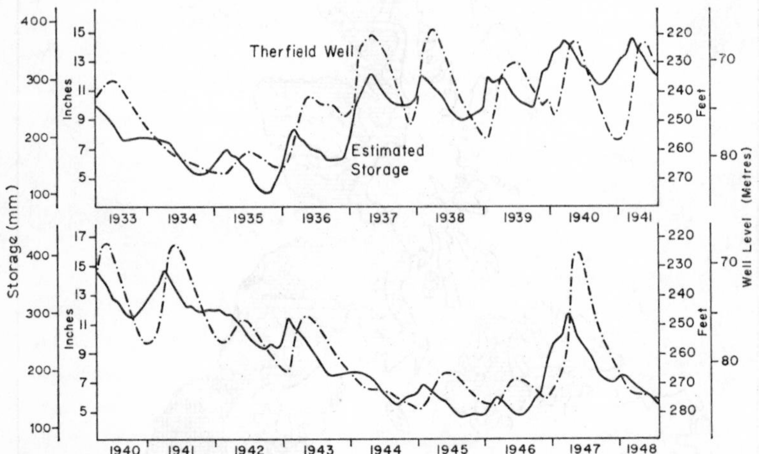

Figure 4.9 Estimated changes in monthly storage for the Stour catchment compared with observed changes in rest water-level in the Therfield well. After Penman (1950).

control of the water balance is precipitation rather than evaporation so that, for example, although some of the highest PE values are found in Devon and Cornwall the relatively large rainfall income in these areas results in only modest water deficits.

In 1950 Penman was the first person to employ water balance techniques on a catchment scale in Britain when he used monthly values of precipitation and calculated PE to estimate changes in groundwater storage over the chalk catchment of the river Stour. Penman was able to compare his estimates of storage with monthly restwater levels in an observation well, and the correspondence over a 16-year period is shown in figure 4.9. The seasonal fluctuations and overall trend of estimated storage are reflected in the well level fluctuations, although there is a slight difference in detailed phasing owing to the delayed response of the water-table to surface events. Subsequently, more sophisticated catchment water balances have been attempted based on a more comprehensive measurement of all phases of the hydrological cycle. A recent example relates to a largely clay catchment on the Holderness Plain of East Yorkshire (Pegg and Ward 1971).

In the dry summer of 1959, Grindley (1960) used the Penman water balance method to calculate the build-up of soil moisture deficit at 73 stations over the United Kingdom in an attempt to predict the elimination of the deficit and the subsequent date when the first sustained increase in runoff was likely to occur in the autumn. Partly as a result of the success of this exercise, the Meteorological Office in 1962 began to make routine calculations of soil moisture deficit for 176 representative stations in Britain, and data are issued in map form at regular intervals to interested organisations (Grindley 1967). The information is used by River Authorities as an aid to flood warning. Water engineers also want to know the likely lag between the first rainfall that ends a dry spell and the start of appreciable runoff, since this can help in the management of reservoir storage and water supplies. An increasing proportion of the farming community is similarly concerned with information on soil moisture conditions, and a precise knowledge of soil moisture deficits provides direct information on the amount of irrigation water which is necessary to bring soils up to field capacity and thus ensure the maximisation of field crop yields.

GROUNDWATER AND STREAMFLOW

Physical Relationships

Groundwater and streamflow are considered together in this section for several reasons. In the first place, they both represent the surplus water arising from the interplay of precipitation and evaporation, and, therefore, complement the above discussion of the water balance. Secondly, these two phases of the hydrological cycle provide the only opportunities for direct exploitation, and so groundwater and streamflow are both utilisable sources of water. The final justification arises from the fact that, although underground and surface waters are often discussed separately for convenience, it is usually most difficult to make a meaningful distinction between them, and there is little doubt that many future developments in water conservation will depend on a greater awareness of the relationships between groundwater and riverflow.

Although all streamflow can ultimately be traced back to precipitation, the volume of water occupying a river channel at any particular moment in time may be derived from a complex series of intermediate sources. After a period of rain the volume of streamflow will increase, and the nature of the resulting storm hydrograph will be closely related to the characteristics of the precipitation. The major component will probably be obtained from fairly intense rain falling in excess of the infiltration capacity of the catchment. Guided by microtopography, this water will make its way by *overland flow* to the nearest accessible watercourse. In addition, some of the rain which does infiltrate below the surface may meet a relatively impermeable horizon, either in the upper soil layers or in the rock mantle, and this water will then move laterally as *interflow* to appear as runoff in a stream channel only a short time after overland flow. During the winter a not dissimilar runoff contribution may result from melting snow, although the exact role of snowmelt is frequently obscured by rain falling at the same time.

Such events are essentially intermittent, depending more or less directly on heavy precipitation, and even with the regular incidence of rainfall in this country would be insufficient to support rivers throughout the year. In dry spells, therefore, runoff is maintained by *baseflow*, which represents the gravity discharge of groundwater to river channels by *effluent seepage*. As shown in figure 3.9, effluent seepage occurs where the stream intersects the water-table. Water will continue to be released slowly from the aquifer to streams as long as the hydraulic gradient is inclined down to the river, and the rate of groundwater discharge will be partially controlled by the slope of the water-table. Effluent seepage is characteristic of most British rivers and is largely responsible for their perennial flow, but, in a few instances, a stream may lie above the water-table which is then itself recharged by *influent seepage* through the bed and channel of the river. A more common, temporary type of influent seepage occurs after a rapid rise in river level following a storm when the hydraulic gradient immediately adjacent to the river is reversed, and for a time the river will be adding to the *bank storage* held mainly in the alluvial deposits flanking the valley sides.

Since baseflow is dependent on water-table conditions, it follows that the proportion of baseflow in total discharge at any time can be obtained from suitable well records. Unfortunately, there are few catchments with a sufficiently developed network of observation wells for such analysis, and baseflow is normally isolated from direct runoff by graphical methods. It has been known for many years that, in general, baseflow recession is exponential in form and therefore produces a straight line when plotted on semi-logarithmic graph paper. This means that for rain-free periods, after surface runoff and interflow have made their contributions, the river hydrograph will assume a linear pattern which represents the upper limit of the groundwater component. There are many problems involved in applying this technique, not least in Britain where the high frequency of rainfall tends to obscure the relationship even during the summer months, but, as shown in figure 4.10, it is usually possible to detect a series of clear recession periods from which the position of the line indicating the baseflow contribution can be interpolated.

Groundwater

As indicated in chapter 3, the occurrence of groundwater depends not only on the existence of a water surplus to recharge the continuous natural depletion of aquifers taking place through spring flow and effluent seepage, but also on the location and nature of the water-bearing strata themselves. Accordingly, following a brief discussion of the water balance aspects of groundwater, reference will be made to the principal British aquifers in order to show the importance of geological condition for groundwater behaviour and utilisation.

Deep aquifers act as large underground reservoirs, and although water-table conditions reflect the water budget situation prevailing at the surface, the response is delayed and smoothed compared with streamflow fluctuations. Over a long period, restwater levels can provide evidence of climatic variations. Thus, the dry spells of 1932–4 and 1943–4, when overall rainfall was well below average, can be picked out in the decline of water-level in the Therfield well shown in figure 4.9.

Such trends tend to be short-lived, and the main variation of the

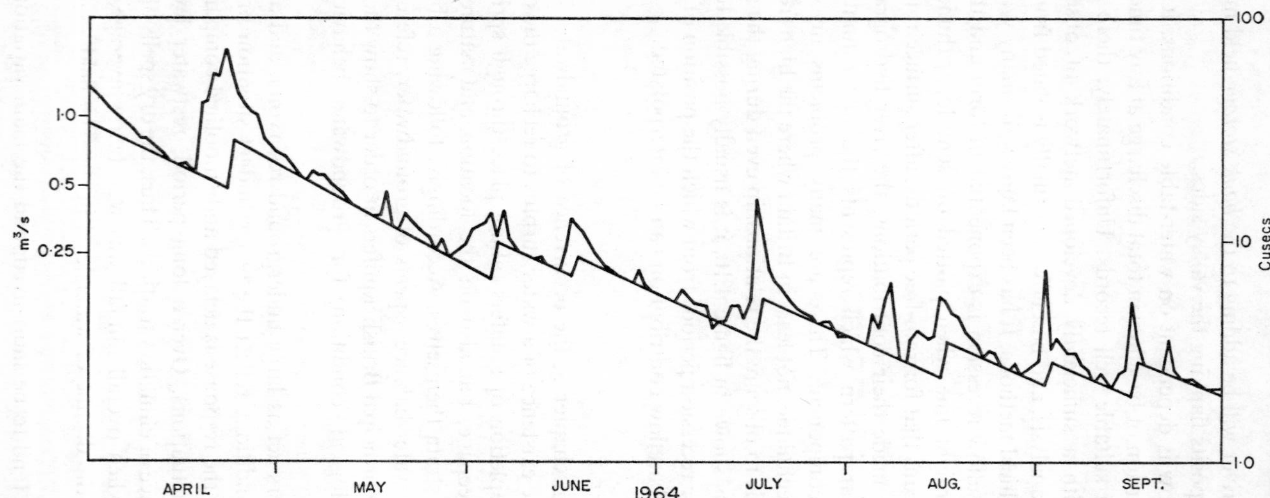

Figure 4.10 Semi-logarithmic plot of the mean daily flow of the Clow Beck, Yorkshire, during the summer half-year 1964. The lower line represents the upper limit of groundwater discharge.

well hydrograph shows a seasonal cycle which is dependent on percolation. The percolation gauge is the only method available for the direct measurement of infiltration to the water-table, and, despite the inherent deficiencies of the instrument, it can provide a reasonable guide to groundwater recharge. The general features of percolation at Harrogate in West Yorkshire are illustrated by the mean monthly values in table 3 compiled over the 35 years from 1916 to 1950. It can

TABLE 3

PERCOLATION AT HARROGATE, 1916–50 (MM)

	Oct	Nov	Dec	Jan	Feb	Mar	Apr	May	Jun	Jul	Aug	Sep	Year
Precipitation	*75*	*79*	*71*	*80*	*62*	*49*	*53*	*62*	*51*	*72*	*74*	*63*	*791*
Percolation	*30*	*53*	*54*	*57*	*47*	*29*	*22*	*15*	*11*	*13*	*14*	*19*	*364*

Winter		Summer	
Winter precipitation	416	Summer precipitation	375
Winter percolation	270	Summer percolation	94

be seen that rather less than half the annual rainfall percolates, and that three-quarters of this total occurs in the winter half-year. In no summer month does the mean percolation reach 25 mm (1 in.). Occasionally, a dry summer month may record zero percolation, and the whole of these data underline the significance of winter precipitation for the recharge of groundwater reserves.

Monthly fluctuations in restwater level follow the percolation regime with maximum elevation of the water-table in February or March and minimum values in September or October after the summer depletion. Figure 4.11 shows this typical pattern for Chilgrove well in the Sussex chalk over a five-year period, but variations do exist in the phasing from year to year. It can be seen that minimum levels have occurred as early as August and as late as December, whilst the maximum water-table height has varied from November to April. Shallow aquifers are even more sensitive to departures from the normal climatic cycle, and often show recharge in late summer due to heavy rainfall in August.

The total seasonal range of restwater levels is determined partially by the composition of the aquifer, since larger fluctuations occur in fine-grained material than coarse-grained rock for an equivalent amount of percolation, but the topographic location of the well is also important. The Chilgrove hydrograph frequently exhibits fluctuations in excess of 30 m (100 ft) and these variations are created not only by the texture of the chalk but also by the position of the well half-way up the dip slope of the South Downs. In the valley bottom the more rapid lateral movement of groundwater will tend to flatten out the seasonal rise and fall, and, for comparison, figure 4.11 shows the hydrograph for another Sussex well over the same period. This well is sunk in the Lower Tunbridge Wells sand of the Wealden Series on the flood-plain of the river Teise. The maximum fluctuation

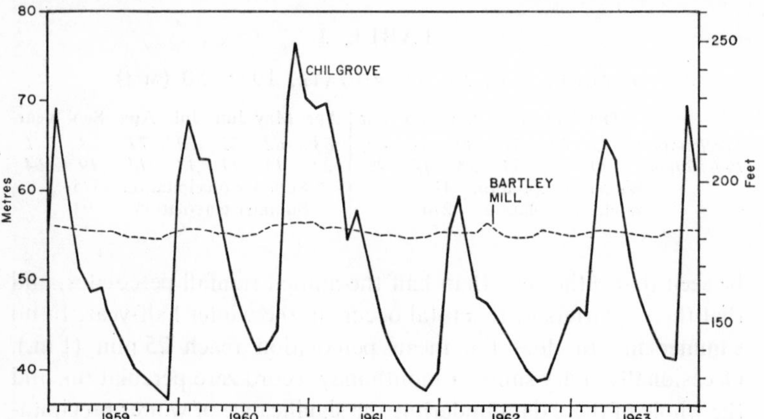

Figure 4.11 Hydrographs for two Sussex wells over the period 1959–63. After Lovelock *et al.* (1967). Crown Copyright Reserved.

shown is little more than 1·5 m (5 ft) owing to the fact that the water-table is in hydraulic continuity with the river thus allowing each to exert a stabilising influence on the other (Lovelock *et al.* 1967).

The discharge of springs and intermittent streams can be taken as an index of groundwater conditions. Most springs are of the gravity type where the phreatic water-table reaches the ground surface, and it is the relatively small variations in water-table height near the spring line which are responsible for the regularity of such flows. Nevertheless, considerable changes in hydraulic gradient have been quoted for fairly short distances within the same aquifer. For example, in the Test and Itchen valleys of the Hampshire chalk gradients from 3 m per 1·61 km (10 ft/mile) to 30 m per 1·61 km (100 ft/mile) have been quoted by Macdonald and Kenyon (1961).

Figure 4.12 outlines the distribution of the principal aquifers in

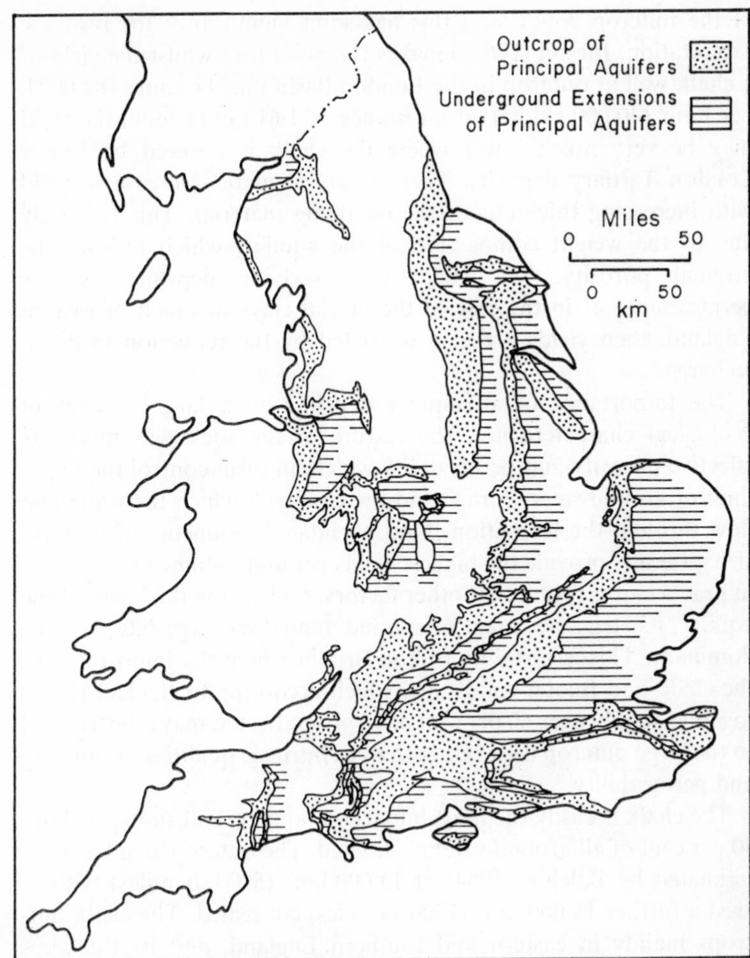

Figure 4.12 The distribution of the principal aquifers in England and Wales. After Ministry of Agriculture, Fisheries and Food (1962).

England and Wales. The most important water-bearing strata are found south-east of a line from Tynemouth to Torquay, and the map also shows that, in addition to the outcrop area, most aquifers have an underground extension where they are confined by younger deposits. The total area of such extensions is probably similar to that of the outcrop zones, and this has some significance for resource exploitation. Ineson (1962*a*) makes the point that whilst the yield of a chalk well at outcrop in the London Basin may be some 182 000 l. per hour (40 000 gal/hr), at a distance of 1·61 km (1 mile) the yield may be very much lower where the chalk is covered by Lower London Tertiary deposits. There is a systematic decrease in yield with increasing thickness of the overlying material. This is largely due to the weight compaction of the aquifer, which reduces the original porosity, but where the overlying deposit has low permeability, as in the case of the glacial clays of much of eastern England, then yields are also restricted by the reduction in direct recharge.

The importance of an aquifer depends on a large number of geological characteristics. The texture of the rock determines its effective porosity and permeability which, in turn, control the upper limit of groundwater storage and the ease with which the water can flow through the formation. Unconsolidated sediments of uniform size generally provide the highest yields per unit volume of rock, but, in practice, it is found that other factors, such as the thickness of the aquifer, its structure, areal extent and annual recharge rate, become dominant. This is certainly true in Britain where the importance of the chalk and Bunter sandstone, which according to Buchan (1963) together supply over 60 per cent of all groundwater, may be attributed to the large outcrop area rather than to intrinsic qualities of porosity and permeability.

The chalk is easily the most important aquifer, and supplies about 40 per cent of all groundwater abstracted. The outcrop area has been estimated by Balchin (1964) at 13 000 km^2 (5000 sq miles) with at least a further 18 000 km^2 (7000 sq miles) concealed. The chalk outcrops mainly in eastern and southern England, and its thickness varies from 90 m (300 ft) in Lincolnshire and Dorset to 510 m (1650 ft) in the Isle of Wight. As an aquifer, the chalk is very porous, but it is fine-grained with a low permeability, and there is little water movement through the pore spaces of the rock. On the other hand, jointing and other structural dislocations have led to numerous deep fissures which become filled by water seeping from the saturated rock. Such fissures greatly increase the ability of the chalk to transmit water, and a well in a fissured zone may yield twenty times more water than one in an adjacent undisturbed area. Similarly, it has been confirmed by Ineson (1962*b*) that the transmissibility of the chalk is greatly increased in certain areas, such as along the line of topographic valleys, where faulting or fissuring has taken place.

The Bunter and Keuper sandstones comprise an important aquifer, and outcrop over some 4500 km^2 (1750 sq miles) with a further 3250 km^2 (1250 sq miles) under more recent deposits. These coarse sandstones attain their greatest development in the Midlands, but extend from Cumberland through to the South-west. They provide large yields, especially in the Bunter Pebble Beds, whilst the high permeability results in only small seasonal fluctuations in restwater levels.

In other parts of England more restricted aquifers may enjoy some local significance. For example, the Oolitic limestones and associated Jurassic sands have been developed in parts of Lincolnshire and Northamptonshire. Coal Measure sandstones provide limited supplies in some industrial districts, but yields are rather unreliable and there is a risk of contamination from surface pollution.

The total volume of water stored in an aquifer is composed of both the *capital stock*, which has accumulated over a long period of time, and the *current recharge* which represents the mean rate of annual replenishment from percolation. The long-term safe yield of an aquifer is usually limited to an amount equivalent to the current recharge rate, otherwise the capital stock will be drawn upon with a consequent lowering of the regional water-table. All pumped wells and boreholes result in highly localised over-development since abstraction is accompanied by drawdown of the water-table immediately round the well in the so-called *cone of depletion*. The water-level usually recovers when pumping stops, however, and it is only when abstraction points are spaced too close together and too much water is pumped that a progressive fall occurs over a wider area.

The increasing demand for water has led to the over-development of some of our most important aquifers, the most publicised case being that of the London Basin where water-levels declined in the central area by 38 m (125 ft) between 1878 and 1911 (Walters 1936). In some coastal districts, over-pumping has resulted in the infiltration of saline water, and a typical example of this is in the chalk of north Lincolnshire around Grimsby. According to Gray (1964) natural artesian overflow through the confining Boulder Clay and other superficial deposits existed in the built-up area before about 1860 when borehole development commenced. With continued abstractions artesian conditions then became seasonal, and now no natural overflow is found within 4·8 km (3 miles) of the town centre. In a few boreholes the pumping level has been lowered more than 15 m (50 ft) below OD, and an artificial hydraulic gradient has been created from the coast to the abstraction zone. Salt water from the Humber estuary has encroached inland, and some water samples have shown that abstracted water near the town is comprised of one-third sea water and two-thirds groundwater.

Streamflow

Streamflow is the most important water resource for the country as a whole, and it has been estimated by Ineson (1966) that the ratio of abstraction from surface sources compared with groundwater supplies is about 9:1 for the United Kingdom, whilst over England and Wales the ratio is still 5:3. The reasons for this situation are not hard to find. The water balance provides a greater surplus in the north and west where the older, harder rocks predominate, and the only extensive aquifers are limited to the relatively dry south-east of England. From a practical aspect, it must also be appreciated that the water yield of rivers is much greater than that from underground sources in terms of point exploitation, and a reservoir, or even a river intake system, can generally provide a much greater volume of water than can be obtained from a single well or borehole.

Since streamflow represents the residual element in the hydrological cycle, its characteristic distribution in space and time depends on the nature of preceding events. These events can be classified into two major categories, namely, *climatic factors* and *catchment factors*. In general, climatic factors operate over wide areas and control the broad monthly regime of rivers, whilst catchment factors are essentially local and influence stream hydrographs on a shorter time-scale. Despite this distinction it is impossible to maintain an absolute separation, and, although relief and aspect may properly be regarded as catchment features, they also exert a significant effect on local climate. In addition, some catchment characteristics are particularly effective in flood production, and a discussion of these will be deferred until the next chapter.

(*a*) *Climatic factors*. The balance between precipitation and evaporation is fundamental in controlling the gross amount of runoff on a regional scale. It has already been noted that the water surplus declines from the North-west towards the South-east, and this results in marked variations in mean annual riverflow. For example, Reynolds (1969) has shown that over an 18-year period the mean runoff from a small catchment entirely above 305 m (1000 ft) in western Scotland was more than 3200 mm (125 in.), whilst some East Anglian rivers have an average flow equivalent to only 127–152 mm (5 or 6 in.) over their drainage basins. Ward (1967) has produced maps of the mean regional runoff variation which shows that this gradient also exists for the *runoff ratio*, or streamflow expressed as a percentage of rainfall, and figure 4.13 indicates that this varies from over 80 per cent in Scotland and mid-Wales to less than 30 per cent in south-east England and along the south coast.

The seasonal regime of rivers, as shown by mean monthly flows, is also dependent on climate. Once again the relationship between precipitation and evapotranspiration is paramount, and this produces a simple regime, classified by Pardé (1955) as *oceanic*, with maximum discharges in winter and minima in summer. Nevertheless, important regional variations can be found within this broad pattern, and while most of the North and West has maximum flows in December, central and eastern England has a peak in January or February (Ward 1968). In most cases a single maximum associated with rainfall surplus is experienced, but in parts of Scotland and northern England there is a secondary maximum, often in March or April, which results from snowmelt.

An even greater variation exists with regard to mean minimum flows which occur in June over Scotland and north-west England, but are progressively delayed towards the South-east where they may be as late as September. This feature has been attributed to the increasing proportion of deep percolation which takes place in the water-bearing strata of the South-east and the subsequent slow release of water to the rivers from contributory aquifers. In general, therefore, the greater the fraction of baseflow in total discharge, the later in the year the runoff regime is likely to be phased.

If the monthly discharge is considered as a proportion of rainfall, it is found that the winter maximum usually has about double the percentage of rainfall appearing as streamflow compared with the month of summer minimum. This underlines the dominance of the winter half-year in the production of runoff, and for many British

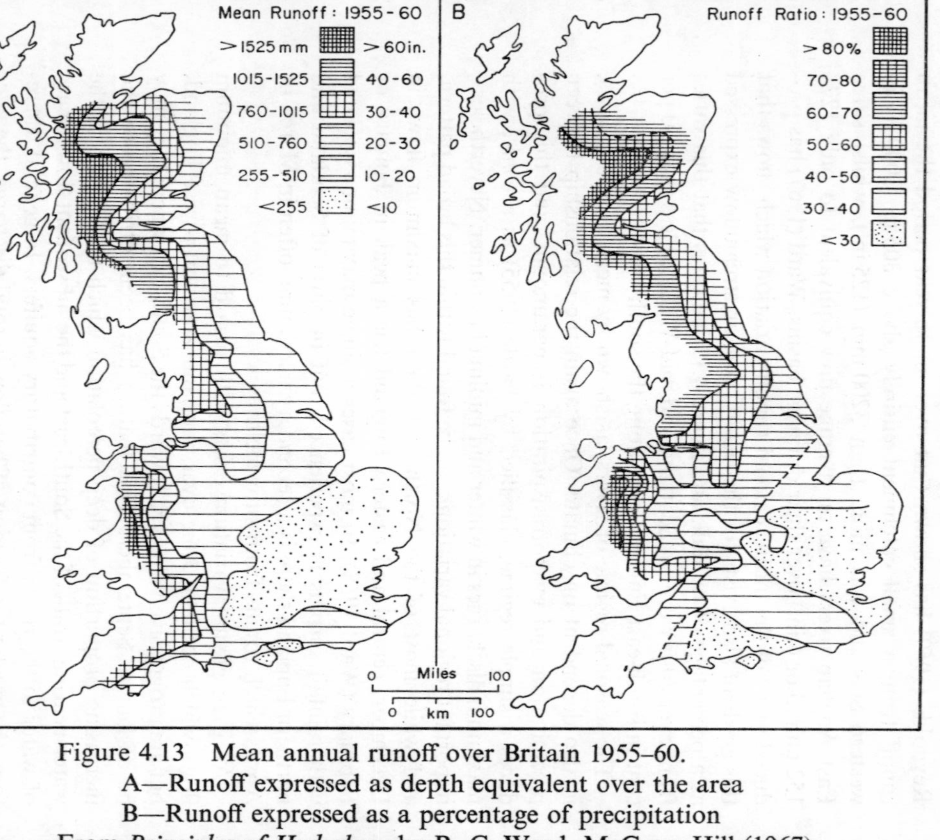

Figure 4.13 Mean annual runoff over Britain 1955–60.
A—Runoff expressed as depth equivalent over the area
B—Runoff expressed as a percentage of precipitation
From *Principles of Hydrology* by R. C. Ward, McGraw-Hill (1967)

catchments approximately two-thirds of the annual discharge occurs between October and March.

Individual years may show considerable differences from the mean pattern of runoff, and unusually wet or dry months can easily modify the seasonal regime. The long-term variation of runoff is probably fairly similar to that of precipitation, and for an upland catchment in Wales the annual extremes of runoff over a 42-year period ranged from 140 per cent to 65 per cent of the mean (Risbridger and Godfrey 1954). The close relationship between rainfall and discharge produced similar variations when the runoff was taken as a percentage of rainfall, and in a year with 125 per cent of the normal rainfall expectation as much as 95 per cent appeared as discharge, whilst with 80 per cent of the mean rainfall only 54 per cent ran off. Other factors being equal it is likely that, as in the case of rainfall, the variability of streamflow will increase with lower totals, but this effect will be compensated to some extent by the permeable rocks of the lowlands which provide regulation through storage.

(*b*) *Catchment factors*. Of all the different catchment factors, *area* is one of the most significant. The perennial rivers of Britain show a systematic increase in discharge from source to mouth, and there is broad accord between catchment size and mean flow. This relationship is particularly close in the English lowlands, as illustrated in figure 4.14, where the low amplitude of relief results in relatively small differences in annual rainfall and runoff conditions. A direct comparison would be much more difficult on a national scale, and table 4 shows the problem of defining the 'largest' river in Britain.

TABLE 4

COMPARATIVE DATA FOR THE THAMES AND THE TAY

	Station	Drainage Area		Mean Discharge		Mean Precipitation 1916–50	
		km²	sq miles	m³/s	cusecs	mm	in.
Thames	Teddington	9870	3810	67	2365	735	28·9
Tay	Ballathie	4580	1770	154	5436	1471	57·9

Thus, the largest gauged catchment is the Thames above Teddington covering 9870 km² (3810 sq miles), but the mean annual discharge is

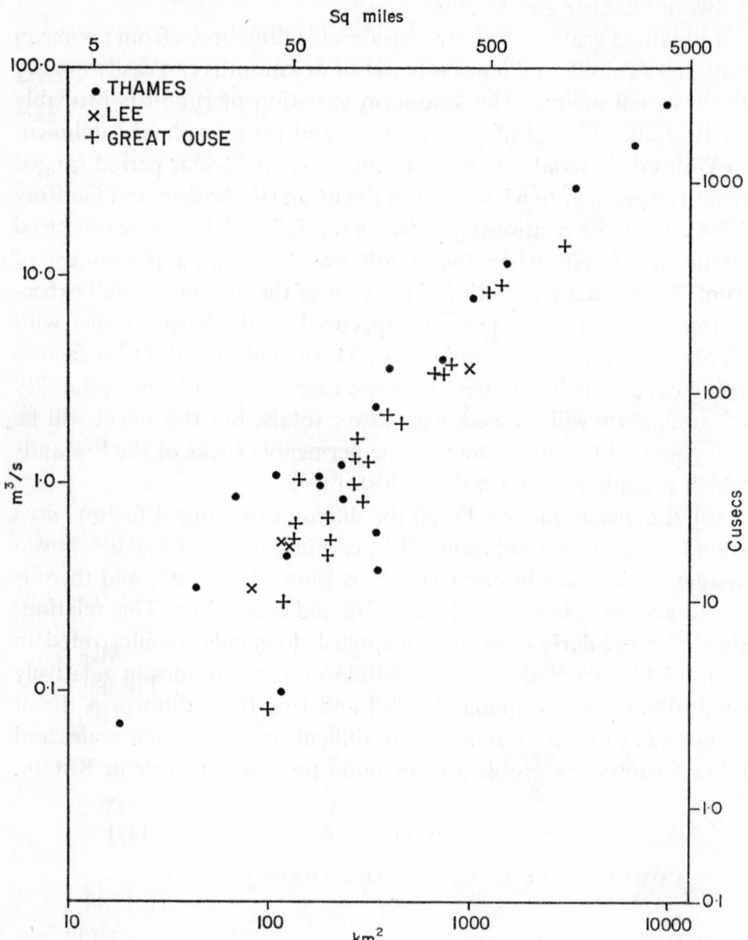

Figure 4.14 The relationship between mean annual discharge and catchment size for three major drainage basins in south-east England. (Compiled from data in *The Surface Water Year Book of Great Britain 1964–65.*)

only 67 m^3/s (2365 cusecs) which is exceeded by several rivers in wetter, less permeable areas, and the largest mean flow of 154 m^3/s (5436 cusecs) is recorded at Ballathie on the Scottish Tay. The Tay rises in the Grampians, and the high rainfall, together with lower evaporation and percolation, produces a discharge which is more than double that of the Thames.

Perhaps the main practical significance of the general trend between catchment size and river flow lies in the possible development of barrage schemes. The overall scale of the country ensures that even our largest rivers are small by, say, Continental standards, but the estuarine grouping of rivers is a characteristic feature which results in some large concentrations of surface water, particularly in the low rainfall zones of the English Plain. The area draining to the Humber estuary totals over 25 000 km^2 (10 000 sq miles) and covers about one-fifth of England, whilst the Wash and the Thames estuary catchments each comprise some 15 000 km^2 (6000 sq miles). Similarly, on the west coast, the Severn estuary drains about 11 500 km^2 (4400 sq miles) covering the greater part of Wales, and, with a high average rainfall, constitutes the largest surface water source in England.

Relief has already been seen to influence discharge by increasing rainfall, but altitude is also important in terms of snow hydrology, and, in conjunction with *aspect*, can materially affect flows. This is frequently the case, not only in Scotland but also farther south, as in the eastward flowing rivers Wear and Tees whose Pennine headwaters are in the snowiest part of England. In spring these rivers may show a regular diurnal variation in flow which is dependent on snowmelt, and, as indicated in figure 4.15, the clearest examples occur under steady anticyclonic conditions with large daily ranges of temperature. An account of the thermal control of discharge in a small upland catchment through both the formation of stream-ice in winter and snowmelt in spring has been presented by Smith (1971).

After altitude, *geology* has the next most important influence on streamflow, although a precise evaluation is impossible due to the general contrast in permeability between the highland and the lowland zones. High values of percolation imply considerable aquifer storage plus the regulation of discharge through baseflow, and this is well developed in the chalk areas of south-east England. Figure 4.16 shows the hydrograph for the chalk catchment of the Hampshire Itchen for the water-year 1959–60, and, despite the contrast in rainfall over the period, the main variation is seasonal with relatively little irregular fluctuation. Restwater levels from an observation well in the catchment permit the groundwater component of flow to be drawn in (Ineson and Downing 1965), and it can be seen that baseflow controls the pattern of discharge through the year. In contrast, figure 4.16 also illustrates the mean daily hydrograph for the

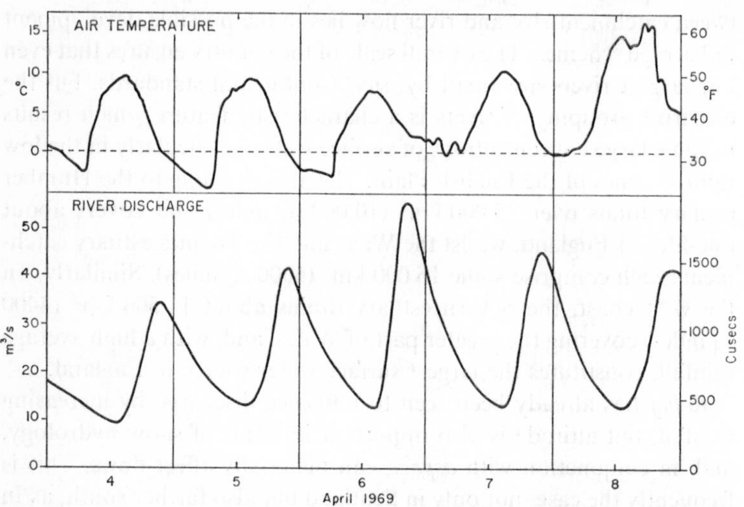

Figure 4.15 The relationship between air temperature and snowmelt discharge on the river Tees during early April 1969. The Dent Bank gauging station measures the flow from 217 km² (83·9 sq miles) of the upper Tees basin.

Trout Beck catchment for the same year. This peat-covered catchment lies entirely above 533 m (1750 ft) in the northern Pennines, and drains an area of only 11·4 km² (4·41 sq miles) compared with a surface catchment of 360 km² (139 sq miles) for the Itchen. The cumulative effect of differences in climate, size and geology is to produce a complete contrast in flow characteristics with large peak discharges per unit area and a rapidly fluctuating or 'flashy' hydrograph for Trout Beck. In such areas there is little aquifer storage and, since runoff is more directly dependent on rainfall, both high and low flows can occur at any season.

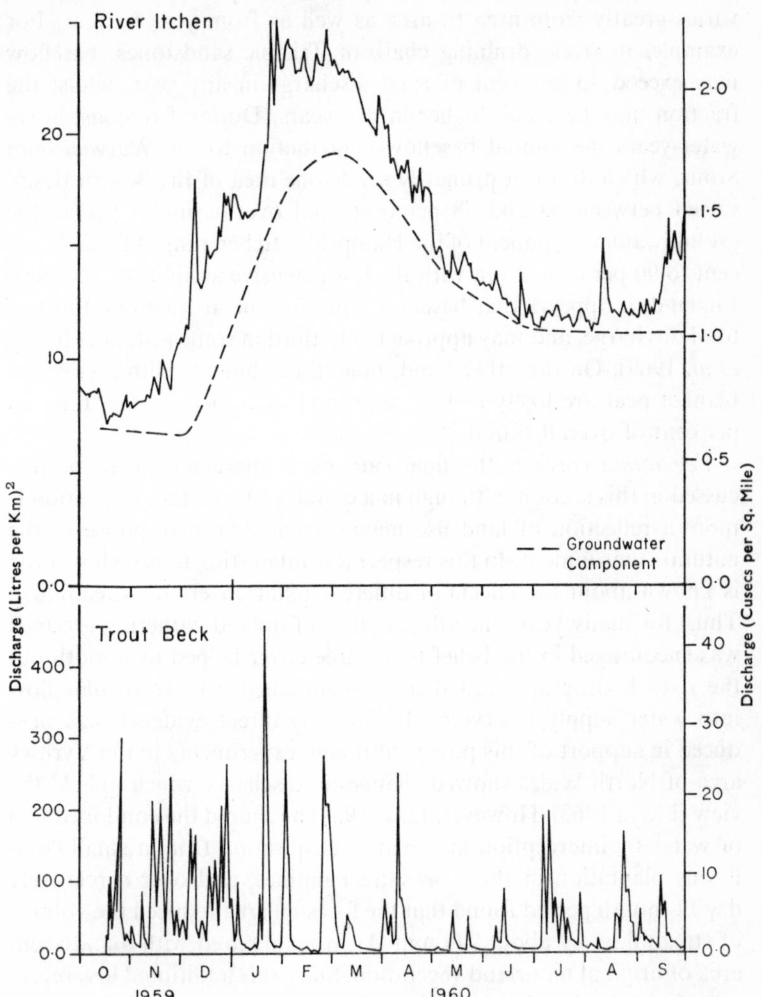

Figure 4.16 Mean daily hydrographs for the river Itchen and Trout Beck catchments during the water-year 1959–60 expressed as discharge per unit area. Itchen hydrograph adapted from Ineson and Downing (1965).

It will be apparent that the proportional importance of base flow varies greatly from area to area as well as from year to year. For example, in rivers draining chalk or Triassic sandstones, baseflow may exceed 75 per cent of total discharge in any year, whilst the fraction may be much higher in dry years. During five consecutive water-years the annual baseflow contribution to the Warwickshire Stour, which drains a primarily sandstone area of the Severn basin, varied between 65 and 78 per cent, and over a similar period the groundwater component of the Hampshire Itchen ranged from 77 per cent to 90 per cent. Even with the less extensive aquifers of northern England, it appears that baseflow will often be at least one-third of total discharge, and may approach one-third in some instances (Gray *et al.* 1969). On the other hand, upland catchments with a cover of blanket peat are likely to have a groundwater element less than 20 per cent of overall runoff.

Vegetation cover is the final catchment characteristic to be discussed in this section, although in a country like Britain vegetation is more a reflection of land use management than a response to the natural environment. In this respect it is interesting to note how little is known about the effects of different plant covers on streamflow. Thus, for many years the afforestation of upland gathering grounds was encouraged in the belief that a tree cover helped to smooth out the river hydrograph and thereby maintained a more regular flow into water supply reservoirs. Hardly any direct evidence was produced in support of this policy, although experiments in the Vyrnwy area of North Wales showed changes in discharge which upheld the view (Lloyd 1963). However, Law (1957) measured the combined loss of water by interception and evapotranspiration from a small coniferous plantation in the Yorkshire Pennines, and over a relatively dry 12-month period found that the forested area reduced the volume of streamflow by about 279 mm (11 in.) compared with an adjacent area of original moorland vegetation. Since this additional loss represented a reduction in reservoir yield of more than one-third, it was concluded that the afforestation of water supply catchments was against the public interest.

Law's work aroused considerable controversy, and although his evaporation losses have been criticised as excessive, it is generally admitted that the results are in line with experience in other parts of the world. The almost complete lack of quantitative information on the effects of vegetation on the water balance was an important factor in determining the Institute of Hydrology's research programme, and several catchment experiments aimed at studying forest influences are now in progress. The main effort is concentrated on the eastern slopes of Plynlimon in central Wales where the forested headwaters of the river Severn are being compared with an adjoining basin on the upper Wye which is in sheep pasture. It is expected that the results will have to be collected for at least a decade before any definitive statement on the influence of forests on streamflow can be made.

5 Floods and Droughts

In many ways, the real practical significance of physical hydrology lies in an understanding of extreme events rather than the average workings of the hydrological cycle. The study of floods and droughts has immediate and obvious applications, and it is remarkable that so little information is available on these themes. Certainly the impact of such extremes increases rather than decreases through time, and with growing concentrations of population and industry the implications of flood damage and regional drought become more and more serious.

FLOODS

Problems of Definition

An initial difficulty in flood studies is that of definition. The only 'physical' flood is a discharge which exceeds the natural channel capacity of a river and then spills onto the adjacent flood-plain. Work by Nixon (1959) has shown that rivers in England and Wales with self-formed channels may reach bank-full discharge on two or three days in an average year, but, although this provides some guide to frequency, it may have only partial relevance for the artificially modified courses of most British rivers. Definitions which concentrate entirely on frequency analysis and which take the largest flow during any twelve-month period as the 'annual flood' will also be unreliable, if only because of the variations in peak discharge from year to year.

Perhaps the best definition of a flood is 'any unusually high discharge', but the size of floods will vary according to the parameters selected. For example, *flood stage* is the most commonly employed factor, largely because it may be measured directly without translation into volume, and also because it is an appropriate yardstick if retaining structures are likely to be overtopped. It is popular in Britain since most flood protection schemes involve embanking lowland rivers rather than the provision of flood storage in the upper reaches. On the other hand, the *inundated area* will be an important factor when assessing the severity of flood damage, and, although this is likely to be related to the maximum river height, the actual duration of the high stage may also be significant. Yet another flood characteristic is the total *flow volume* and the *peak discharge*, but the unreliability of river measurements under flood conditions means that flood flows often have to be re-constructed after the event from trash marks and other evidence of the height which the flood reached. Although much accurate flood data will always be unobtainable through the occurrence of floods in ungauged areas, there has undoubtedly been too much false economy in the past with the construction of gauging structures which are incapable of measuring the peak flow of a major flood.

Natural Flood Mechanisms

A study of flood producing factors does little to clarify definition since British floods are due to a variety of causes, although in each case there is an excess of precipitation over infiltration capacity which produces surface runoff. Mention has already been made of the sequence of runoff processes in response to heavy precipitation, and figure 5.1 illustrates a typically asymmetrical flood hydrograph from an isolated storm over a small upland catchment. The importance of surface runoff can be gauged from the rapid rise to the peak discharge, which represents the point in time when the tributary stream network is making its maximum contribution to flow. Following the peak, there is an equally well defined recession limb which, although steep in the early stages, gradually flattens out to assume an exponential shape as baseflow progressively replaces surface runoff. This is the usual shape of the flood hydrograph, but almost infinite variations can occur, particularly under snowmelt conditions or as a result of multiple storms.

The factors which lead to flooding are not dissimilar to those which influence overall discharge, and, once again they can be subdivided into *climatic* and *local* causes. As might be expected, the immediate cause is invariably climatic, and is dependent on either storm rainfall or snowmelt, or a combination of both. It was shown

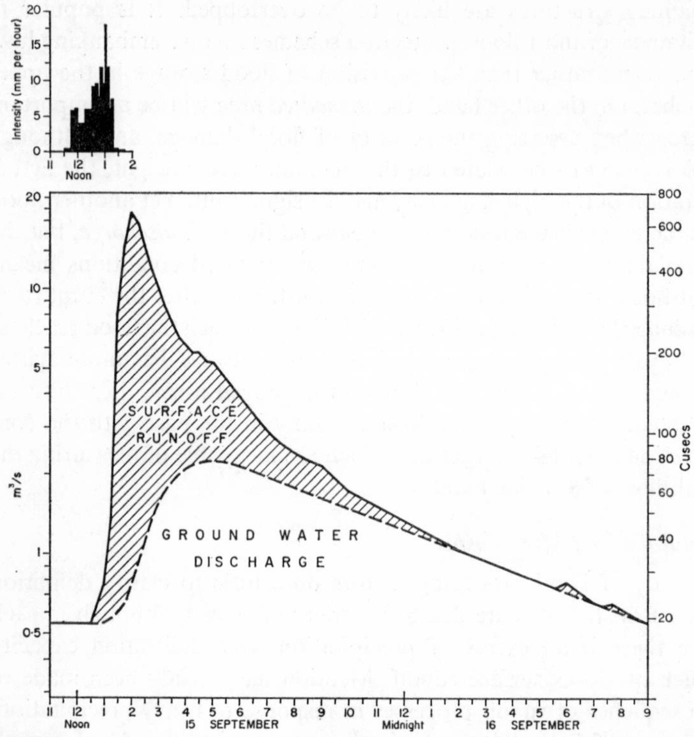

Figure 5.1 A typical flood hydrograph resulting from a single rainstorm over a Pennine catchment in September 1961. Drainage area 15·3 km² (5·9 sq miles) and altitude of gauging station almost 305 m (1000 ft) OD.

in chapter 4 that most of the intense daily falls of rain over Britain are caused either by Atlantic depressions, often with well-developed warm fronts, or by convectional activity in the summer, and there is no doubt that these two factors account for most of the major floods over the country. There is a general lack of data on rainfall intensity and the relationship between the magnitude and duration of particular excessive falls, but figure 5.2 taken from Rodda (1970) summarises the largest falls recorded over Britain for periods of up to two years compared with observed world maxima. It can be seen that, although the British falls have the same general relationships, they are much less intense than those recorded elsewhere, and even the heaviest is only about one-quarter of the global extreme. This difference is a measure of the equability of our climatic regime.

Precipitation characteristics are, of course, only a partial explanation of floods since catchments will respond quite differently to equivalent rainfalls according to the prevailing local conditions.

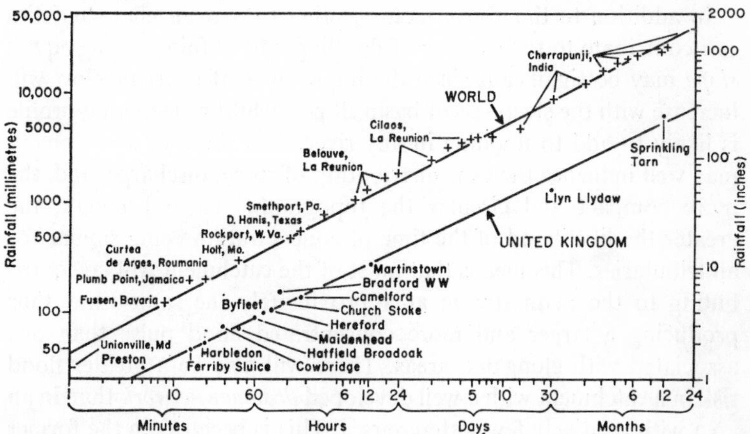

Figure 5.2 The relationship between magnitude and duration for extreme rainfalls in the United Kingdom compared with observed world maxima. After Rodda (1970).

Again, some of the catchment factors have already been mentioned. Thus, *drainage area* is a significant element of floods since not only does it influence the size of the peak discharge but it also determines the *time of concentration*, which is the period required for water to travel from the most remote portion of the basin to the gauging station at the outlet. Clearly, this will affect the time lag between storm rainfall and the subsequent flood peak. For small catchments, such as the one shown in figure 5.1, the period of rise may be an hour or less, whilst for large catchments, such as the Thames, several days will be necessary. *Altitude* is an important factor, not only because slopes tend to steepen with increasing height, but also because higher catchments will receive a greater rainfall. This means that they are likely to be saturated more frequently than lowland areas, and consequently less soil storage will be available for storm rainfall. The *geology* of catchments must be considered since a more impervious basin will produce a greater proportion of surface runoff than an area with larger groundwater reserves. Similarly, *vegetation* can be expected to have a material influence on flood flows, and, for example, a mature forest cover will delay and reduce flood peaks compared with either herbaceous vegetation or bare soil surfaces.

In addition to the above factors, other catchment characteristics can contribute to the severity of flooding. Other things being equal, *slope* may be significant since the importance of overland flow will increase with the steepness of basin slopes, whilst a steep long-profile is likely to add to flooding in any river. The *shape* of a catchment may well influence the time distribution of storm discharge, and, the more compact and circular the topographic basin becomes, the greater the likelihood of the time of concentration being similar for all tributaries. This means that most of the catchment will be contributing to the main stream at approximately the same time, thus producing a larger and more concentrated flood pulse than one associated with elongated areas. There will also be a greater flood risk in a catchment with a well developed *drainage network* than in an area with relatively few watercourses. This is because, in the former case, overland flow will have only a short distance to travel before it reaches a stream channel, whereas, in a basin of sparse drainage, longer overland flow will not only delay peak discharge, but also provide a greater opportunity for infiltration which will result in a reduced flood flow.

Infiltration is obviously a key factor in rainfall-runoff relations. It will be largely influenced by the nature of the *soil*, and Edmonds *et al.* (1970) have prepared a tentative hydrological grouping of soils in north-east England based on the effect of minimum infiltration rates on flood hydrographs from twenty-six catchments. Although differences in soil type and structure modify flood patterns to some extent, the principal soil variable in Britain is undoubtedly the fluctuation in infiltration capacity which results from existing climatic conditions. In particular, antecedent soil moisture status can be related to flood behaviour since any saturated soil will be unable to absorb any further precipitation, and there will be a very high ratio of runoff to rainfall. Conversely, following a dry spell, soil moisture storage will be available and the early part of even an intense storm may produce little surface runoff, depending on the infiltration capacity of the soil surface. An especially effective reduction of infiltration capacity occurs as a result of prolonged periods of freezing temperatures which, by freezing the water in the upper soil layers, create a virtually impermeable surface.

Despite the fact that intense and continued rainfall can occur at any time of the year, there is a marked seasonal concentration of flooding in Britain. Table 5 has been prepared by taking the month

TABLE 5

PERCENTAGE MONTHLY INCIDENCE OF EXTREME PEAK FLOWS

Oct	Nov	Dec	Jan	Feb	Mar	Apr	May	Jun	Jul	Aug	Sep
3·3	11·6	26·3	11·3	6·7	18·8	0·5	0·5	2·6	2·4	5·9	10·1
Winter 78·0 per cent						Summer 22·0 per cent					

of absolute peak discharge over the entire period of record listed for the 388 gauging stations in the *Surface Water Year Book 1964–5* and expressing the frequency in percentage terms. It can be seen that over three-quarters of the floods occur in the winter half-year and that the monthly values reflect the regime of mean flows throughout the year. It is noteworthy that March has the second highest frequency after December, a fact which may almost certainly be attributed to snowmelt.

Winter conditions are more conducive to flooding because of seasonal contrasts in infiltration opportunity. In other words, lower evaporation during winter will cause more extensive saturation of catchments which will then become very responsive to heavy rainfall. Such seasonal contrasts in flood hydrology have been identified by Harvey (1971) for the river Ter which drains some 78 km^2 (30 sq miles) of central Essex. The application of unit hydrograph techniques to this boulder-clay catchment showed that intense storm rainfall produced floods of only relatively short duration in the summer months compared with the winter pattern. Apart from the possible effects of seasonal variations in crop cover, this distinction was primarily attributed to the fact that soil moisture deficits on the flat watershed plateau become so large that summer runoff is effectively restricted to the lowest part of the catchment. In the summer, therefore, the small contributory area is capable of sustaining only short-duration flood hydrographs.

Because of the interplay of such factors, winter floods tend to be of more complex origin than those of summer, and the variety of causal mechanisms can best be illustrated by case studies of some past flood events. These examples have been organised seasonally for the sake of convenience, but it should be appreciated that a rigid distinction is not possible. For example, although widespread heavy rains are treated mainly in a winter context, they can occur during summer as shown by the exceptional flooding of August 1829 in the Moray Firth area of Scotland and, more recently, by the floods which affected south-east England in September 1968.

Some British Floods

(*a*) *Winter floods.* It is not difficult to find examples of major floods during the winter half-year, and a primary distinction can be made between those resulting solely from prolonged heavy rainfall and those in which snowmelt or frozen ground played a distinctive role.

One of the best documented series of floods in the former category is that which afflicted east Devon in the autumn of 1960, and, although the flooding occurred right at the beginning of the winter, it is illustrative of the cumulative nature of many floods at this season. The calendar year 1960 was the third wettest on record for England and Wales, but the main excesses were confined to southern England, particularly the South Coast and the West Country (Booth 1961). Most of the rainfall occurred in the period from July to November, and in the ten-week spell between 27 September and 5 December 561 mm (22·09 in. of rain), which is equivalent to two-thirds of the mean annual total, fell in Exeter.

During this ten-week period, five serious floods were recorded on the river Exe which rises on Exmoor and drains a catchment area of 1518 km^2 (586 sq miles) consisting largely of relatively impermeable slates, grits and shales of Devonian and Carboniferous age (Brierley 1964). Each flood was caused by fairly widespread frontal rain falling on an already saturated catchment, and considerable damage ensued. An important fact is that, whilst rivers in east Devon reached higher stages than at any time earlier this century, the rainfall intensities and storm durations were not rare. The maximum recorded intensity was 29 mm (1·125 in.) per hour for a thirty-minute period at Exmouth on 6 October, and it has been estimated by Harrison (1961) that the return period for this storm, and also for the storm of 30 September, is as low as $2\frac{1}{2}$ years.

These Devon floods provide a good example of the significance of antecedent catchment conditions during winter, and this is an important consideration with regard to snowmelt and frozen ground. The contribution of melting snow to flood peaks is more complex in Britain than in those countries where the progressive seasonal accumulation of snow is followed by one major spring-thaw release. Here the vicissitudes of a normal winter result in several small falls of snow, but, with a rise in temperatures a few days later, much of the snow is removed. This removal is normally accompanied by rainfall, which itself frequently occurs when a milder westerly airflow is re-established. Through the winter a series of snowmelt floods may be produced, which are complicated and increased by rainfall. Only rarely does snowmelt form the sole flood contribution, and these occasions are limited to snowfalls which are melted in late spring by high maximum temperatures.

In severe winters the chance of snowmelt flooding increases, particularly if a thick snow cover is maintained into March, and in March 1947 and 1963 snow caused appreciable flooding in eastern England. Between 14 and 21 March 1947, sixteen stations listed in the *Surface Water Year Book 1964–5* had their highest recorded flows. The floods were largely confined to the Nene and Great Ouse catchments, and the main damage was in the Fenlands. Similarly, in the period 5 to 15 March 1963, nineteen other rivers experienced their maximum discharges. This time most of the flooding took place farther north within the basins of the Yorkshire Ouse and the Northumbrian rivers, although several stations in Devon and Somerset recorded absolute peak flows in mid-February at the end of the 1962–3 winter.

Rainfall and snowmelt often combine to produce floods, but little is known about the interaction of these processes. A major problem is created by the ability of a ripening snow cover to absorb rainfall, and, whilst the snow may afford initial storage for both rainfall and meltwater, the rapid release of water caused by the collapse of the snow blanket can produce very high floods. For example, a study of flooding in Glen Cannich by Wolf (1952) indicated that a snow cover about 305 mm (12 in.) thick on the upper part of the catchment was able to absorb heavy rainfall for a period of three hours before releasing the accumulated water to give a flood peak some 35 per cent greater than anticipated.

The associated winter flood problem of frozen ground can dramatically reduce the infiltration capacity of a catchment. These effects are particularly significant on catchments which are normally permeable, such as those on chalk, and some interesting figures have been quoted for the Thames. Two precipitation/runoff situations were studied according to Wolf (1966), one for a winter period in 1929, which was the wettest recorded spell before a flood, and the other for a period in the spring of 1947 when the ground was frozen. The results were as follows

		Precipitation	Discharge	Runoff Coefficient
1929	22 Nov–15 Dec	194 mm (7·63 in.)	70 mm (2·75 in.)	0·36
1947	5 Mar–26 Mar	128 mm (5·06 in.)	80 mm (3·14 in.)	0·62

The evidence suggests that, even with a saturated catchment, the 'infiltration loss' amounts to the equivalent of 5 mm (0·2 in.) per day, but with frozen ground this is reduced to some 2 mm (0·085 in.) per day. It is estimated that, if the 1929 precipitation had occurred on frozen ground, the runoff coefficient would have reached 75 per cent and exceptionally severe floods would have resulted.

Special mention must be made of the winter floods which arise near the east coast largely as a result of tidal forces. The chief cause can be traced to a coincidence of high spring tides with severe northerly gales in the North Sea, and often these factors are sufficient to produce flooding alone, although they can also work in conjunction with high river discharges inland. An example in the latter category is the Thames flood of 7 January 1928 as reported by Brooks and Glasspoole (1928). Heavy rain and snowmelt at the beginning of January created some flooding above London, and the flow of 500 m^3/s (17 655 cusecs) at Teddington on the 7th, approached the all-time record of November 1894. Below London the passage of the flood crest was impeded by a spring tide given extra height by gale-force winds from a depression which had passed over Scotland on the 6th, and the water was almost 1·8 m (6 ft) above the expected level. An even more disastrous event occurred purely as a result of tidal factors on 31 January 1953, when over 803 km^2 (310 sq miles) of the east coast were inundated between the Humber estuary and Dover with the loss of more than 300 lives (Steers 1953). It has been shown by Douglas (1953) that on this occasion a deep North Sea depression resulted in the strongest northerly gale on record and the tidal surge exceeded 2·4 m (8 ft) in some coastal areas. Much of lower Thameside, including Central London, is highly vulnerable to such storm surges and it has been estimated that the surge which has a statistical recurrence once in 1000 years would flood about 116 km^2 (45 sq miles) of the Thames valley and directly affect some 1¼ million people. After much discussion about the merits of alternative schemes, the design of a flood barrier to be constructed near Woolwich has now been finalised, and the scheme should be completed by the late 1970s (Stubbs 1971).

(*b*) *Summer floods*. The most characteristic summer flood is probably associated with thunderstorm development over the flatter land along the east coast of England. There are some historic examples of such events, such as the Norwich floods of 25 August, 1912, and the flood of the river Lud in Lincolnshire on 29 May, 1920, when twenty-three people were killed. On the other hand, the severity of summer floods is normally increased by the addition of an orographic factor to the rainfall and the effects of a steep catchment in promoting rapid discharge, which means that it is often in the uplands where the catastrophic floods are found. Thus, a more recent upland event was the flooding of 8 August, 1967, in the Bowland Forest and Pendle Hill localities of the Lancashire Pennines. It has already been shown, however, that the South-western Peninsula is particularly prone to heavy rainfall such as that which produced the Mendip floods of 1968 (Hanwell and Newson 1970), but one of the best documented examples is the Lynmouth flood of August 1952.

On 15 August, 1952, an extremely severe thunderstorm occurred over Exmoor and was the culmination of four months of thundery weather in the West Midlands and the South-west. One of the heaviest daily rainfalls on record was observed at an altitude of 473 m (1550 ft) when the Longstone Barrow gauge gave a reading of 229 mm (9 in.) for the 24 hours beginning at 09.00 GMT on the 15th, and according to Bleasdale and Douglas (1952) evidence from the surrounding lowland suggests that the non-orographic component of precipitation was less than half of this total. Like many other moorland areas, the Lyn river system, which drains some 101 km^2 (39 sq miles), has a low permeability. It is mainly composed of peat, thin soil and bare rock, and whatever natural storage exists in the catchment must have been eliminated by heavy rainfall in the two weeks preceding the 15th. In addition, the rivers on the northern slopes of Exmoor have a particularly steep topography resulting from rejuvenation and vigorous fluvial erosion, and this characteristic was important in creating rapid surface runoff. No flow records are available for the area, but it has been estimated by Dobbie and Wolf (1953) that the extreme peak flows exceeded the equivalent of 63 mm (2·5 in.) depth from the catchment, whilst for short periods the runoff intensities were as high, or even higher, than the rates of rainfall.

The Influence of Man

It is sometimes claimed that floods in this country are increasing, although it is extremely difficult to find reliable evidence which either confirms or disproves this theory. A genuine increase in flooding would normally be measurable in terms of larger and more frequent peak discharges, but the short data-run for most British gauging stations provides an inadequate time-sample. Rainfall records are, of course, available over a much longer time span, but the information rarely relates to specific storm events. At the present time it is impossible to state whether any real secular variations in rainfall intensity have taken place in the period of instrumental record, but an analysis of extreme daily values observed since 1881 at Oxford quoted by Rodda (1970) suggests a recent increase in the frequency of heavy rain at this site. Figure 5.3 shows that large daily falls have occurred most often in the period from 1941 to 1965, but it is not certain that the increase is representative of the country as a whole, whilst it is even more difficult to assess the significance of such a change in terms of resulting flood flows.

The runoff response to heavy rainfall is complicated by continued land-use changes which alter the natural physical characteristics of most catchment areas. In the absence of directly measured flood discharges, recourse is often made to flood stage marks which have been placed on bridges and riverside buildings to record the maximum height reached by previous floods. However, even if a tendency to higher flood levels can be detected from such historical records, as possibly for the upper parts of the Severn and the Wye since 1840 in a study by Howe *et al.* (1967), this evidence does not necessarily imply greater flood peak discharges. Most stage records are available for populated areas, and are frequently obtained near to, or even within, large towns. It is exactly these stretches of river which have

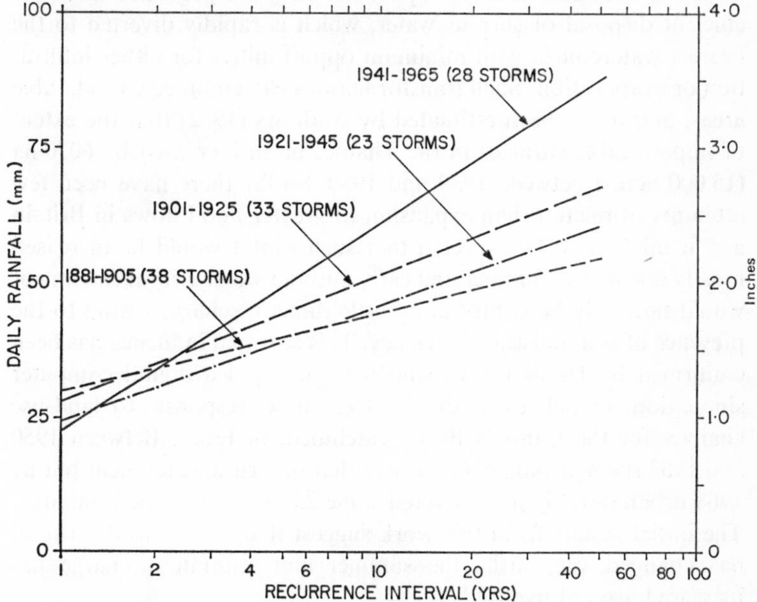

Figure 5.3 The change in magnitude-frequency relationships for daily rainfall totals exceeding 1 inch (25·4 mm) at Oxford. After Rodda (1970).

undergone the greatest alterations in the recent past through urban expansion, and most riverside development tends to reduce the effective channel capacity with the construction of embankments, bridges and other works. This means that river stage may well be increasing in urban areas without an attendant rise in actual discharge.

Although the question of possible climatic change cannot be resolved, it is likely that human activity is a more important factor in modifying the nature of the flood hazard. For the most part the changes will occur through Man's inadvertent effects on the hydrological cycle. These take a variety of forms, and building expansion, for example, has wider implications than the reduction of channel capacity in natural river channels. Thus, the spread of urbanisation converts former rural land to artificial and often totally impermeable surfaces. The entire drainage system of a town is geared towards the efficient disposal of surplus water, which is rapidly diverted to the nearest watercourse with minimum opportunities for either infiltration or evaporation. Such transformations can embrace considerable areas, and it has been estimated by Andrews (1962) that the extent of impermeable surfaces in the Thames basin increased by 6070 ha (15 000 acres) between 1939 and 1960. So far there have been few attempts to relate urban expansion to greater flood flows in Britain and it might well be expected that such runoff would be increased mostly during the summer and early autumn when a rural catchment would normally be contributing little direct discharge owing to the presence of soil moisture deficiency. This seasonal influence has been confirmed by Hollis (1970) who has employed a digital computer simulation model to evaluate streamflow response to land-use changes for the Canon's Brook catchment in Essex. Between 1950 and 1953 the hydrologic record was that of a rural catchment but by 1968 urban development covered some 25 per cent of the total area. The initial results from this work suggest that, whilst winter runoff has changed very little, the summer and autumn discharge has increased around five-fold.

Building development can also bring about changes in river water quality, particularly during the actual construction phase, and some work on small catchments in Devon by Walling and Gregory (1970) has shown that suspended sediment concentrations may occasionally be up to 100 times greater than the concentrations measured in undisturbed conditions.

In addition to influencing the runoff process, it has also been suggested that urban areas can bring about a net increase in the total amount of precipitation recorded locally. Barrett (1964) has drawn attention to an apparently anomalous rise in rainfall in the Manchester region and shown that the area of largest increase may be related to the outline of the conurbation. Other workers have claimed that the heat island effects associated with large cities may be sufficient to cause greater instability in the lower atmosphere and thereby act as a trigger mechanism for thunderstorms. Atkinson (1968 and 1969) has found a distinct maximum of thunder rainfall located over the central part of the London conurbation. This urban maximum of precipitation appears to be almost entirely a summer characteristic

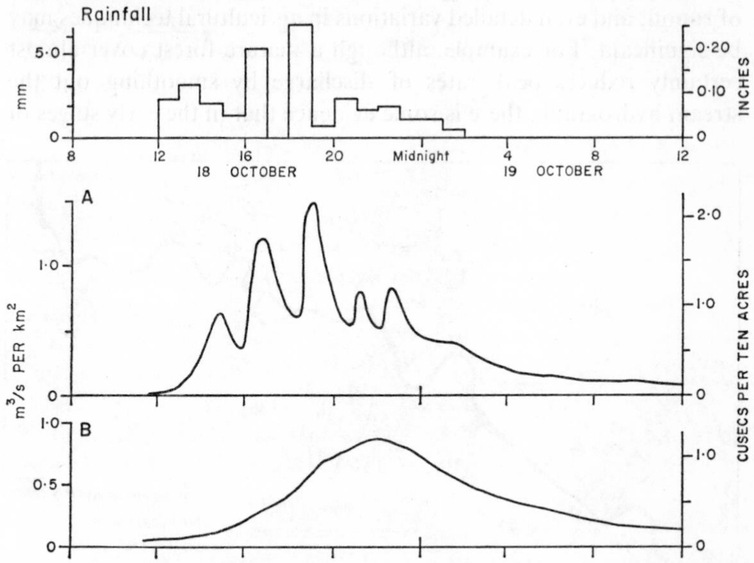

Figure 5.4 A contrast in hydrograph response to rainfall over two small peat-covered catchments in the Westmorland Pennines during October 1957.

Catchment A—area 4·8 ha (11·9 acres). Peat surface severely burnt and drained by erosion channels and moor gripping.
Catchment B—area 5·5 ha (13·5 acres). A virtually untouched *Sphagnum* bog with little surface drainage.

After Conway and Millar (1960).

associated with warm frontal storms, attributable to a number of possible causes including higher daytime temperatures and increased air turbulence in the lower atmosphere arising from the greater 'roughness' of the city centre. A specific urban thunderstorm over Reading has been described by Parry (1956) and it will be clear that the accumulating evidence from both hydrology and meteorology hints at the growing flood-producing potential of urban areas during the summer months.

Man's influence on the hydrological cycle is no less potent in the rural areas, although here changes probably take place over longer periods. Any land-use change is likely to modify the time-distribution of runoff, and even detailed variations in agricultural techniques may be significant. For example, although a mature forest cover almost certainly reduces peak rates of discharge by smoothing out the stream hydrograph, there is some evidence that in the early stages of

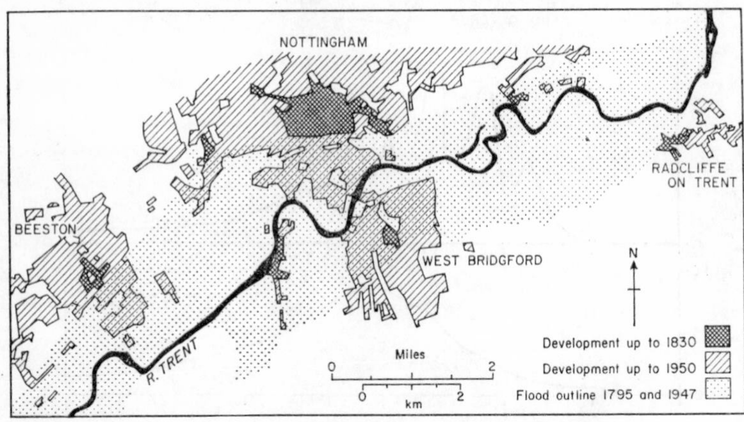

Figure 5.5 Increasing building development on the flood-plain of the river Trent near Nottingham. After Nixon (1963).

afforestation the reverse may be true. In particular, the Forestry Commission's practice of deep ploughing prior to planting plus other management operations involving access roads, drainage and soil compaction could actually lead to a temporary increase in surface runoff according to Reynolds (1967).

If flooding is becoming a greater hazard in rural areas, the most important single cause is likely to be the spread of agricultural drainage systems, either in the form of open ditches or buried tile drains. Once again, very little is known about the influence of such land management practices on runoff, but results obtained for some small, peat-covered catchments in the high Pennines of northern England by Conway and Millar (1960) suggest that drainage of the peat, together with the traditional burning-off of the moorland vegetation, may produce an appreciable rise in peak discharges. Figure 5.4 shows comparable storm hydrographs for two of the catchments, and the area subjected to draining and burning has a larger and more rapid response to rainfall which must be chiefly dependent on the land-use contrasts.

Quite apart from Man's physical interference with the hydrological cycle, there is also the possibility of changing mental attitudes to flood risk. In the past it was more or less willingly accepted that river flood-plains fulfilled a natural function, and such zones were avoided by settlement. More recently the growing scarcity of building land has encouraged building on flood-plains without the protection of adequate river training works. The extent of building which has taken place on washlands in the Nottingham area is shown in figure 5.5 in relation to the encroachment of major floods, and a similar picture could be presented for the lowland reaches of many of our rivers (Nixon 1963).

Flood Reduction

The spread of flood-plain occupance gives some urgency to the problem of flood hazards. There is relatively little data available on which a flood prevention policy may be based, and in 1968 it was announced that the Natural Environment Research Council had decided to undertake a comprehensive investigation into the flood hydrology of the United Kingdom based on recommendations of the Institution of Civil Engineers (1967). Some of the hydrological deficiencies have already been outlined, but the difficulties involved in the measurement of flood damage and the evaluation of flood risk are probably even greater. There is, of course, always the impossibility of ascribing a specific value to human life, but this country still lacks a uniform systematic policy towards the collection of more tangible flood loss information. The need for centralised data on direct structural and agricultural damage as well as on indirect losses caused by the interruption of communications has been stressed by Harding and Porter (1969). Flooding is as much an economic problem as a hydrological one, and without basic information on the economic consequences of flooding it is doubtful if a rational attitude can be formulated. Any flood could be prevented given sufficient investment, but the necessary engineering works have a high capital cost, and it will become more and more important for land-use planning on flood-plains to be determined on a reliable estimation of cost: benefit ratios.

From a hydrological standpoint, flood reduction involves two different approaches, both of which may be required in certain instances. These are flood *prediction* and flood *protection* and *control*.

(*a*) *Flood prediction*. Strictly speaking, the estimation of future peak riverflows operates in two quite different ways with essentially separate aims and methods. Flood *prediction* proper makes use of a long time-period, usually the total span of records, and concentrates on the more extreme events. It is largely based on mathematical theory, and attempts to predict the statistical frequency of flood occurrence. The results are expressed in terms of average probability or return period, but there is no indication of *when* a flood of a particular magnitude will occur. Thus, a flood with a calculated return period of 100 years may arrive either this year or be delayed for a century. Flood *forecasting*, on the other hand, deals with specific events in the short-term as they arise, and, by using current information on weather conditions, state of the ground, etc., an attempt can be made to provide a warning not only of the magnitude of the river peak but also the timing of the event.

In Britain accurate flood prediction is hampered by the lack of long-period flow records, and, although techniques do exist whereby a series of flow data can be either extended or even synthetically generated from existing information, they lie outside the scope of this book. Where a long record is available, as for the Thames, the situation is more straightforward, and Wilson (1969) has shown how the annual maximum daily discharges for this river may be analysed for predictive purposes. In recent years, however, there has been a growing tendency to base flood prediction at least partially on physical considerations, and more attention is now being given to the role of meteorology in flood prediction. This method works on the assumption that there is a physically prescribed upper limit to the depth of precipitation which can fall over a given area in a specified time, and the concept of *probable maximum precipitation* has given rise to that of the *probable maximum flood*. The number of variables involved and their complex relationships make for considerable difficulties in the direct application of this approach, but it may eventually provide a reasonable guide to the extremely rare and catastrophic flood.

In the immediate future, greater benefits are likely to derive from developments in river forecasting. A special forecasting problem is created in Britain by the small size of our drainage basins since so little time is available for warning between the onset of rainfall and the arrival of the flood crest in the densely settled lowlands. It is clear, therefore, that any improvements which the Meteorological Office is able to make with regard to storm warnings and the quantitative forecasting of heavy rainfall will be of substantial benefit in flood protection. In addition, it has already been shown that the most severe floods with the swiftest rise originate in the uplands where few human observers are available. This means that a really efficient flood warning system will have to be based on a network of automatic raingauges and river recorders which are capable of supplying data by telemetry to a central office where the information can be assimilated and then possibly be re-distributed in the form of a regional flood warning.

Most forecasting techniques depend on the interpretation of present events in the light of previous catchment responses to analogous situations, and antecedent conditions over the drainage basin are of great importance. For example, the Devon River Authority has used a daily antecedent precipitation index for forecasting purposes in the Exe valley, whilst the Thames Conservancy has developed a method of flow forecasting which depends on the isolation of the baseflow component of discharge (Sutcliffe 1964). It was found that baseflow contributes so much of the total discharge of the Thames that groundwater conditions, as well as soil moisture content, had to be taken into account for flood forecasting as well as for the estimation of low flows. Although it has been traditional practice in this country to use daily precipitation values as a measure of antecedent storm conditions, it is certain that calculated soil moisture deficits will become employed to a greater extent in future operational forecasting.

(*b*) *Flood protection and control.* This aspect of floods comes essentially within the province of the civil engineer, since it is through the construction of hydraulic works that peak discharge can be deliberately modified. All such schemes have the common principle of providing storage by means of which flood peaks may be reduced and possibly delayed, but, for our purposes at least, a distinction may be made between the *river training works*, which are designed mainly to protect the lowlands, and the *reservoir works* of the uplands which attempt to regulate and control flood discharges throughout a river system.

River training works are constructed at specific points where a flood risk exists, and Nixon (1963) has demonstrated something of the variety in the techniques used. One of the simplest solutions is to build flood embankments to increase the capacity of the river channel, although in some cases it is possible to improve the natural channel directly by dredging. In densely populated areas it may be impossible to increase the size of existing rivers, and use is then made of flood relief channels. In effect, these channels duplicate the river course, and in the most favourable situations the channel can be made to by-pass the built-up area as in the case of the river Welland relief channel which avoids Spalding.

Although river training works can provide effective flood protection for the areas immediately concerned, they do nothing to reduce the flood hazard further afield and may possibly direct surplus waters to increase flood stages elsewhere. A more fundamental approach is to control floods in the uplands where they start, and to use large impounding reservoirs to trap flood discharges and then release the excess water downstream in a more uniform flow. This attractive solution is widely employed in some countries, but no large flood control dams have been constructed in Britain. It is felt that the total flood risk does not warrant such an expensive measure, since, in order to be really effective, such reservoirs would have to be very large indeed. On the other hand, it is recognised that future water conservation will depend to an even greater extent on controlling the flow of our rivers for multiple benefits, and the current policy trend is towards river regulating reservoirs which have flood reduction as one of their basic aims.

At the present time, however, almost all upland reservoirs are for direct water supply purposes only and have no flood control function. Nevertheless, if some spare storage capacity does exist in such reservoirs before a storm, then, almost by accident, some flood reduction may be achieved. One example of this occurred in January 1960 on the Derbyshire Derwent below the reservoirs of the Derwent Valley Water Board. As shown in figure 5.6, three flood peaks caused by heavy rain in the latter part of January were absorbed before the reservoirs became full and started overflowing on the 29th. Immediately downstream of the reservoirs at Yorkshire Bridge it is estimated that the two largest flood flows were reduced by a total of 94 m^3/s

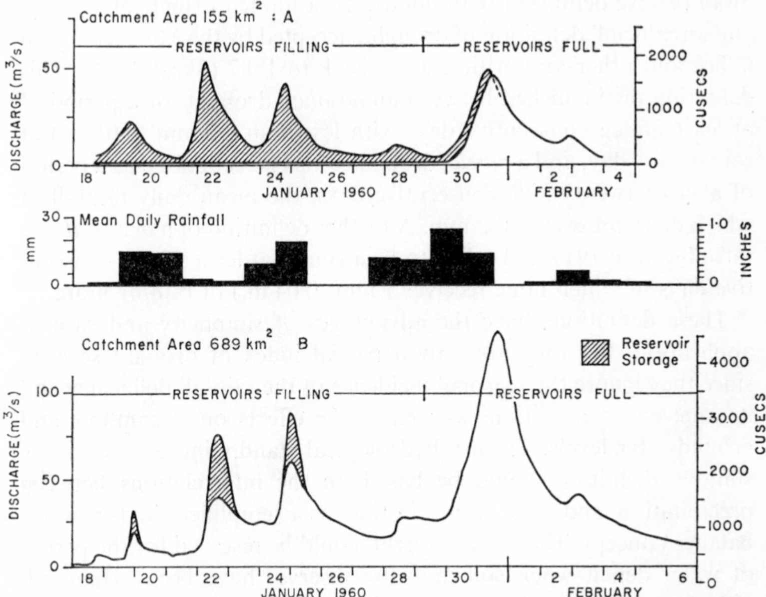

Figure 5.6 The effect of reservoir storage on flood flows of the river Derwent, Derbyshire, in early 1960. After Nixon (1963).
Hydrograph A relates to the flow at Yorkshire Bridge.
Hydrograph B relates to the flow at Matlock.

(3325 cusecs) whilst at Matlock, about 30 km (19 miles) downstream, the reduction was only 57 m^3/s (2030 cusecs). This illustrates the fact that both the absolute and proportional flood benefit decreases downstream as a progressively smaller fraction of the total catchment is reservoired, and is an indication of the great difficulty in providing sufficient flood storage to protect the lowland reaches of our rivers.

DROUGHTS

Definition of Drought

Since droughts are caused essentially by a single factor, namely rainfall deficiency, it is tempting to think that they are amenable to a more precise definition than floods. To a limited extent this is true, and an 'official' definition of drought, accepted by the Meteorological Office and other authorities, dates back to 1887 (Skeat 1961). This definition distinguished between an *absolute* drought, or a period of at least fifteen consecutive days with less than 0·2 mm (0·01 in.) of rain on any day, and a *partial* drought which is recognised as a period of at least twenty-nine consecutive days, the mean daily rainfall of which does not exceed 0·2 mm. A further definition of a *dry spell* was introduced in 1919 and taken to be a run of at least fifteen consecutive days of which none receives 1 mm (0·04 in.) of rain or more.

These definitions have the advantages of simplicity and ease of application, but they are only a partial index of drought severity since they ignore the seasonal incidence of the rainfall deficiency and its antecedent conditions as well as the effects on streamflow and groundwater levels. From a hydrological standpoint, a much more suitable definition would be based on the interrelations between precipitation and evapotranspiration as exemplified in the water balance concept. The term 'drought' could be reserved for the period of water deficit when soil moisture reserves have been exhausted, although this is partially dependent on local soil profile characteristics. On the other hand, an assessment of drought satisfactory for water resource purposes should involve a more direct reference to the reduced yield of surface and underground sources, and it is here that the problem is complicated, as in the case of floods, by local catchment characteristics.

Ideally, a definition of drought should take into account the dry weather discharges of rivers, for even the effects of a water balance drought will vary according to the nature of the low flow behaviour of different drainage basins. Thus, a river with a high proportion of baseflow will be cushioned against lack of rainfall to a far greater degree than a river with little groundwater storage where, for equally sized catchment areas, the low flows will be smaller both in absolute terms as well as in relation to the mean discharge.

Although the significance of dry weather flows may appear

self-evident, little attention has been given to the evaluation of such discharges. No generally acceptable definition is available, although it has been suggested by the Surface Water Survey (1960) that, where adequate records exist, frequency analysis could be employed and the term 'dry weather flow' could then be defined as all rates of flow which are exceeded for, say, 95 per cent of the time. A major obstacle arises from the difficulty of making accurate low flow measurements on many of our rivers. In the first place many gauging stations are not equipped for the precise measurement of extreme minima when a relatively small absolute error in measurement will make a considerable difference in proportional terms. Secondly, and more important, is the fact that dry weather flows in Britain are dependent to only a limited extent on natural conditions, and often the most important controls are man-made. Artificial manipulations of river-flow take a number of forms and operate on an almost infinite number of time-scales. For example, streamflow may be depleted or enhanced regularly by abstractions of water or discharges of effluent which are fairly constant on an annual basis, but which are highly intermittent over shorter periods. The effect of these modifications can be considerable in dry weather when perhaps most of the natural flow is being pumped for irrigation or when the discharge may be more than doubled by effluent disposal. In addition to the actual changes in volume, human interference also includes the effects of artificial structures such as lock gates, weirs and mill sluices which may exert a temporary influence on the timing of low flows.

Even when reliable low flow data are examined, it is found that, unlike the case with floods, little regional pattern emerges. A schedule of observed dry weather flows was prepared by the Surface Water Survey after the dry summer of 1959, and, to facilitate direct comparison, the discharges were expressed as runoff per unit area of catchment. Average values ranged from 0·25 l. s^{-1} km^2 (0·023 cusecs per sq mile) in Essex to as much as 6·8 l. s^{-1} km^2 (0·620 cusecs per sq mile) in South Wales, although the latter figure was influenced by the discharge of water from coal mines. Most of the values were between 1·1 and 2·2 l. s^{-1} km^2 (0·1 and 0·2 cusecs per sq mile). Despite the importance of individual catchment characteristics, the lowest values were found in south-east England. In parts of Sussex, Essex and Kent, as well as London and the Thames Valley, extreme minima on rivers draining flat, clay catchments reached zero, although it must be appreciated that many of these rivers are characterised by large summer abstractions.

The Nature of Drought

Droughts in Britain are caused by a dislocation of the normal atmospheric circulation which favours the regular passage of mid-latitude depressions across these islands, and spells of settled weather are invariably associated with anticyclonic situations. The most frequent and prolonged droughts generally result from north-eastward extensions of the Azores high pressure cell, which then raises pressure over at least the southern part of the country (Brooks and Glasspoole 1928). The high pressure can become extremely effective in displacing the track of Atlantic storms well to the north, but northern Scotland often remains under the influence of the migratory lows. Drought can also be caused by a development of high pressure to the north-east of Britain when a Scandinavian anticyclone will bring a steady easterly flow to most of this country. This air, which blows directly off the Continent, is dry and its restricted path over the North Sea rarely allows the take-up of precipitable moisture, although some light orographic rainfall may be experienced near the east coast.

Dry spells are more widespread than heavy rainstorms, but it is unusual for no part of the British Isles to record rainfall during any one day, and Glasspoole and Rowsell (1947) have confirmed there is a marked regional variation in the incidence of rainfall deficiency. Figure 5.7 shows that the average number of absolute droughts recorded between 1906 and 1940 decreased from over one per year in southern England to less than one in every five to ten years in the extreme north of Scotland. A similar picture emerges with respect to partial droughts, and such contrasts might be expected in view of what has already been said about rainfall variability over the country. In the 35-year period under review, there was no year with more than one absolute drought in north-west Britain, the Pennines and Snowdonia, but it is also clear that no part of the country is immune from at least fifteen consecutive days without rain. On the other hand, whilst the longest recorded rainless spells over most of Scotland, northern England and upland Wales hardly ever reach thirty days according to Glasspoole and Rowsell (1950), this drought duration has been doubled in southern England, where the longest

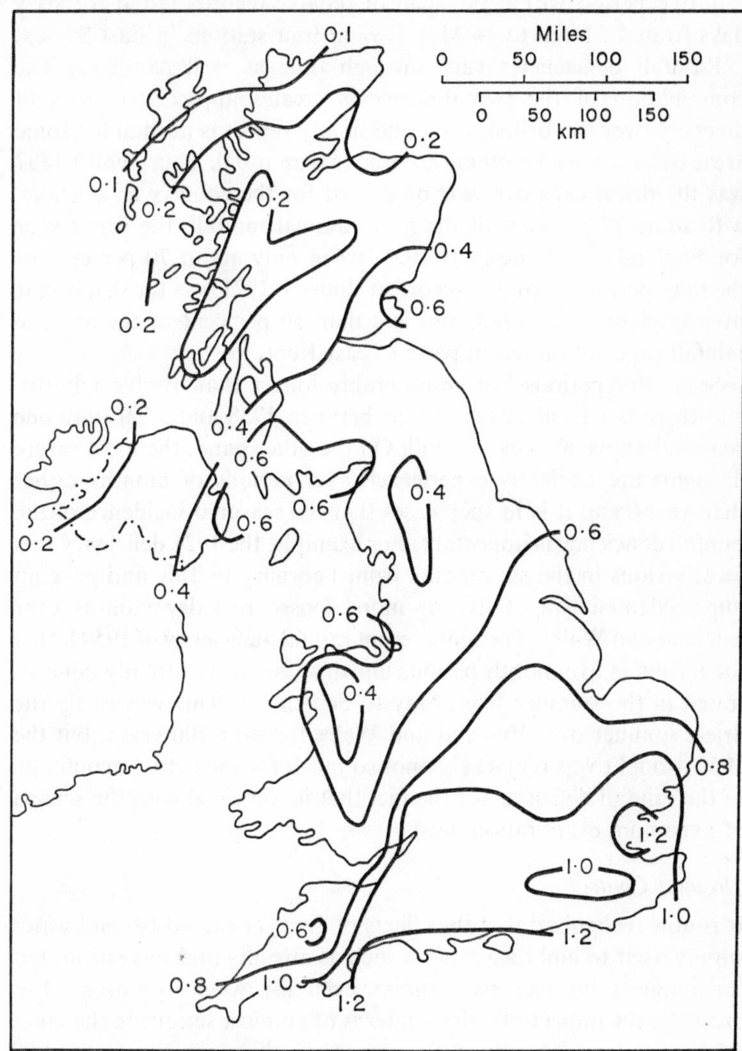

Figure 5.7 The regional distribution of mean annual absolute drought between 1906 and 1940. After Glasspoole and Rowsell (1947).

rain-free period within the span of reliable records lasted for sixty days from 4 March to 14 May 1893 at four stations in East Sussex.

Rainfall deficiencies vary through time as well as space. The combination of the two dimensions creates appreciable drought diversity over the British Isles, and in any year it is normal for some areas to be dry whilst others are wetter than usual. Thus, whilst 1887 was the driest calendar year on record for the country as a whole, with some 77 per cent of the mean annual rainfall, the driest year for England and Wales was 1921, when only about 70 per cent of the long-period mean was recorded. Indeed, 1921 was the driest year over England since 1788, and less than 50 per cent of the average rainfall expectation fell in parts of east Kent.

Some dry periods last considerably longer than twelve months, and there is partial evidence that between 1738 and 1760 only one year had above average rainfall. On the other hand, the most severe droughts are normally experienced over periods of months rather than years, and it is in such cases that the seasonal incidence of the rainfall deficiency is important. For example, the 1921 deficiency was most serious in the six months from February to July and gave an unprecedented run of five or more consecutive dry months over England and Wales. The more recent rainfall deficiency of 1959 lasted for a similar five-month period, but this time it was totally concentrated in the summer from May to September. This was easily the driest summer over England and Wales for over 200 years, but the 1959 drought was remarkable not so much for the actual magnitude of the rainfall deficit as for the fact that it coincided with the season of maximum evaporation need.

Drought Control

It is now recognised that the effects of drought extend beyond water supply itself to embrace aspects such as amenity and recreation, but the implications can be complex even for water resources. For example, the impact of a dry winter is often most serious in the areas relying on deep groundwater sources since these reserves are replenished by the rainfall excess at this season, whilst surface reservoirs tend to remain full from near the beginning of the winter and have insufficient capacity to store most of the winter rainfall. The reverse is true of summer and autumn droughts, which have a more immediate effect on surface storage, since the dry spell comes at just the time of year when streamflow is at its lowest level. Not surprisingly, therefore, the response to drought differs over the country as in 1959 when most of the supply restrictions introduced by the water supply authorities were in the north of England.

Drought prediction depends on much the same sort of principles that underlie flood estimation. Some reliance is placed on statistical and probability methods, particularly in connection with the prediction of rainfall deficiencies, but the most useful techniques for forecasting low river discharge depend on the analysis of the exponential depletion curve of groundwater runoff. The advantage of this method is that the forecasts relate specifically to the catchment under consideration, and, by extrapolating the depletion curve forwards from the early summer period, an estimate can be made of low flows later in the year. Similarly, extreme drought conditions can be simulated by extending the baseflow plot through a rainless period of any assumed length. Work conducted along these lines shows the important effect of geological characteristics on rates of depletion and ultimate dry weather flows. In the Scottish Lothians it has been found by Wright (1970) that the slowest recessions and highest drought flows are associated with extensive areas of sand and gravel or coarse sandstone, whilst areas of crystalline rock, boulder clay and peat show directly opposite effects. It is interesting to note that the flow from peat catchments was less sustained than for any other formation. This is in accord with evidence from elsewhere, and suggests that blanket peat is probably a good deal less effective in regulating the discharge into upland reservoirs than many water supply authorities have believed in the past.

Droughts cannot be prevented from occurring, and the only protection against them involves the construction of engineering works to alleviate the full effects. As in the case of floods, storage is again the vital key, whether it is achieved underground or in surface reservoirs. The delayed response of groundwater reserves to rainfall deficiency compared with surface supplies makes the interchangeability of different sources an attractive proposition which is under increasing investigation in this country. Similarly, the use of storage to maintain dry weather discharges above an agreed minimum flow, which is acceptable to all river interests, is a fundamental principle underlying recent trends in water conservation, and as such is more appropriately considered as an aspect of river regulation in chapter 9.

6 Public Water Supply

At the present time, rather more than half of the total water utilised in Britain is supplied by the statutory water undertakings. Most of this water is used for domestic purposes, but the water industry is also facing a growing commitment towards industrial supplies, and it is the purpose of this chapter to examine both spheres of the public supply system.

THE EVOLUTION OF PUBLIC WATER SUPPLIES

The existing public water undertakings have grown from the first organised attempts to provide a reliable drinking supply for local communities, and it is impossible to appreciate the role of these authorities without some reference to the past. In detail, local factors of geology, rate of settlement expansion or personal initiative have often contributed greatly to the evolution of supplies, but, for the country as a whole, certain broad trends can be distinguished.

Early Developments

It is probable that some degree of co-operative effort has always been necessary to secure communal water supplies. In Roman times the more important towns, such as Lincoln, had organised water supplies which were frequently dependent on underground sources. References to urban schemes become increasingly numerous in the medieval period. Thus, at Kingston-upon-Hull a Royal Charter of 1447 allowed for the enlargement of the newly created County to incorporate a spring-fed supply which was urgently required to replace the arrangement whereby fresh water was conveyed to the town by boats crossing the Humber from Lincolnshire (Aylwin and Ward 1969). In London early supplies obtained by direct abstraction from the Thames and adjacent springs were distributed by water carriers, but after 1236 a system of conduits was constructed to convey water into the urban area from farther afield.

In most towns the direct abstraction of water from local underground or surface sources sufficed until the eighteenth or early nineteenth century, by which time the rapid increase in population, together with the attendant pollution, was making such supplies inadequate. Where a town had a Royal Charter the water supply was sometimes provided by the Corporation, but in the majority of cases the growing demands were met by private water companies. For example, the Sheffield, Ashton and Bolton waterworks were all founded by joint-stock companies in the period of financial speculation around 1825. It has been claimed by Stern (1955) that out of a total of 190 local authorities operating in 1846, only ten possessed their own waterworks, whilst two others – Liverpool and Leeds – held shares in their respective undertakings and exercised some direction over policy. The private companies obtained Acts of Parliament which gave them authority to supply their townships, and such legislation often provided initial piped supplies to sizeable urban communities. This was particularly the case in the industrial North as at Sheffield where the water company, formed in 1830, was responsible for supplying no less than 90 000 consumers (Sheffield City Water Committee 1961). Most of these water companies suffered from poor technical and financial resources, and the supplies were unreliable. It was also common for piped supplies to be restricted to one part of a town. In 1837 only about one-third of Bradford's 35 000 population was receiving regular supplies, and water carts still provided a door-to-door service in the less fortunate areas (Bradford Corporation Water Department 1955).

Such unsatisfactory conditions persisted in many areas until the Municipal Boroughs were established later in the century. On the advice of the newly-created Water Committees, the Borough Councils almost immediately bought up the existing works and assets of the private companies, and it is usually from this time that larger and more distant sources of supply were appropriated. This change in policy was made possible by the greater financial resources now available, but the general attitude was also conditioned by the growing awareness of the importance of a wholesome water supply in relation to public hygiene and sanitation.

Asiatic cholera became epidemic in England in 1831, and further outbreaks took place until 1866. The first outbreak alone was responsible for 50 000 deaths, and there was virtually no knowledge at this time of the role of water in the transmission of disease. Existing sanitary provision by the local authorities simply involved the discharge of raw sewage and other wastes to the nearest watercourse with the inevitable contamination of local water supplies. In London, for example, it eventually became clear that the supply obtained from river intakes below the major sewage outfalls was polluted despite the early introduction of filtration in 1829, but it was several years before the intakes were moved upstream. By the middle of the nineteenth century some of the true squalor of urban life was revealed, as in the report of the Royal Commission of 1845 on the Health of Large Towns written mainly by Edwin Chadwick, the social reformer. The Commission visited fifty large towns and only six were found to have an adequate water supply, whilst not one was served with a proper drainage system. In Manchester and Liverpool over 40 000 people lived in cellars with a complete absence of sanitation, and in Birmingham some 80 per cent of the houses had no water supply according to Evans (1950).

As a result of such reports the public health movement became strongly identified with the search for new sources of potable water in the moorland valleys which surrounded many of the industrial towns. Manchester Corporation, for example, was greatly influenced by the Chadwick report, and initiated the first of the large upland impounding schemes. In 1846 the Corporation promoted a Bill to acquire the existing Manchester and Salford Waterworks Company, and to authorise new impounding works along the river Etherow some 24 km (15 miles) to the east of Manchester. Seven reservoirs were constructed by 1877 providing an overall yield of 1·26 m^3/s (24 mgd). The scheme was designed by J. F. La Trobe Bateman, who was personally responsible for water supply projects for no less than thirty major towns and cities in Britain. These included the important Glasgow scheme whereby the storage capacity of Loch Katrine, over 48 km (30 miles) from the town, was increased to provide a supply of 2·63 m^3/s (50 mgd) to the city.

The latter part of the nineteenth century saw the widespread establishment of upland reservoirs for the gravitational supply of water to the expanding manufacturing towns. In view of the early industrial rise of Lancashire and Yorkshire, it is not surprising that the Pennines became the first major upland source to be exploited. These moorlands have retained their importance to the present day, although additional demands later in the nineteenth century caused many cities to look further afield as local dam sites became more difficult to find. For example, in the 1880s Liverpool Corporation obtained a large supply from the Vyrnwy valley in North Wales, whilst about ten years later Birmingham began reservoir construction in the Elan valley of central Wales 121 km (75 miles) away from the city. This trend towards long-distance piped supplies is admirably illustrated by Manchester Corporation. About 1875 the growing demand threatened to overtake the available supply from the Longdendale works in the Etherow valley and, in 1879, Parliament authorised the use of the natural storage afforded by Lake Thirlmere about 161 km (100 miles) distant in the Lake District. In 1923 Manchester took over Haweswater some 129 km (80 miles) from the city, and so became the largest undertaking dependent on surface supplies in the country.

All these nineteenth century urban schemes had much in common. They were dependent on the direct-supply reservoir capable of storing ample supplies of soft, upland water draining from extensive moorland gathering grounds. The water was conveyed from the reservoirs, largely by gravitational influences, to treatment works and associated service reservoirs on the higher outskirts of the town. From here the water was subsequently distributed to individual consumers through service mains. In order to safeguard the purity of the supplies, most authorities purchased the gathering grounds around their reservoirs, and thus prohibited public access to large areas of upland Britain. Hill farming in the catchment areas was strictly controlled by the water undertakings, with restrictions on human and sheep populations, and many hill farms were eventually abandoned. A wider vision did become apparent, however, towards the end of the nineteenth century. In 1878 the Manchester Corporation Act for Thirlmere made specific provision for public access to the reservoir gathering grounds, and similar clauses were incorporated into the 1892 Birmingham Act for the Elan valley. The Thirlmere Act is also significant in that it contained the provision, subsequently applied in later schemes, for smaller water undertakings to obtain a supply from the aqueduct *en route* to Manchester provided they were sufficiently close to it and had no other adequate source of supply.

This was a first step towards the principle of bulk supply agreements and co-operation rather than rivalry between water authorities.

On the other hand, real progress in the direction of better supplies for essentially rural areas did not materialise for many years. Even during the early years of the present century, rural areas were considered purely in terms of water export, and it was common for large aqueducts to carry water across zones without reliable piped supplies. Early examples of regional co-operation between undertakings are notable because of their rarity. One illustration is the Derwent Valley Water Board which was created in 1899 by the amalgamation of five constituent authorities – Leicester, Sheffield, Derby, Nottingham and Derbyshire County. The aim as described by Lockyer (1957) was to develop the ample resources of the Derbyshire Derwent in order to improve supplies over a large area of the north Midlands, and the formation of the Board prevented any one local authority from controlling all of the river. Subject to supplies totalling a maximum of 0·34 m^3/s (6·5 mgd) to various local authorities in Derbyshire, each of the remaining four Corporations is entitled to receive the following bulk supply percentage from the Board for detailed distribution within the individual supply areas – Leicester 35·72 per cent, Sheffield 25 per cent, Derby 25 per cent and Nottingham 14·28 per cent. To facilitate these supplies the Board constructed three large reservoirs on the Derwent – Howden 1912, Derwent 1916 and Ladybower 1945 – and the whole project shows the economies of scale which might have been achieved by similar co-operation in other areas.

In general, however, the first decades of the present century saw few important changes in the policies of the statutory water undertakings. By this time the allocation of the upland gathering grounds was mostly complete and rising demands, which were partially created by extensions of urban supply areas to cover adjacent rural areas, were often satisfied by the consolidation of existing resources rather than the appropriation of new sources.

This consolidation was made possible by original errors in the yield assessments of the early reservoirs. Ideally, these yields should have been based on actual runoff records but normally only limited rainfall data were available. The urgency with which many of these schemes were undertaken, either to cope with rapidly growing demands or to forestall a rival authority from developing the source, meant that standardised procedures were adopted. This standardisation applied to both the calculation of supply yield and also the estimation of compensation water. In a situation where quick decisions had to be made on inadequate evidence, and where no pressure or incentive existed for the careful utilisation of water as a limited resource, it is hardly surprising that the water engineers allowed over-generous safety margins by under-estimating the true discharge from the gathering grounds. The riparian interests were normally allocated one-third of the estimated yield, irrespective of their real needs, whilst the reservoirs, constructed on the same yield basis, had a storage capacity too small to ensure efficient use of the total resources. In theory, at least, a direct-supply reservoir should be capable of supplying well over three-quarters of the average catchment runoff for supply purposes, but most schemes fell well short of this. For example, even with later additions to supply, it has been estimated by Smith (1966) that the yield taken by Bradford Corporation from a total area of about 114 km^2 (44 sq miles) in upper Nidderdale, Yorkshire, represents only about one-third of the mean flow from the area.

As the true yield of many of these reservoired catchments became clear during this century, some of the original schemes were modified to take a greater quantity of water into supply, either by statutory reduction of the compensation discharge or by further engineering works. Risbridger (1963) has quoted several examples of compensation reductions amounting to over 50 per cent, whilst other authorities improved water yields by raising the height of planned or existing dams so that more water could be stored. Much use was also made of *catchwaters.* These are open conduits which intercept the drainage from small streams in adjacent catchment areas and divert the flow into the existing reservoir, thereby artificially increasing the topographic limits of the supply catchment. The transmission of these additional supplies to the consumption area was often achieved by the duplication of aqueducts and the installation of pumping stations to boost the flow of water through the trunk mains.

Post-war Changes

The Government White Paper of 1944 drew attention to certain defects in the public water supply industry. The subsequent Water Acts of 1945 and 1948 attempted to reduce the multiplicity of small undertakings, and ensure better supplies to both rural areas and industry. Thus, the Minister of Health was given powers to create new Joint Water Boards and to vary the limits of supply of existing authorities as he thought best. Provision was made for more bulk supply arrangements, either compulsorily or by agreement, and for the first time a statutory obligation was placed on the undertakings to furnish a supply of water, if so requested, to premises for other than domestic purposes as long as domestic requirements were not jeopardised. Despite this important legislation, little real improvement had been achieved by the middle 1950s when it became increasingly clear that the structure of the supply industry was in urgent need of fundamental reform.

The main problem was the fragmentation of supply authorities, and, even as late as 1956, there were over 1050 separate water undertakings in England and Wales. Most of these were local authorities, some of whom were supplying populations of only a few hundred, whilst almost half of the total population was served by fifty-five undertakings. Many authorities were too small to operate efficiently. In the rural areas, especially, they had neither the financial nor the technical resources to extend piped supplies, prevent waste or keep proper records. Many were dependent on either traditional rural sources such as wells and springs, which were sometimes inadequate in both quantity and quality, or on bulk supplies from larger neighbouring authorities. A typical example is the Isle of Anglesey, which has a population of over 50 000 within its area of 444 km^2 (276 sq miles). In 1943 mains water was available to only 25 per cent of the island's population, and was supplied from thirteen separate sources by no less than eight undertakings. One year later entire responsibility for the supply passed to the Anglesey County Council. Since then two impounding reservoirs have been constructed, and an extra 34 km (21 miles) of water main has been laid (Anonymous 1967).

The situation was no less confused in the urban areas, despite the universal availability of piped supplies, and Gregory (1958*a*) has shown something of the complexities of supply which existed into the late 1950s in the British conurbations. Because of the piece-meal growth of undertakings, no conurbation was served by a single authority, and considerable administrative contrasts existed between the different population centres. Thus, Greater London's thirteen undertakings were mainly private companies lying around the dominant central Metropolitan Water Board, whilst West Yorkshire consisted of only one private company with local authorities comprising the remaining thirty undertakings. Similarly, Tyneside was mostly supplied by two private companies, although eight of the ten undertakings on central Clydeside were local authorities.

There was also a marked variation in the supply sources used by different conurbations. In Greater London relatively local river and groundwater sources were utilised, but, although groundwater from the Triassic sandstones was important in the West Midlands and on Merseyside, all other conurbations showed a clear reliance on upland reservoirs. On a national scale the uplands provided less than half of all the water supplied by statutory undertakings in England and Wales, but they were dominant in the densely populated industrial areas of the North, the Midlands and South Wales (Gregory 1958*b*). Altogether, three-quarters of all upland water was used away from the source area, whilst the association of particular conurbations with specific upland regions, which is still evident, illustrates just how enduring the nineteenth century supply legacy has been.

Despite encouragement from the central Government, the water industry showed little initiative in rationalisation. Eventually, in September 1956, the Minister of Housing and Local Government adopted a firmer attitude with the issue of the first of several official circulars pressing the need for regrouping and amalgamation on the undertakings (Ministry of Housing and Local Government 1956). Gradually the movement gained momentum. Within a decade the number of undertakings had been reduced to one-third in England and Wales, and by 1970 there were only 315 undertakings in the United Kingdom (Wilkinson and Squire 1970). The changes which amalgamation has brought in England and Wales are summarised in table 6. It can be seen that the trend has been towards a reduction

TABLE 6

NUMBER AND TYPE OF WATER UNDERTAKINGS IN ENGLAND AND WALES IN 1954 AND 1970

Type of undertaking	*1954*	*1970*
Local Authorities	906	83
Water Boards and Joint Committees	43	105
Water Companies	98	36
Others	7	9
Total	1054	233

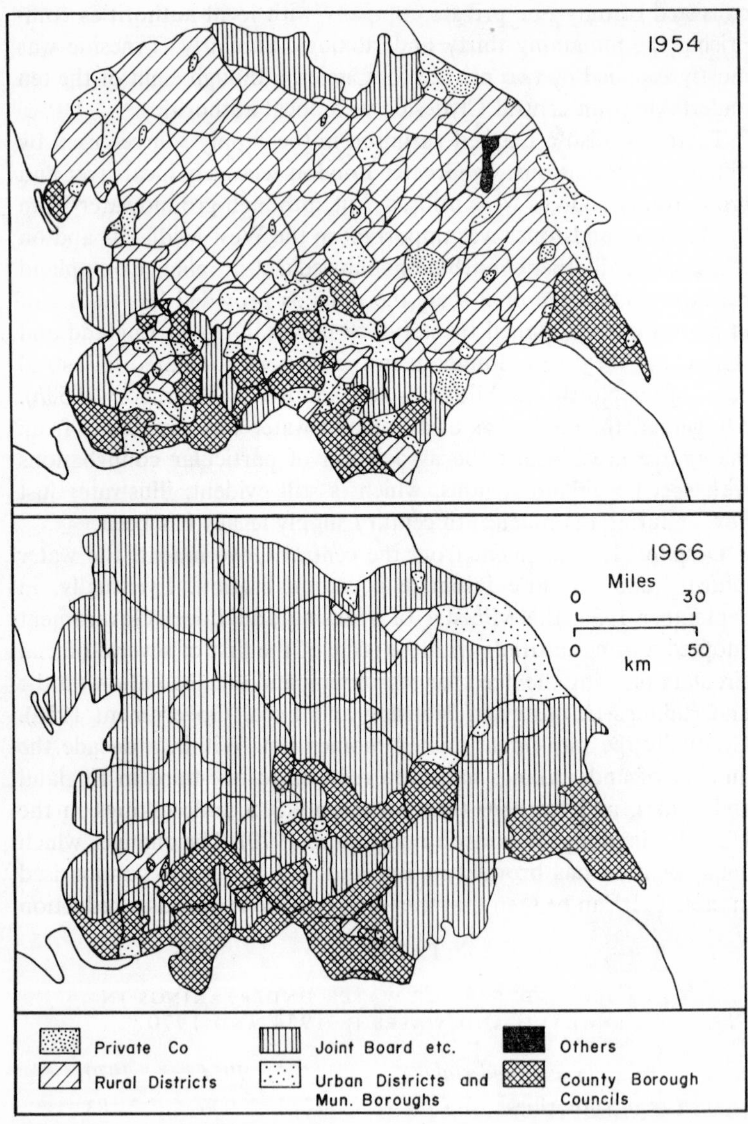

Figure 6.1 The regrouping of statutory water undertakings in northern England between 1954 and 1966. After Gregory (1969).

in the number of local authority undertakings and water companies together with the formation of more water boards. The way in which this affected the administrative structure of the industry in northern England between 1954 and 1966 is shown in figure 6.1 which has been taken from Gregory (1969). It can be seen that in the urban areas the former Municipal Boroughs and Urban District authorities have been largely absorbed by the expanded County Borough areas of supply which now incorporate satellite towns and suburbs. In the rural areas the former Rural District authorities have been replaced by the Joint Water Boards who now have extensive supply functions over large areas, including some important towns. In southern England a similar reduction in administrative units has been achieved by a real expansion of both private Water Companies and Joint Boards, including the Metropolitan Water Board. This is the largest undertaking in the country, and supplies well over six million people. The total supply delivered amounts to over 20 m^3/s (380 mgd), most of which is distributed within the detailed supply area of 868 km^2 (539 sq miles).

Regrouping in Scotland was achieved by the Water (Scotland) Act of 1967. As from May 1968 this Act transferred the functions of about 200 existing local water undertakings to thirteen regional water boards and a Central Scotland Water Development Board. The regional boards are responsible for supplying water to consumers and will, in general, develop and maintain the necessary sources of supply. The Water Development Board has wide powers to develop sources to supply two or more of the regions, whilst it also supplies water in bulk to the regional water boards for detailed distribution. In Northern Ireland amalgamations have been much more piece-meal. There were still 68 undertakings serving the area in 1970, with a majority of local authorities (56) compared with twelve water boards.

THE NATURE OF DEMAND

At the start of this decade the statutory water undertakings were supplying between 131 and 158 m^3/s (2500 and 3000 mgd), of which no more than two-thirds was taken by the *domestic consumer*. This water is paid for by a fixed initial charge or *water rate*, which is levied on the rateable value of the householder's premises, and therefore bears no relation to the amount of water used. Thus, apart from a few check meters installed by the undertakings to prevent waste in distribution, all domestic supplies are unmetered. Until April 1969 the Malvern undertaking was the only exception to this rule, but this anomaly has since disappeared with the incorporation of the authority into the newly-formed South-West Worcestershire Water Board. The remaining supply goes to industry, and this *trade consumption* is metered to individual industrial establishments – from large factories to laundries and fish shops – and is paid for according to the quantity taken. Since the domestic and trade sectors of consumption differ in many respects, it will be convenient to treat them separately.

Domestic Consumption

The dominance of domestic consumption has its origin in the nineteenth century public health movement and the subsequent development of water undertakings as a social service. As a result of the emphasis on potable supplies, about 97 per cent of the population has an individual piped supply.

Before the introduction of the River Authority licensing system, the records of the undertakings themselves formed the only available information on consumption trends. The first national study was carried out by the Ministry of Health (1949). This report selected twenty-six large and geographically representative undertakings in Britain, which, together, were responsible for supplying 43 per cent of the population with about half of the nation's recorded water consumption. It was found that in the decade 1938–48 the total quantity of water supplied in England and Wales rose from 34 to 41 m^3/s (651 to 778 mgd), which represented an average increase of about 2 per cent per annum. It was further shown that, if the Metropolitan Water Board was excluded from the analysis of the twenty-two English and Welsh undertakings, the increase amounted to some 3 per cent per year, which, if continued, would result in a doubling of the 1938 demand by 1970. The rate of increase in Scotland, calculated for four undertakings over the same decade, was only 1 per cent per annum. It was later suggested that the forecast for England and Wales was an underestimate, and that some undertakings were already supplying twice the 1938 amount. However, a further review by the Central Advisory Water Committee indicated that the mean annual increase in the decade 1955–65, as predicted by the supply authorities themselves, was likely to remain within the 2–3 per cent range. This growth rate was in fact maintained up to 1965 and still appears to be a reasonable general estimate despite more rapid increases, particularly in metered consumption, in certain areas.

The continued rise in domestic water consumption is, of course, partially explained by the growth in population numbers, but the major influence is the progressive improvement in living standards. It has been claimed by Balchin (1958) that domestic consumption in 1830 averaged less than 18 l. (4 gal) per person per day, whilst present demand is about ten times higher. The individual components of domestic demand in south-east England are set out in table 7

TABLE 7

ESTIMATED AVERAGE DAILY CONSUMPTION PER HEAD IN SOUTH-EAST ENGLAND

After Sharp (1967)

Demand component	*Year 1967* (l.)	(gal)	*Year 2000* (l.)	(gal)
Drinking and cooking	4	1	4	1
Dish washing and cleaning	14	3	18	4
Laundry	14	3	23	5
Personal washing and bathing	45	10	59	13
W.C. and refuse disposal	50	11	59	13
Car washing	—	—	4	<1
Garden use and recreation	4	1	27	6
Waste in distribution	23	5	36	8
Total	154	34	230	51

together with estimated increases for the end of the century. It can be seen that personal hygiene and sanitation together account for about two-thirds of current domestic use, and that these components are expected to represent over half the total demand by A.D. 2000 (Sharp 1967). On the other hand, owing to regional differences in climate and personal income levels, this projected trend may not be representative of the country as a whole.

In the past, domestic consumption has risen as a result of access to a reliable water supply, the subsequent increased use of water-using appliances and the ease with which water can be heated. Thus, the introduction of piped supplies in rural areas always causes an abrupt upsurge in demand whilst, in urban areas, slum clearance and rehousing is the principal factor influencing demand. The provision of taps, indoor water closets and fixed baths is important in itself, but the type of housing scheme can also be significant. Table 8 details

TABLE 8

WATER CONSUMPTION RELATED TO WATER HEATING SYSTEMS IN BRADFORD

After Bradford Corporation Water Department (1957)

Type of property	*Water heating system*	*Consumption litres/head/day*	*Consumption gal/head/day*
Back-to-back	None	35	7·8
Semi-detached and modern terraced	Fireback boiler	59	13·0
New semi-detached	Independent boiler	77	17·0
Flats	District system	100–139	22·0–30·5

consumption figures obtained from parts of the City of Bradford in 1957. There appears to be some relationship between *per capita* consumption and the ease with which water can be heated in the home. In particular, the constant supply of hot water to large blocks of flats at a fixed price from centralised heating schemes produces a considerable increase in demand over more traditionally served premises.

The upward trend in domestic consumption eventually creates problems of providing additional sources for all undertakings, but many urban authorities have further difficulties resulting from old works and distribution systems. In the central parts of many towns the water-mains have been laid for well over a century. Corrosion, plus the effects of vibration from heavy traffic, often cause appreciable wastage from mains and service pipes, and such leakage is increased if the water is supplied at high pressure. In addition, rehousing schemes usually involve a relocation of domestic demands as population is transferred from central areas to peripheral housing estates, and this may necessitate a reorganisation of the distribution system with new treatment plants and service reservoirs. The major problem in rural areas, however, is usually the cost of financing the extension of piped supplies to small, dispersed communities.

Industrial Consumption

Although some water undertakings were selling water to industrial consumers as early as the mid-nineteenth century, trade demands have always been of secondary importance to the water supply authorities. The bias towards the domestic consumer has meant that the public undertakings treat virtually all their supplies to a uniform standard of potability before distribution. Since potability is rarely a major criterion of quality for industrial supplies, industrial consumers have, in the past, found it cheaper and more convenient to develop their own sources of raw water.

In the period following the Second World War, a changed situation has prevailed. The 1945 Water Act, which placed a qualified obligation on the supply authorities to provide industrial water, also introduced controls on the sinking of new wells and boreholes in certain areas. As a result, the industrial consumer turned to the water undertakings for the new supplies which were required by the increased consumption during the post-war industrial expansion. At the same time, similar increases in agricultural demands, notably for dairying and irrigation, led to further demands on the undertakings. Thus, the trade sector of consumption began to grow more rapidly than domestic demands. In 1959 the Central Advisory Water Committee noted that it was in the industrialised areas, where metered requirements were already a high proportion of the total demand, that the greatest future increases were to be expected. This was confirmed by the 1962 report of the Committee which showed that, in some districts, the mean annual increase in metered consumption during 1955–60 was 5·2 per cent, or more than double the rate of increase for the total quantity of water supplied by all authorities. In south-east England, for example, total metered consumption has more than doubled since 1946 (Sharp 1967), and this trend is likely to continue owing to the further controls on the development of private supplies introduced by the River Authorities' licensing system.

There is a considerable variation in the proportion of industrial water supplied by different undertakings. Expressed in terms of per capita demand, trade supplies range from as low as 23 litres/person/day (5 gal/person/day) in some rural areas, or in industrial areas where alternative supplies may be available, to as much as 227 litres/person/day (50 gal/person/day) in districts of concentrated industry with high water demands (Skeat 1961). Almost without exception, however, industrial establishments rely on the statutory undertakings to supply the sanitation requirements of their employees. At present the average amount of water taken for these purposes is between 45 and 68 litres/person/day (10 to 15 gal/person/day) but this accounts for only a small fraction of metered consumption. As in the case of domestic consumption, trade supplies may be subject to high peak demands. This can be a particular problem in rural areas where irrigation water is drawn from the public mains since Prickett (1963) has pointed out that the maximum rate of demand is as high as the public water demand per unit area of dense urban development. On a diurnal scale, shift-working may be a significant factor, whilst in dairying areas the village service reservoir may be full at 06.00 hr but exhausted one hour later owing to the demands of milk cooling.

TRENDS IN WATER SOURCES

The growing demand for water places an increasingly difficult obligation on the statutory undertakings to provide additional supplies, and new sources of supply have become especially difficult to develop. With increased abstractions and the progressive deterioration of water quality through pollution, convenient sites for reservoirs or groundwater pumping are rarely available. In addition to physical restrictions on water availability, the supply industry is also faced with opposition from public opinion when certain sources are proposed for development, and the location of new impounding reservoirs is now a highly controversial issue in our crowded island.

Disputes between the water authorities and preservationists, farmers and scientists have become common over the last few years. Recreationists have also become more vocal about the rights of public access to existing gathering grounds, especially when these extend over a large area of a National Park as in the Peak District where according to Darby (1967) reservoired catchments comprise about one-third of the total area. It is because of such difficulties, both internal and external, that the water industry has re-appraised not only its search for new sources but also its utilisation of existing schemes. Many of these re-appraisals would not have been possible formerly because they depend on co-operative effort on the part of several undertakings, and one of the most significant trends in recent years has been the replacement of the old spirit of inter-authority competition by a policy of collective responsibility.

With regard to existing sources, much of the co-operation has been achieved through the re-grouping policy and a more flexible use of the supplies. Many of the new undertakings have their own independent sources but, in certain areas, the distribution of bulk supplies is important. This is the case in north-west England, which is dominated by the Manchester C.B.C. undertaking. Although this undertaking provides a detailed supply of about 5 m^3/s (97 mgd) over an area of 678 km^2 (262 sq miles), a further 1·3 m^3/s (25 mgd) is provided as bulk supplies to twelve other undertakings in the area (Wilkinson and Squire 1970). No less than eight of these undertakings are Water Boards created by the re-grouping policy. Although their reliance on Manchester is only partial, the situation reflects the regional importance of Manchester's aqueduct leading north–south from the Lake District through an area traversed by relatively minor westward flowing rivers. An important advantage of bulk supplies is that they reduce the vulnerability of an undertaking which relies entirely on one source of supply. Thus, the Lancashire undertakings served by Manchester may be able to draw on a Lake District source if more local supplies become exhausted.

Some undertakings achieve similar flexibility through the development of both surface and underground sources which may be utilised at different times of the year. A typical example from the same area is the Fylde Water Board. Traditionally this undertaking relied on upland catchments in the Lancashire Pennines near Bowland, the water being transferred by aqueduct across the Fylde area to the main consumption centre around Blackpool on the coast. Like all tourist resorts, the Lancashire coast has high peak demands during the summer holiday season at precisely the time of year when surface reserves are low. Largely to meet this demand, the Water Board has augmented its surface sources from boreholes in the Fylde sandstone, which may be drawn upon during dry spells in summer. In addition to the seasonal balancing of surface and groundwater supplies, the Board is able to call on Manchester for bulk supplies, and thus achieves a high degree of diversification in terms of water sources.

Co-operation between undertakings has now become accepted for the development of large new sources of supply which have regional significance. For example, in 1961 a river abstraction scheme was sanctioned on the Yorkshire Derwent to provide additional supplies over a large area of south Yorkshire (Baldwin 1961). The scheme involved co-operation between the Sheffield, Leeds, Rotherham and Barnsley undertakings, and provided for an ultimate maximum rate of abstraction of 1·3 m^3/s (25 mgd) from the Derwent at Elvington near York. Although a 59 km (37 miles) long aqueduct had to be constructed to the terminal reservoir, the large discharge and good quality of the Derwent permitted this development without the need for capital expenditure on storage. A slightly different co-operative venture followed the creation of the Great Ouse Water Authority in 1961 (Anonymous 1966). This undertaking was given powers to construct a storage reservoir known as Grafham Water near Huntingdon into which water is pumped from the river Great Ouse. These works came into operation in 1966, and the Authority now provides bulk supplies to the five constituent undertakings – the Bedfordshire Water Board, the Lee Valley Water Company, the Luton Water Company, the Mid-Northamptonshire Water Board and the Nene and Ouse Water Board – plus a temporary supply to the Bucks Water Board. The first-stage works now in use have a capacity of 1·3 m^3/s (25 mgd) and serve a population of about 1·5 million, but the second-stage works, estimated to be required by 1972, will raise the peak output to 3·9 m^3/s (75 mgd).

An even larger project, which is also capable of being developed in stages but is based on natural loch storage, has been designed to meet the requirements over most of Central Scotland (Anonymous 1971). Here responsibility for developing new regional schemes now rests with the Central Scotland Water Development Board with a membership drawn from the seven constituent water boards in the area. In 1971, after a decade of planning, the Central Scotland Water Development Board opened the Loch Lomond water supply scheme which has a potential yield of 5·2 m^3/s (100 mgd). Water is abstracted from the loch through two major pumping mains and then distributed as far east as Grangemouth on the Firth of Forth and into Renfrewshire south of the Clyde via the Erskine bridge. The level of Loch Lomond is automatically maintained at a constant height by a barrage on the river Leven, and this barrage also controls the flow of compensation water down the river. The first phase of the scheme generally provides for about half of the estimated future requirements in any area and it is anticipated that pipelines, pumps, storage reservoirs and treatment works will be duplicated as demand increases.

The Yorkshire Derwent, the Grafham Water and the Loch Lomond schemes illustrate some of the advantages of collective effort, but the most fruitful outcome of co-operation between undertakings has been in the use of river regulation reservoirs which has led to a complete change in water resource evaluation. During the past twenty years there has been growing dissatisfaction with the traditional direct-supply type of reservoir. The first criticisms came from the general public seeking access to gathering grounds for recreational purposes, and the water supply industry then became obliged to re-examine the standard policy of total sterilisation of reservoired catchments. Gradually it became clear that, in the light of recent advances in water treatment, many authorities were employing unnecessarily stringent precautions in order to prevent contamination of drinking supplies. With an increase in river abstraction schemes, engineers realised that the existing river channels offered natural opportunities for the transportation and storage of water which could be transformed into a reliable potable supply if the river was regulated by storage. From a water supply viewpoint, a main advantage of a river regulating reservoir is that, with pumping directly from the river near the area of demand, the construction of expensive trunk mains is avoided. Furthermore, the downstream abstraction means that the runoff from a much larger catchment area is available for supply, and regulating reservoirs provide a substantial increase in yield over direct-supply schemes based on identical reservoir capacity. Since the passing of the Water Resources Act, river regulation has become a major instrument associated with wider conservation measures, but the early regulation schemes were originally developed almost exclusively for public supply purposes.

The first British river to be regulated was the Dee, which drains part of north-east Wales before reaching the Irish Sea below Chester as shown in figure 6.2. The water resources of the river Dee were first utilised on a large scale by the construction of the direct-supply Alwen reservoir, authorised by the Birkenhead Corporation Act 1907, to meet demands on Merseyside. As detailed by Rowntree (1963) the next development took place in 1950 when the Mid and South-east Cheshire Water Board and the West Cheshire Water Board independently sought permission from the then Dee and

Clwyd River Board to abstract from the Dee at Llangollen and Chester weir respectively. The River Board sanctioned these proposals in return for financial assistance with a scheme for using Lake Bala (Llyn Tegid) as a flood control reservoir, since the regulated discharge would improve low flow conditions sufficiently to support the proposed withdrawals. Under the Dee and Clwyd River Board

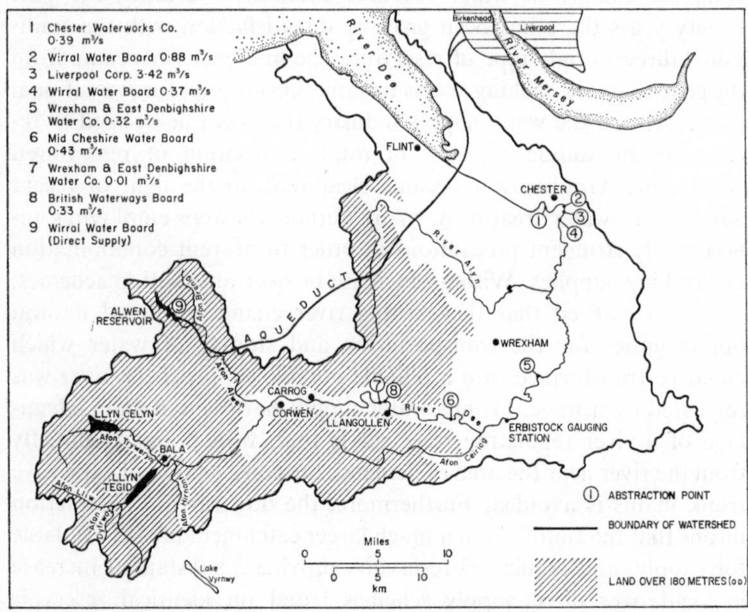

Figure 6.2 The river Dee catchment showing the location of reservoirs and water abstraction points.

Act 1951, new sluice gates were installed to vary the water-level at Bala and so provide some $17{\cdot}27 \times 10^6$ m³ (3800×10^6 gal) of storage. Of this total storage, $4{\cdot}55 \times 10^6$ m³ (1000×10^6 gal) was to be used for increasing dry weather flows, a further $2{\cdot}05 \times 10^6$ m³ (450×10^6 gal) was reserved for extreme droughts whilst the remainder was allocated for flood storage. Other engineering works included the diversion of the river Tryweryn from its previous course where it became confluent with the Dee below Bala so that the whole headwaters of the Dee came under the control of the outlet valves on Lake Bala.

The original agreements were subsequently modified by further abstraction applications from water undertakings and other water-using interests. Eventually a scheme was drawn up whereby the additional abstractions were permitted as long as a flow of at least 2·9 m^3/s (102 cusecs) was maintained at the Erbistock gauging station. If the discharge fell below this level the abstractions were to be progressively reduced until, with a flow of 0·79 m^3/s (28 cusecs) or less, no water could be withdrawn. A further complication was introduced in 1956 when Liverpool Corporation put forward independent plans to build a large reservoir on the river Tryweryn. It was envisaged by Liverpool that the new Tryweryn reservoir (Llyn Celyn) would further regulate the Dee so that abstractions of up to 3·4 m^3/s (120 cusecs) could be taken from the river near Chester, but, after opposition from the River Board, the new reservoir was integrated more closely into the Bala scheme. Liverpool achieved its desired abstraction rate of 3·4 m^3/s, and the prescribed flow at Erbistock has been increased to 7·9 m^3/s (279 cusecs). Since the mean flow of the Dee at this point is only 31 m^3/s (1095 cusecs), the entire control scheme has resulted in a guaranteed discharge in the lower reaches of 25 per cent of the average flow. In addition, the Tryweryn reservoir also provides some flood-storage capacity, whilst hydro-electric power is generated by the water released from the reservoir into the river.

The river Tees in north-east England was the second river in the country to be regulated by headwater storage. This river has been developed solely for water supply purposes by a single undertaking – the Tees Valley and Cleveland Water Board – and is particularly interesting because regulation has been necessitated by industrial demands.

Like the Dee, the river Tees was originally developed by a number of direct-supply reservoirs constructed on tributaries of the main stream, as shown in figure 6.3, around the beginning of the century. However, as described by Smith (1967), the water demands of the expanding iron and chemical industries on Teesside gradually began to dominate water consumption in the area. By 1965 the Water Board delivered 77 per cent of its total supplies to industry, which is about double the average national proportion, and this will probably rise to over 8 per cent in the 1970s. Some years ago it became apparent that the Water Board would be unable to meet the demands with treated mains water, and a separate trade supply was developed by

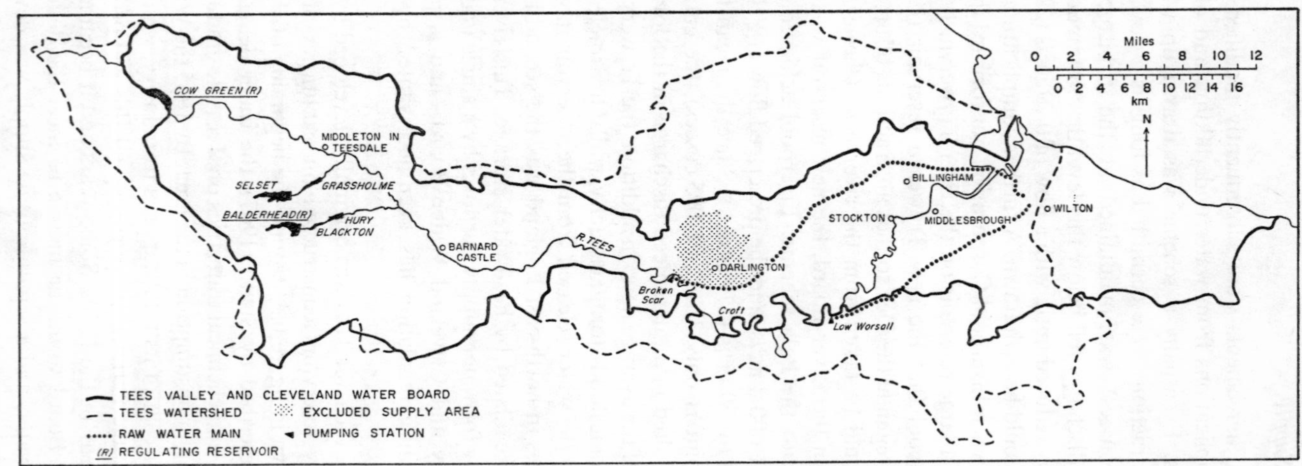

Figure 6.3 The development of the water resources of the river Tees.

pumping raw water from the lower reaches of the river. In 1950 a pumping station was erected at Low Worsall near the tidal limit to deliver untreated water to the newly constructed chemical works at Wilton, and, following the success of this scheme, it was decided to abstract a better quality trade supply upstream at Broken Scar. From 1963 raw water has been conveyed by special main to ICI (Billingham), Dorman's (Lackenby) works as well as ICI (Wilton), and in 1969 the Water Board was supplying over 1·7 m^3/s (33 mgd) of untreated industrial water. This type of trade supply is likely to be adopted more widely since it enables the supply authority to cater for further industrial demands without investment in treatment works, and, if the requirements are concentrated within a small area, a minimum of separate new trunk mains is required.

On the other hand, abstraction on this scale can only be supported by river regulation. To meet the large upsurge in demand during the early 1960s the Balderhead reservoir was proposed, and was originally conceived as a direct-supply reservoir. However, when it eventually came into use in 1965 the reservoir was operated on a river regulating basis. As a direct-supply system Balderhead would have yielded only 0·6 m^3/s (12 mgd), but operated to improve the reliable flow of the lower Tees, as well as supplementing the existing reservoirs on the river Balder, the new reservoir provided a total increment of 1·2 m^3/s (24 mgd) to the Water Board's supplies.

With the Balderhead reservoir in use, provision was made for a total abstraction of 1·7 m^3/s (33 mgd) from the lower Tees, whilst a further 1·7 m^3/s (32 mgd) from the Board's existing reservoirs gave an overall yield of 3·4 m^3/s (65 mgd). The scheme also enabled Darlington Corporation to withdraw 0·4 m^3/s (7 mgd) of potable supplies from a separate river intake at Broken Scar, whilst a minimum flow of 0·5 m^3/s (18·6 cusecs) was scheduled to pass downstream from this point. Subsequent estimates of water consumption up to 1980 by ICI showed that further river regulation would be required, and a larger regulating reservoir has been built at Cow Green. This is the first reservoir to be constructed on the main stream of the Tees, and has a calculated yield of 1·8 m^3/s (35 mgd). It is expected that, when the Cow Green reservoir becomes operational in 1971, the guaranteed low flow of the Tees at Broken Scar will be raised to 0·8 m^3/s (28 cusecs), although increasing demands in the area suggest that even these reserves will be outstripped by 1975.

7 The Non-domestic Demand for Water

This chapter considers the utilisation of water which is, in general, obtained from sources independent of the public supply system. Such a survey embraces a wide field, including the requirements of industry, agriculture, electricity power, navigation and recreation, and a number of initial problems must be recognised.

In the first place, the gross demand to be considered involves a larger volume of water than that discussed in the previous chapter, coupled with a more diverse pattern of use and development. Some water demands, such as those of manufacturing industry and agriculture, are similar to public supply in being mainly *abstractive*, whilst navigation, recreation and amenity comprise *non-abstractive* requirements and are dependent on an adequate volume of water being left in rivers and other watercourses. Another important non-abstractive use is, of course, effluent disposal, but since this relates directly to water quality and pollution it is more conveniently dealt with in the following chapter.

In addition to the enormous variations in the quantity and quality of water needed for the various purposes outlined above, there is also the problem of defining exactly what the term 'use' implies. So far in this book, the terms 'water use' and 'water consumption' have been introduced as synonymous in order to indicate the gross demand. This convention is reasonably adequate when dealing with domestic supplies, which show a relatively uniform *per capita* demand, but it is much less satisfactory when considering more diffuse requirements. For example, very large volumes of water are needed for both direct cooling purposes in industry and for irrigation, but, whereas only a small proportion of the former is totally 'consumed' or 'lost' by evaporation, the efficient application of irrigation water necessarily implies that all the water is evaporated with no possibility of re-use. Even where re-use does occur, there is a progressive deterioration in water quality which renders the water less suitable for other purposes, and, although it may be technically possible to reclaim such water by treatment, the extent to which this is done depends on a number of economic and social variables. Therefore, whilst some attempt will be made to distinguish between gross water requirements and the amounts returned to source, the situation is so complex that a valid distinction between 'consumption' and 'use' is not yet possible for many sectors of demand.

Another basic difficulty arises from the lack of statistical information relating to private water abstractions, and even some water undertakings fail to sub-divide their metered consumption between principal demand components such as industry and agriculture. The 1945 Water Act placed a qualified requirement on abstractors to keep records, but few such returns were officially required. Most of the information on groundwater abstractions was collected under Section 14 of the 1945 Act, which required a licence for the sinking of new boreholes or wells in the specially delimited conservation areas. Surface abstractions were governed by Section 9 of the River Boards Act (1948), but the River Boards were only interested in this information if the quantities involved were substantial in relation to the riverflow, and no complete inventory of abstractions was available until the introduction of the licensing system under the 1963 Act. With certain exceptions, all abstractions, irrespective of source, are now notifiable to the appropriate River Authority, and permission for such abstractions may be granted under licence or withheld. Only when all licence registers are complete will a comprehensive picture of private abstractions be available.

Manufacturing Industry

Apart from staff hygiene and certain universal purposes, such as fire fighting, which are often supplied from the public system, manufacturing industry requires water for a wide range of uses as demonstrated by Lea (1967). These uses can be grouped into three broad categories

(i) Energy production from boilers. Some boiler-feed water is needed by most industries for steam raising. In most cases relatively small, low-pressure boilers are used, but, for the production of electrical power on a large scale, massive high-pressure units are employed.

(ii) Processing and production. This is the most complex category of industrial uses. It includes water used for cleansing at all stages of manufacture, as a chemical medium for dissolving and diluting soluble substances, as a transporting agent for substances in solution or suspension (particularly for waste disposal), and as a basic raw material which is incorporated into the final product as, for example, in the food, drink and pharmaceutical industries.

(iii) Cooling water. Water is the most economical and efficient medium for the removal of excess heat generated by industrial processes, and cooling water is the largest single gross requirement of manufacturing industry. Nevertheless, large differences exist between individual industries, and a high proportion of the water is returned to source.

It will be clear that variations in the quantity and quality of water required for the above purposes, operating in conjunction with the local availability of supplies, will determine both the type of source employed and the amount of water purification which is undertaken. Whilst the statutory undertakings give priority to the bacteriological purity of supplies, manufacturing industry is more concerned with mechanical and chemical quality. Thus, the general trend to higher pressure boilers is producing a demand for a better quality feed-water with a low total dissolved solids content (Hopthrow 1963). In turn, this tends to restrict the source of supply to either the public mains or suitable rivers or boreholes depending on the initial quality of the water and the amount of treatment which is judged to be economic since, with the highest pressure boilers, some demineralisation is necessary irrespective of source. A lower quality of water is tolerable for much process work, especially waste disposal. Here a greater use is made of direct abstractions from private sources, and, in some instances, mine water with a permanent hardness may be pumped from collieries. Where it is obtainable, there is a distinct industrial preference for soft upland water, which has even been a locational factor for some industries such as textiles. But there are also notable exceptions, such as brewing, which appears to favour hard water, whilst a high bacteriological standard will also be necessary for water used in the processing of food and drink.

Cooling water is normally of low quality, mainly because the large volumes required frequently limit the source to direct abstractions from the lower reaches of major rivers. Indeed, some riverside and coastal industrial plants are able to function only because of the almost unlimited supplies of cooling water available from estuaries and the sea. Such water has a high total dissolved solids content, ranging from 5000 mg/l in some estuaries up to 35 000 mg/l for sea-water. Estuarine water may be more corrosive than sea-water owing to the discharge of industrial effluent. It may also be heavily laden with tidal silt and, although utilisation is possible in certain cooling systems on a 'once-through' basis, little re-circulation can be achieved. In addition, the operation of the tides may cause a large mass of water to oscillate up and down the estuary before eventually being dispersed out to sea, and, in these circumstances, large-scale heat rejection from power-stations and industrial premises may raise the water temperature so that it is not a fully effective cooling agent, particularly at low tide.

Mention has already been made of the lack of reliable information on the amounts of water required by individual manufacturing industries, but the limited data which are available suggests that the largest demands are made by some of the traditional, heavy industries. After the electrical supply industry, the main users in Britain are probably the chemical, steel and paper industries, and Balchin (1958) showed the size of water input necessary for these industries. A large chemical complex may consume more water than a million people. Thus, in 1959 the ICI chemical factories at Billingham on north Teesside were using some 0·37 m^3/s (7 mgd) of mains water, 0·18 m^3/s (3·5 mgd) of medium quality water from local streams and boreholes, plus 12 m^3/s (230 mgd) of water from the Tees estuary (Cooper and Smith 1960). More recently, a survey of water-use in the production of British iron and steel during 1968–69 reported by Speight and Davis (1970) has shown that this industry is currently taking 28 m^3/s (535 mgd) of which almost 60 per cent is drawn from tidal sources. The overall dominance of tidal sources is due to the large number of integrated works in coastal locations, plus the fact that most of the water is used for cooling in the blast furnace and power generation departments. Of the total fresh water intake, 46 per cent is obtained by direct abstraction from streams and rivers, 24 per cent from canals and 21 per cent from the statutory undertakings.

On the other hand, variations within particular industries often destroy the validity of much generalisation, as in the paper industry which probably takes less than 5 per cent of its total water requirement from the public mains. A study of forty paper mills in north-west England by Gibson (1958) showed that, whilst three-quarters of the firms used less than 0·06 m^3/s (50 000 gal/h), one establishment drew in as much as 0·32 m^3/s (255 000 gal/h), which was more than any of the surrounding water undertakings were then supplying. The size of the firm and the amount of production were not the sole determinants of water-use, and consumption ranged from 14 m^3 (3150 gal) to over 1818 m^3 of water (400 000 gal) per ton of paper manufactured. In this case, the types of raw material used, the quality of the finished paper and the amount of water re-circulation practised at individual mills were other relevant factors.

Similar findings have emerged from a more ambitious study of industrial water use in south-east England by Rees (1969). This investigation rested largely on the results of a questionnaire distributed to manufacturers, and table 9 indicates the wide variations

TABLE 9

INTER-INDUSTRY VARIATION IN WATER USE IN S.E. ENGLAND

After Rees (1969)

	Percentage of Firms taking Water for Specified Uses					
Industry Group	Cooling	Washing	Process work	Steam raising	Staff hygiene	Other uses
Food	64·7	64·7	76·5	88·2	100·0	29·3
Drink	100·0	88·9	100·0	100·0	100·0	44·4
Clothing and textiles	0	40·0	20·0	60·0	100·0	20·0
Leather and fur	0	25·0	100·0	100·0	100·0	0
Furniture and timber	57·2	14·3	71·4	100·0	100·0	57·2
Paper	50·0	36·4	77·3	86·4	95·5	13·6
Printing	75·0	100·0	50·0	50·0	100·0	0
Plastics and rubber	54·5	18·2	54·5	72·7	100·0	18·2
Chemicals	76·0	40·0	82·0	76·0	100·0	16·0
Non-metallic minerals	26·7	46·7	73·3	46·7	80·1	13·2
Metal and metal products	84·6	38·5	61·5	53·8	92·3	30·8
Mechanical engineering	57·2	14·3	57·2	42·9	100·0	14·3
Precision engineering	50·0	75·0	37·5	62·5	100·0	12·5

between industries with regard to the use of water from all sources, including local undertakings. It was found that cooling water accounted for between 65 and 70 per cent of all water used, compared with 14 per cent for manufacturing, 8 per cent for sanitation and 4 per cent for steam production. The type of manufacturing was an important variable in explaining the volume of water used, and regression analysis revealed that the tonnage of raw material inputs and the number of employees were the two factors most closely related to water consumption within the industrial groups. In general, raw materials provided the best explanation when water entered the manufacturing process or was used for cooling, whilst employment became more significant when most of the water was taken for staff hygiene.

As might be expected, the sources of private industrial abstractions differ, whilst the total quantity of water abstracted is almost double the 42 m^3/s (800 mgd) of metered water taken from the public undertakings. Local conditions dictate the actual availability of supplies, but the largest quantities tend to be abstracted from surface sources, one of the most important on a national scale being the British canal system. Although metered consumption is rising rapidly, private abstraction seems to be expanding much more slowly at present, partly as a result of the increasing difficulty of finding new sources and also because of the controls contained in the River Authorities' licensing system. According to Rees (1969), about 80 per cent of the firms questioned in south-east England have either already been refused permission to extend their abstractions or fear that the licensing system will decrease the range of options open to them. From the sample survey, it appears that the firms themselves expect an increase in the overall industrial use of water of less than 2 per cent per annum, which is less than half the annual increase predicted for the South-east by the Water Resources Board (1966). Such discrepancies illustrate the real difficulty of extrapolating industrial demand. Furthermore, it must be emphasised that, owing to the particular structure of manufacturing industry in south-east England and the general problem associated with water supplies in that region, neither estimate may be directly applicable in other parts of the country.

Agriculture

As in the case of industry, the agricultural demand for water covers a wide spectrum of use. Undoubtedly the major utilisation, and one which is frequently overlooked, occurs quite inevitably as a result of natural evapotranspiration from outdoor crops. This water, usually regarded as 'loss' by the water engineer, enables the growth of most field crops and, through herbage, provides approximately half the total water intake of farm stock (Penman 1967). However, this chapter is concerned solely with the controlled supply of water to agriculture, and this can be conveniently considered as either general requirements or irrigation usage.

General Needs. In addition to ordinary domestic use, the general demand for water on the farm is mainly associated with dairying and stock-drinking, although smaller quantities are used for other purposes such as vegetable washing (Prickett 1963). Because of this, most consumption estimates depend on broad *per capita* allocations to the various livestock populations as follows:

Cows in milk	136 litres/day (30 gal/day)
Other cattle and horses	46 litres/day (10 gal/day)
Sheep and lambs	6·8 litres/day (1·5 gal/day)
Pigs	13·6 litres/day (3 gal/day)
Poultry	0·23 litres/day (0·05 gal/day)

The largest overall consumption is for dairying. Of the 136 litres/day for milking cows, half is allocated for drinking purposes, and the remainder for cleaning and milk cooling. In practice, however, the amounts taken into supply are usually less than this, and some early work on dairy consumption in Cheshire by Griffiths (1954) showed a range of actual usage between 14 and 104 litres/day (3 to 23 gal/day) for each milking cow, with a mean of only 57 litres/day (12·5 gal/day).

Traditionally, farms have relied on small, privately developed sources of supply, but the spread of grant-aided piped supply schemes since 1945, firstly to improve domestic amenities and then in response to statutory requirements for cleanliness in dairying, has led to the present situation described by Prickett (1970) where a mains supply is available on two-thirds of the 350 000 farms in England and Wales. Private sources are still retained for many purposes, and public supplies probably provide less than half of the gross demand, but in dairying especially a mains supply is usually the only means of obtaining a reliable quantity of water with the good bacteriological quality and low temperatures necessary for cleaning milking equipment and for milk cooling.

About £1 million is invested annually in new or improved farm water supply schemes, and about 60 per cent of this expenditure is for non-irrigation purposes. It has been estimated by Prickett (1963) that in 1962 about 10·5 m^3/s (200 mgd) was required for all agricultural needs other than irrigation, and, since this total includes herbage moisture, the effective demand will be only about half this quantity. Although such agricultural requirements have undoubtedly expanded over the last decade, they still form a very small absolute load on Britain's water resources. The load is also spread fairly evenly over the country so that further growth in demand is unlikely to create serious difficulties. In this respect, general farm requirements contrast markedly with irrigation demand.

Irrigation. Irrigation is most usually associated with arid countries where it is vital for crop production, and is therefore known as *basic irrigation.* Since 1950 there has been a remarkable growth of *supplemental irrigation* in more temperate, humid latitudes of the developed world such as Britain, where irrigation water is applied to increase and guarantee yields from crops which the natural climate will already support. Within recent years irrigation has ceased to be used solely for restricted application on high-value horticultural produce, often grown under glass, and the development of spray irrigation techniques suitable for field crops has effectively created an entirely new demand for water on a regional scale.

The spread of successful irrigation was initially dependent on a clear understanding of moisture balance principles, and the subsequent demonstration of the practical benefits to be derived from more precise soil water management. In Britain irrigation developed from the application of Penman's 1948 evaporation formula to the calculation of soil moisture deficits. There was a steady growth in sales of irrigation equipment throughout the 1950s, and purchases were considerably stimulated by the low yields experienced by many farmers in the dry summer of 1959.

The aim of irrigation in this country is to supplement natural rainfall so that water availability is never a limiting factor in crop production. In the absence of such growth checks, an increased flow of nutrients will ensure additional leaf development which benefits overall yields. Ideal conditions occur when soil moisture is maintained within the range available to the plant rooting system, that is between *field capacity* and the *wilting point*, although the actual availability of water, plus the amount and frequency of irrigation applications, will depend to some extent on soil type. The physical characteristics of the soil are especially significant, and light, sandy soils require more careful attention than heavier clays on which crops are able to withstand soil moisture deficits more easily.

Irrigation must, therefore, be applied before drying reaches the permanent wilting point, whilst any water supplied in excess of field capacity is wasted and can lead to water-logging in the soil. In theory, irrigation applications should maintain the average moisture content of the top 300 mm (12 in.) of the soil between 50 and 80 per cent of field capacity. Thus, crops with roots capable of tapping a reserve of 100 mm (4 in.) of water can normally be irrigated when the soil moisture deficit has reached 50 mm (2 in.).

If irrigation is applied carefully, it acts as a fertiliser, and substantial improvements in yield have been noted (Ministry of Agriculture, Fisheries and Food 1962). Increases of about 50 per cent in the total yield of potatoes have been recorded over a wide range of conditions, with a doubling of yields in dry years. Experimental results for sugar-beet have shown increases of 30 per cent, whilst it is also known that cereals will respond markedly to irrigation, especially during a dry spring. Grassland is very sensitive to growth checks caused by lack of water in summer, and experiments have indicated yield increases of more than 100 per cent in dry years with improvements of 30 to 50 per cent in a normal growing season. All these results, of course, refer to standing field crops, and are additional to the response of vegetables and other market garden produce to controlled watering either in the open or under glass.

The extent of irrigation practice is basically determined by the net economic return resulting from the improved yields, but demand can only be met within the context of available supplies. Most irrigation schemes apply water through overhead spray lines, the water usually being pumped from the nearest private source. Apart from being too expensive, a mains supply rarely has the capacity for irrigation on a field scale, and the most common source is surface streams, although larger farms may have deep boreholes or even small storage reservoirs. In the past, the detailed distribution of spray irrigation has depended on the availability of free water sources. Thus, a survey of irrigation in the Great Ouse Basin by More (1964) showed that most farmers pump directly from small tributary streams and irrigate land less than 1·6 km (1 mile) from the source. Where fairly large quantities of good quality water are required, as in the area of intensive horticultural production under Dutch lights on north Humberside, deep borehole supplies are frequently employed as shown by Aylwin and Ward (1969).

It was estimated by the Natural Resources (Technical) Committee (1962) that farmers had purchased sufficient equipment to irrigate 52 611 ha (130 000 acres) of land, and that the average rate of increase was 6070 ha (15 000 acres) per annum. Given the continued availability of low-cost water, it was anticipated that this rate of expansion would result in the irrigation of 202 350 ha (500 000 acres) by 1980. In addition, it was suggested that about 607 000 ha ($1{\cdot}5 \times 10^6$ acres) could theoretically benefit from irrigation, and thereby create a potential annual peak demand for water of 454×10^6 m^3 ($100\,000 \times 10^6$ gal). However, in 1967, just over 101 000 ha (250 000 acres) were being irrigated, with the use of some 54×10^6 m^3 ($12\,000 \times 10^6$ gal) of water per season.

Table 10 shows the areas under different crops in England and

TABLE 10

AREAS OF CROPS IRRIGATED IN A DRY SEASON: ENGLAND AND WALES

After Prickett (1970)

	1965		*1967*	
Crop	*Hectares*	*Acres*	*Hectares*	*Acres*
Grass	34 158	84 404	33 323	82 339
Second early and main crop potatoes	16 328	40 347	17 598	43 483
First early potatoes	8 273	20 443	8 506	21 019
Vegetables	16 371	40 453	16 954	41 892
Sugar beet	14 948	36 936	12 754	31 514
Orchard fruit	4 006	9 898	3 982	9 839
Cereals	4 066	10 046	2 818	6 964
Small fruit	2 240	5 536	2 602	6 430
Hops	1 081	2 671	1 205	2 977
Other crops	6 324	15 626	4 509	11 142
Total	107 795	266 360	104 251	257 599

Wales, which, on the basis of purchased equipment, were capable of being irrigated in 1965 and 1967. It can be seen that there was an overall decline between the two years, mainly in the lower value crops of grass, sugar-beet and cereals which total almost half of the irrigated area and are principally supplied from direct abstractions.

It will be several years before the full effects of the River Authorities' licensing system and the abstraction charges introduced on 1 April 1969 become clear, but it seems likely that the rate of increase may well be less than formerly envisaged and that irrigation will become increasingly associated with the higher value field crops. Prickett suggests that the increasing necessity for over-season water storage, either to utilise a small source efficiently or to take advantage of the lower winter charges levied by the River Authorities, will be a critical factor in irrigation economics, and that only the higher value produce will be able to support the capital outlay necessary for the construction of small reservoirs.

Although the rate of irrigation expansion appears to be slowing down and the overall annual demand is less than 20 per cent of all the other agricultural uses, including herbage moisture, spread throughout the year (Smith 1970), it is the regional location of demand and the peak seasonal load which creates real supply problems. Almost all of the water is consumed without any return to source at precisely the time of year when other demands are high and surface supplies especially are short. Most important of all, the greatest demand is concentrated in the driest parts of south-east England, and it has been stated by O'Riordan (1970) that in parts of East Anglia the potential irrigation demand could well exceed the dry weather flow of the rivers. Figure 7.1 taken from Ministry of Agriculture and Fisheries (1954) illustrates the frequency with which potential evapotranspiration exceeds rainfall by more than 76 mm (3 in.), which is a fairly reliable index of the irrigation threshold for most crops. It can be seen that south-east of a line from about Hull to Torquay irrigation could be beneficially applied in at least one year in every two, whilst around the Thames estuary and along the South Coast into Hampshire some irrigation is required every year.

Electricity Power

Water availability has a dual significance for the electricity supply industry since it is required for both the generation of power at hydro-electric stations and for cooling purposes at thermal power sites. It is the distinctive nature of these demands, as well as the large gross demand for cooling purposes, which makes it necessary to consider electricity generation separately from manufacturing industry as a whole.

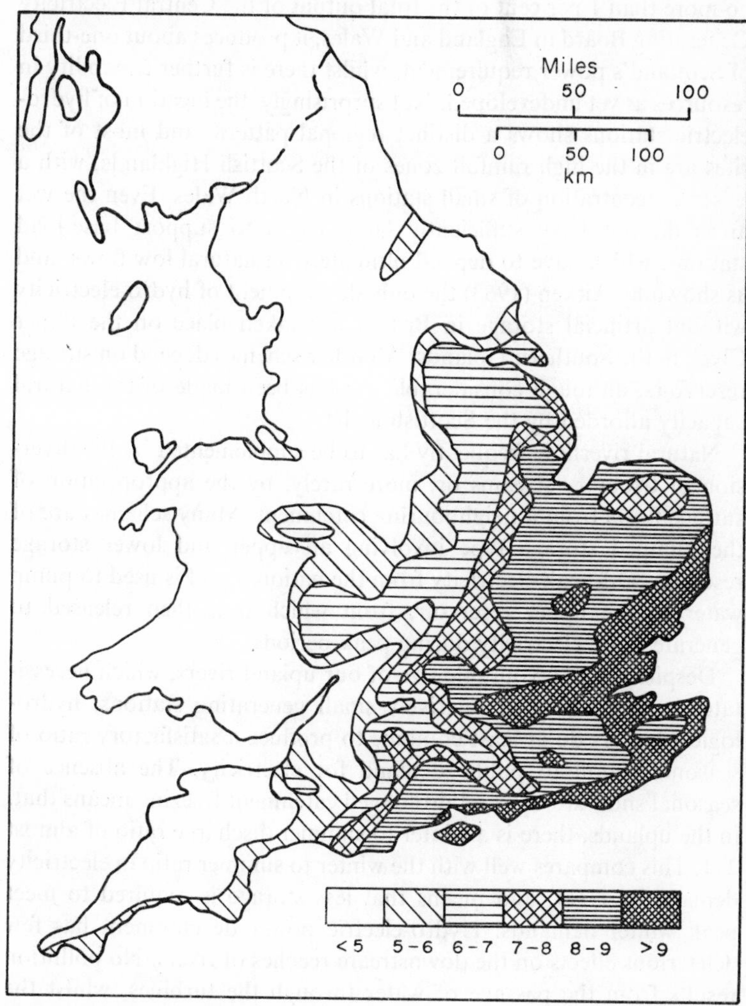

Figure 7.1 The frequency of irrigation need over England and Wales expressed as number of years out of ten. After Ministry of Agriculture and Fisheries (1954).

Hydro-electric power. Although hydro-electric power accounts for no more than 1 per cent of the total output of the Central Electricity Generating Board in England and Wales, it produces about one-third of Scotland's power requirement, whilst there is further capability in resources as yet undeveloped. Not surprisingly, the location of hydro-electric stations shows a distinct regional pattern, and most of the sites are in the high rainfall zones of the Scottish Highlands, with a lesser concentration of small stations in North Wales. Even the wet areas do not have sufficiently large rivers to support base-load stations, which have to depend ultimately on natural low flows, and as shown by Aitken (1963) the only development of hydro-electricity without artificial storage in Britain has taken place on the upper Clyde in the Southern Uplands. All other schemes depend on storage reservoirs, although considerable use has been made of the natural capacity afforded by the Scottish lochs.

Natural riverflow frequently has to be supplemented by the diversion of tributary streams or, more rarely, by the appropriation of surface flows from a neighbouring catchment. Many schemes are of the pumped storage type involving an upper and lower storage reservoir. Off-peak electricity from the national grid is used to pump water to the upper reservoir, from which it is then released to generate more electricity during peak periods.

Despite the unfavourable size of our upland rivers, which necessitates a multiplicity of relatively small generating stations, hydrological factors do at least combine to produce a satisfactory ratio of seasonal runoff to public demand for electricity. The absence of seasonal snow storage and prolonged catchment freezing means that, in the uplands, there is a winter to summer discharge ratio of almost 2 : 1. This compares well with the winter to summer ratio in electricity demand of 1·7 : 1, and means that less storage is required to meet peak winter demands. Hydro-electric power development has few deleterious effects on the downstream reaches of rivers. No pollution results from the passage of water through the turbines, whilst the smoothing of the natural regime of the river by means of storage control is a direct benefit in most cases.

Cooling water. The demand for cooling water at thermal power-stations is the largest gross abstractive water requirement in the country and is responsible for more than half the licensed withdrawals from all sources. It has been estimated by Calvert (1967) that in 1967 about 210 m^3/s (4000 mgd) was used for direct cooling purposes, with a total evaporative loss of 2·6 m^3/s (50 mgd), and it was predicted that by 1971 the figures would be 158 m^3/s (3000 mgd) and 4·3 m^3/s (82 mgd) respectively.

The reduction in gross demand for cooling water is due to the progressive change-over from direct cooling in power-stations to the use of cooling towers with internal re-circulating systems. There has been a long-term trend of reduced circulating water requirements in relation to unit production of electricity, but the national demand for electrical energy is growing much faster than the use of cooling water can be brought down, and there is, therefore, a growing net demand for cooling supplies. At the present time according to Clark and England (1963) at least two new 2000 megawatt coal or oil-fired stations are needed each year, plus one nuclear station. Each 2000 megawatt installation has a maximum cooling water circulation of about 63 m^3/s (50×10^6 gal/hr) which is in excess of the dry weather flow of any British river, and thus re-cycling of water is essential. In nuclear power-stations the water requirement per unit of generated electricity is greater than at thermal stations. It is partly for this reason that most nuclear plants are sited on the coast, although the Trawsfynydd station in Merionethshire depends on the water in a large lake originally used for hydro-electricity generation.

The immense quantities of cooling water required should allow the dissipation of excess heat without the water itself becoming warmed more than 7° to 8°C (13° to 14°F) whilst the temperature of the effluent must be carefully controlled in order to prevent thermal pollution. In a modern cooling tower the evaporation loss is only slightly more than one per cent of the total amount of water being circulated, but for a 2000 megawatt station working at full output this means a total of 0·74 m^3/s (14 mgd) which must be sustained by direct abstractions. Fortunately, as a result of the seasonal variations in electricity demand, cooling water requirements are at a minimum in the summer when riverflows are low, but, even so, large thermal stations have to be restricted to the lower reaches of our major rivers such as the Trent.

Navigation

The small size of the British rivers has generally precluded their utilisation for commercial inland navigation. Nevertheless, some river estuaries, such as the Humber and the Mersey, are commercially significant, and it is important that river discharge should be maintained at a sufficient level to prevent siltation from impeding traffic in the navigable channels of these estuaries.

Most inland navigation is associated with canals, which originated in the late eighteenth and early nineteenth centuries. Many of the later canals were dependent for their water supply on artificial feeder reservoirs, and responsibility for more than ninety of these reservoirs, together with some 3200 km (2000 miles) of canal system, now rests with the British Waterways Board. It has been estimated that the Board has between 136 and 182 $\times$ 10^6 m^3 (30 000 and 40 000 $\times$ 10^6 gal) of water annually available, and, with the decline of commercial navigation on these waterways, the sale of this water represents an important source of revenue (British Waterways Board 1964). In many areas, canal water is of low quality, but this is often compensated by accessibility and ease of abstraction in built-up areas, and it is likely that canals represent the largest single source of water for manufacturing industry in Britain.

Canal reservoirs are mainly located in the uplands. As a result of the dense canal network in certain parts of the country, stored water can be transmitted by gravity for long distances from the source. Figure 7.2 shows that water held in Whaley Bridge and other reservoirs in the southern Pennines serves a total of 296 km (184 miles) of canal, and can be conveyed by different canals to widespread river systems such as the river Trent at Alrewas, the river Mersey at Runcorn, the river Tame at Glascote and Curdworth or the river Sow at Tixall. Similarly, water stored in the Lancashire Pennines north of Burnley can be distributed to either side of the Pennine watershed by the Leeds and Liverpool canal, whilst just four intake points on the canal system can supply water for an overall length of 990 km (615 miles) in north-west England.

So far the regional co-ordination necessary for large scale water transfer by the canal system has been lacking, but some water undertakings have taken advantage of this ready-made distribution network. Thus, as shown by Marsh (1963) the Mid and South-east Cheshire Water Board uses the Llangollen canal to transfer water from North Wales to industrial Cheshire some 72 km (45 miles) distant.

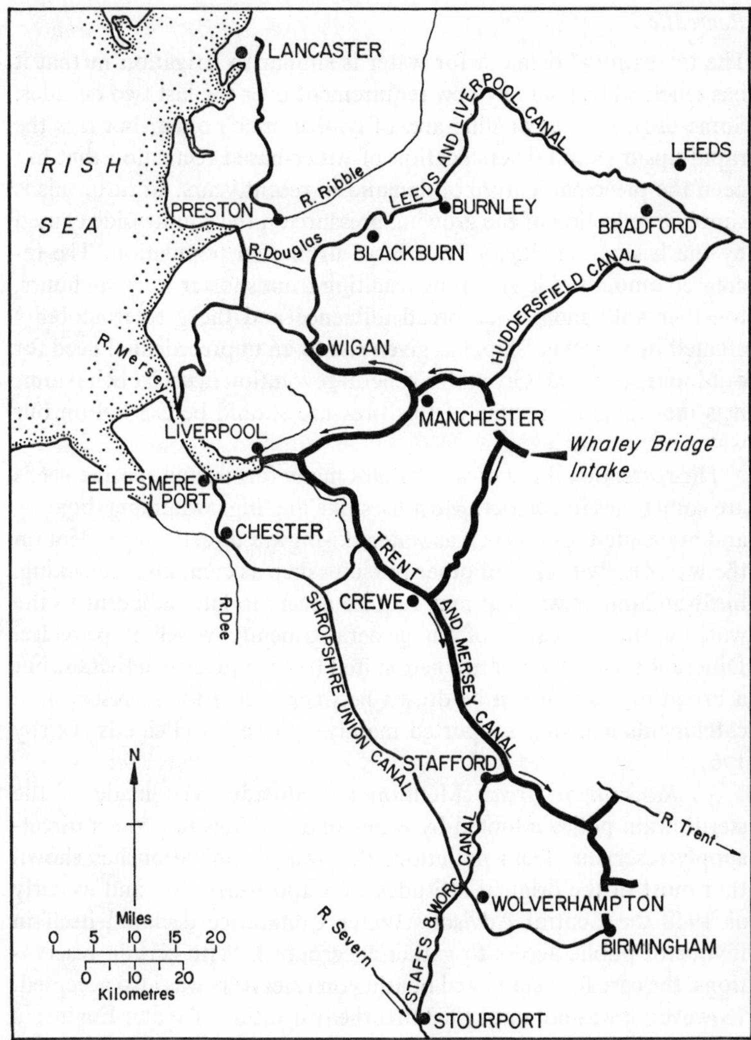

Figure 7.2 The potential distribution of water from the Whaley Bridge intake via the canal system of north-west England. After Marsh (1963).

Recreation

The recreational demand for water is similar to irrigation in that it has emerged as a largely new requirement over the last two decades. Some uses, such as angling are, of course, much older, but it is the rapid upsurge and diversification of water-based recreation that has been the principal feature of demand in recent years. In turn, this is simply a reflection of the growing pressure on the countryside caused by the leisure activities of our large urbanised population. The increased amount of leisure time resulting from shorter working hours, together with more widespread affluence and the greater mobility created by car ownership, has given rise to an unprecedented need for outdoor recreation. Given this general revolution in social behaviour, it is inevitable that some of this pressure should be exerted on our water resources.

The recreational use of water takes many forms, and specific needs are sometimes in conflict. Most uses like angling, swimming, boating and associated sports such as water ski-ing are directly dependent on the water body itself, but other pursuits such as camping, picnicking, birdwatching or walking may require access to land adjacent to the water surface because of the general amenity which it provides. Different types of water are best suited to such diverse activities, but a broad distinction can be drawn between recreation in reservoired catchments and that supported mainly by rivers and canals (Darby 1967).

(*a*) *Reservoired Areas*. Mention has already been made of the sterilisation policy adopted by water undertakings to protect direct-supply reservoirs from pollution. Post-war examination has shown that most of the original attitudes were too restrictive, and as early as 1948 the Central Advisory Water Committee declared itself in favour of public access to gathering grounds. With certain reservations, the case for fishing and boating on reservoirs was also accepted. However, it was not until 1963 that the Institution of Water Engineers fully accepted these proposals by issuing a tentative code of practice dealing with waterworks recreation (Institution of Water Engineers 1963). By this time, the needs of public access were gaining statutory recognition. Section 80 of the 1963 Water Resources Act empowered the River Authorities to meet any reasonable demand for recreation on reservoirs under their control to the extent of providing physical facilities and levying charges for the use of such facilities. More recently, the Countryside Act 1968 required water undertakings to allow public recreation on their reservoirs as far as possible, whilst the authorisation for most new reservoirs includes recreational clauses dealing with the formation of fishing and sailing clubs.

One of the most ambitious recreational projects developed by a water undertaking has been that organised on Grafham Water by the Great Ouse Water Authority as reported by Saxton (1969). This man-made lake first overflowed in February 1966, and since then a wide range of recreational activities has been provided. Access is available for the general public, and there are three picnic sites with parking facilities for 1500 cars. A sailing club has been formed with a membership in 1969 of about 1500 adults and 200 juniors with a total of 640 boats on the club register. Little conflict between sailing and fishing interests has been apparent, and the lake has been artificially stocked with brown and rainbow trout. During the trout fishing season over 20 000 daily fishing permits are issued. In addition, at the western end of the lake, a nature reserve has been established with access granted by day permits.

The success of the Grafham Water scheme illustrates the benefits which can accrue from the planned recreational use of reservoirs, but some of the older direct-supply reservoirs, with outdated treatment works, would be unable to support such intensive use without some reduction in the quality of water supplied. There is, however, some scope for the recreational use of reservoirs storing water solely for compensation purposes. The potential contribution of reservoired catchments to recreational facilities is greatest in northern England where extensive moorland gathering grounds are near to industrial conurbations. Indeed, such areas sometimes constitute the most accessible open spaces, and many are within the National Parks. Angling has been allowed on some of these waters for many years, but before the Second World War only three water undertakings allowed their reservoirs to be used for regular sailing. This situation has now changed and boating facilities are much more widely available, but little information is yet available on the economic aspects of such developments (Kavanagh 1968).

(*b*) *Rivers and Canals.* Current restrictions on the recreational use of rivers and canals are totally different from those affecting water supply reservoirs, and the major limiting factor is the existence of water pollution rather than the need to prevent contamination. As with reservoirs, multiple recreational use is practised, but the most important single leisure activity is fishing. Estimates of the total number of anglers in Britain range from 2 to 3·5 million, and each year over 1 million rod licences for fishing in inland waters are issued by the River Authorities (Boddington 1967). Most of these licences are used for coarse fishing along canals and the lower reaches of rivers where water quality is relatively low. Only a minority of anglers engage in trout fishing, but it is probable that the greatest angling pressure is felt on good trout streams, which have declined in number, especially in England and Wales, owing to the effects of pollution. Angling demand is also in excess of supply for migratory fish, since pollution in the estuaries and tidal reaches of many rivers has led to the virtual extinction of salmon and seatrout in some areas as emphasised by Baxter (1963).

Overall responsibility for the preservation of fisheries rests with the River Authorities, and it is probably true to say that most of the improvements they achieve arise more or less indirectly from the controls on river pollution. More specifically, however, the Authorities can regulate the use of fisheries to a considerable extent. Through the issue of licences and the use of powers of prosecution related to legal restrictions, covering aspects such as the length of the closed season or fishing by means of a prohibited instrument, the Authorities can prevent over-fishing. As a more positive measure, they are also involved in the re-stocking of angling waters and the maintenance of fish farms and hatcheries.

The volume of water in a stream, as well as its quality, is known to affect fish populations. It is generally accepted that, in addition to simply maintaining fish survival, riverflows should be sufficient to facilitate migration and spawning as well as successful angling. A river spate, or rapid river discharge, tends to stimulate migration, whilst spawning appears to depend more on the depth of the water and the velocity of flow. Work on upland rivers, principally in Scotland by Baxter (1961), has shown that the overall flow requirements of migratory fish are not excessively large. Little more than 12 per cent of the average daily flow is adequate, which is similar to the natural dry weather flow of many rivers. Where rivers are reservoired there seems to be a case for a variable seasonal discharge of compensation water rather than a regular flow throughout the year.

Few attempts have been made to control riverflows in order to produce the most favourable angling conditions, and the limited evidence available suggests that discharges would have to be fairly high. For example, a study of salmon catches over five seasons on the river Avon, Hampshire, reported by Brayshaw (1967) showed that most fish were taken when the river was flowing between 70 and 125 per cent of the average daily discharge.

Although canals cannot provide the variety of fishing found on rivers, the proximity of canals to the built-up areas makes them popular for recreational activities. About three-quarters of the national canal system, amounting to some 2415 km (1500 miles) is suitable for fishing, whilst there is also a growing demand for pleasure boating and cruising, particularly on the more rural inland waterways.

8 Effluent Disposal and Pollution Control

In the preceding chapters it has been shown that, for most purposes, it is necessary to consider water resources in terms of quality as well as quantity, and passing reference has been made to the adverse effects of pollution. Water pollution occurs almost entirely as the result of effluent disposal, which is sometimes overlooked as a major water demand because it is a *non-abstractive* requirement. But, in order to remove our liquid waste out to sea, vast quantities of water are needed as a transporting agent in our river systems. Since the output of both domestic and industrial effluent is increasing more or less directly in relation to the growing abstractive demand, the pollution load becomes progressively harder for water resources to absorb. Thus, effluent disposal and the subsequent deterioration in water quality influence both the use and conservation of water because, as the pressure on resources continues to build up, so the degree of pollution and the amount of feasible re-use of water will, in many respects, determine the real availability of supplies.

The Nature of Water Quality

Water may be classified according to its physical, chemical an biological composition

(1) Physical factors – colour, clarity, taste, odour, temperature, suspended solids content.

(2) Chemical factors – reaction, dissolved solids, hardness, nitrogenous matter.

(3) Biological factors – bacteriological content, dissolved oxygen, biochemical oxygen demand.

The relative importance of the above variables depends largely on the use which is to be made of the water as pointed out by Tebbutt (1971), but there are also differences in the ease and reliability of measurement of some of the parameters. Taste, for example, is entirely subjective. However, the most significant deficiency in terms of water resources is the lack of any systematic sampling network for water quality on a national scale. Most sampling is done on a routine but intermittent basis by the River Authorities and water undertakings. Sampling is often undertaken only on a fortnightly or monthly basis, and the sample normally has to be removed to the laboratory for analysis. The development of automatic systems capable of continuously monitoring variables such as pH, suspended solids and dissolved oxygen is still at an experimental stage as described by Briggs *et al.* (1967), and even relatively simple measurements like temperature were recorded at only nineteen sites in 1965 (Water Resources Board 1968). More detailed information will certainly be required in the future, whilst there is an urgent need for the automatic transmission of water quality data to central offices in order to provide the earliest possible warnings of pollution.

Even in its 'natural' state, water shows marked differences in composition according to the type and location of the source. Normally, deep groundwater will be clear and odourless. Groundwater circulation will produce a low suspended solids content owing to the filtration of mechanical and other impurities in the aquifer, but this sub-surface movement will also cause an alkaline reaction and a high degree of mineralisation. Typical chalk water may have a pH of 8 or over with perhaps 400 mg/l of total hardness, whilst Magnesian Limestone water may have a hardness up to nearly 3000 mg/l. The temperature regime of groundwater is virtually constant throughout the year, whilst the always low dissolved oxygen content will decrease even further away from the outcrop as the water becomes progressively de-oxygenated. On the other hand, an upland stream draining a moorland catchment may be discoloured with peat particles or silt, particularly after a storm, and will have a decidedly acid reaction with a pH of 6 or perhaps less. The total hardness is likely to be below 20 mg/l. In further contrast to groundwater, it will show considerable temperature fluctuations, both seasonally and diurnally, and will have a high content of dissolved oxygen, especially in turbulent sections of the channel.

It will be clear, therefore, that there is effectively no such thing as pure water in nature. Pure water can only be created by distillation in the laboratory, and the absence of any meaningful standard makes the concept of pollution difficult to define. In practice, pollution is generally understood as a *Man-made* modification of water quality, which renders the water less suitable for use than in its original state. The emphasis on human interference is essential, not only because this is the only type of pollution which is really preventable, but also because water is sometimes *naturally* polluted as demonstrated by Townend and Lovett (1963). Thus, surface streams carry silt, plus waste animal and vegetable products from the land, whilst groundwater may be excessively hard in limestone districts or suffer from the presence of iron in sandy formations. Most of these natural effects cause the presence of impurities, but they are restricted in occurrence and the consequences are limited by the self-purifying action of rivers. It is only when Man introduces substances on a scale sufficient to disturb this ecological balance that the system becomes overloaded and real pollution sets in.

Sources of Pollution

Pollution can occur in an almost limitless number of ways, and a classification of causes can never be entirely satisfactory. Thus, Klein (1962) has shown that pollutants can be classified according to whether they are solid or liquid, on the basis of origin, or whether the effects are physical, chemical or biological. A major problem is that cause and effect can rarely be isolated owing to the complex composition of many effluent discharges. Sometimes a chain reaction may be established, as when a rise in temperature affects the dissolved oxygen in a stream and also accelerates biochemical reactions. For our purposes, it will be sufficient to outline the general sources of pollution and show the broad effects these have on water quality. We distinguish five such sources

(*a*) *Sewage Effluent*. Theoretically *sewage* is the general name given to all forms of liquid waste, but the term is often used solely for domestic effluent. This restriction is hardly justified, however, since almost half of the total volume of waste comes from industrial sources, and in manufacturing regions the proportion may be much higher. Nevertheless, it has been estimated that the total quantity of liquid waste received for treatment at sewage works in England and Wales amounts to $14{\cdot}1 \times 10^6$ m^3/d (3100 mgd) of which $7{\cdot}3 \times 10^6$ m^3/d (1600 mgd) is from domestic sources and $6{\cdot}8 \times 10^6$ m^3/d (1500 mgd) is industrial effluent (Working Party on Sewage Disposal

1970). The domestic proportion is equivalent to just over 135 l./d (30 gal/day) per head of population and may be related directly to the volume of domestic consumption.

At present about 94 per cent of the population, comprising 46 million people, are served by main drainage. Of these, 40 million have drainage to sewage works followed by the subsequent disposal of treated effluent in rivers or estuaries, whilst the remainder discharge waste directly to estuaries.

Domestic sewage effluent is the most important source of water pollution in Britain. It is normally discharged to rivers after treatment by means of outfalls on the downstream side of settlements. After rainfall, washings from streets and roofs add appreciably to the overall total, although in some areas the sewerage system may discharge this storm water directly to the streams. Sewage is largely organic in character, and it is the breakdown of constituent proteins, fats and carbohydrates which is responsible for pollution.

The overall effect of organic pollution depends not only on the nature of the pollutant but also on the ability of the river to re-purify itself. In its natural, unpolluted state, a river has considerable resistance to local pollution. This resistance is dependent on the process of *self-purification* which, although controlled by a complex interaction of factors, is largely a function of the dissolved oxygen content of the stream. Flowing water will derive, by direct solution from the atmosphere, a certain amount of dissolved oxygen, and this oxygen is held in equilibrium with the overlying air. In addition, according to Lovett (1957) further dissolved oxygen may be released within the stream at relatively high partial pressures by the photosynthetic activity of plants and algae. There is often a marked diurnal concentration of this oxygen supply, especially during the summer when the water may be supersaturated with dissolved oxygen owing to photosynthesis under conditions of bright sunlight.

When organic pollution occurs, the river tries to eliminate it biochemically through the action of micro-organisms. Bacteria feed on the organic matter and, using the dissolved oxygen, break the polluting substances down into relatively simple and harmless end-products. As a result, the condition of the river will progressively improve as long as the bacterial demand for oxygen does not exceed the supply, but if the stream's oxygen content becomes exhausted, the river will lose its capacity for self-purification. Eventually the water may become anaerobic and septic. Under these conditions the organic matter is reduced to a different set of end-products. Putrefaction may then occur along with objectionable smells and the extinction of most of the aquatic life of the stream.

Although the processes of de-oxygenation and re-oxygenation take place simultaneously, purification is slow, and the maximum de-oxygenation of a stream may take place many kilometres downstream of the effluent entry point (Klein 1962). The rate of oxygen recovery

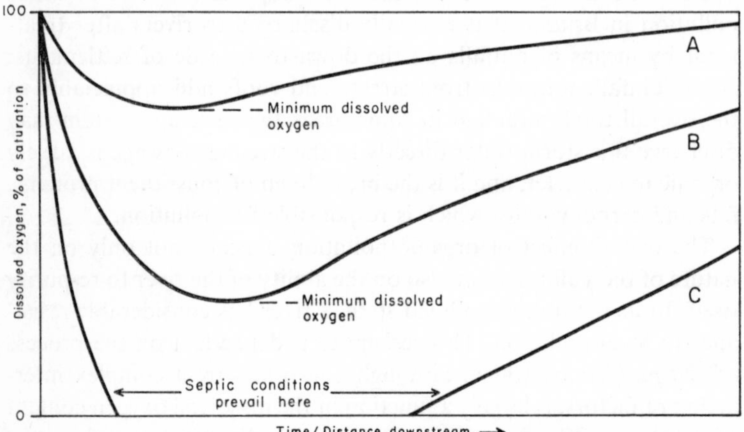

Figure 8.1 Diagrammatic sag curves illustrating the de-oxygenation and subsequent recovery of a stream after (A) slight, (B) heavy and (C) gross organic pollution. After Klein (1962).

is more gradual than that of depletion, and figure 8.1 diagrammatically illustrates typical oxygen curves according to the severity of the pollution involved. Where gross pollution occurs the curve may be interrupted by septic conditions.

The detailed reaction of a river to a given load of organic pollution depends on the variety of factors which control the oxygen balance. The ratio of effluent to the dilution afforded by clean, well-aerated water will clearly be significant, and this relationship is often determined by streamflow characteristics. In addition, a given volume of flow will experience considerable contrasts in re-oxygenation rates as a result of turbulence. A shallow stream flowing over a rocky bed will re-aerate more quickly and hold a larger proportion of dissolved oxygen than a deep sluggish river. On the other hand, re-oxygenation may be quite efficient in ponds or shallow lakes, where a large surface area is exposed to the atmosphere relative to the total mass of water, and where the time-lag associated with storage may also be important. The input of dissolved oxygen from photosynthesis is a less predictable element because, although it may comprise an important source on a warm summer day, the increase in temperature also speeds up bacterial activity and the self-purification process. This creates a heavy demand for oxygen and, since warm water can hold less oxygen than cold water, photosynthesis may be unable to keep pace with demands. Taking into account the greater probability of low seasonal riverflows under such conditions, it follows that the risk of serious pollution will be appreciably greater in summer than winter.

In addition to pollution through de-oxygenation, sewage waste is, of course, the main source of *biological* pollution. Even treated sewage contains a large number of bacteria and, although many are harmless, other organisms can lead to water-borne illnesses such as dysentery, cholera and typhoid. The main danger from bacterial pollution occurs when the river is used as a potable supply as emphasised by Houghton (1967), and further treatment has to be adopted in which chlorination plays an important role.

(*b*) *Industrial Effluent*. Unlike domestic sewage, the quantity and composition of industrial waste can be highly variable, and the nature of trade effluent reflects the pattern of manufacturing industry over the country. Thus, certain industries such as wool processing or brewing may have a large volume of effluent which varies little in composition while the chemical industry, on the other hand, will tend to have a more variable output depending on the range of products manufactured and the higher rate of technical innovation in the industry (Southgate 1969). Some industrial effluents, particularly the less objectionable ones, may be discharged directly to streams or estuaries either with or without prior treatment. In other cases the factory may be connected to the public sewage works, although there may well be pre-treatment at the industrial premises if toxic wastes are discharged. The collective treatment of domestic and industrial effluents has a number of advantages, including economy of cost and effort with a minimum of pollution points on the river, and in the highly industrial parts of the country more than half the discharge from sewage disposal works may have originated as trade effluent. It is the largely organic industrial wastes which are most suitable for treatment at the local authority works. Many of these industries are of the food processing variety, such as vegetable canning and brewing, whilst the drainage from slaughterhouses, dairies, paper mills, tanneries and the wool textile industry is often similarly treated. Occasionally specific problems arise from organic solids and sludge released in these discharges.

Another type of industrial pollution stems from substances which are directly toxic to stream life. Some toxic chemicals discharged in trade waste may be organic, and are often associated with gasworks or the manufacture of chemicals or insecticides. Phenols, tar bases and cyanides are important here as is oil, which creates a film on the water surface thereby preventing re-aeration. In extreme cases a fire risk may exist. Other dangerous inorganic compounds include the salts of heavy metals, since copper, zinc, chromium and lead can cause damage to plant life and fish in extremely low concentrations (Klein 1962). Excessive acidity or alkalinity is a further problem. Acid wastes are produced mainly by the chemical industry and by metal plating and pickling. The chief constituent is sulphuric acid, which is highly corrosive. Alkaline waste waters can have pH values of 12 or even more, and include caustic soda from cotton processing and sodium carbonate from wool scouring effluent. Many trade wastes are objectionable because they increase the turbidity of water through material held in suspension, whilst the introduction of colour itself is usually in the form of organic dyes.

(*c*) *Agricultural Waste*. Agricultural pollution has increased significantly in recent years. With the trend towards greater units of livestock production, plus higher standards of cleanliness, a large dairy or piggery may have to dispose of as much sewage as a small town. Although most agricultural pollution does occur in mainly rural areas, where other pollution sources are small, some problems do still arise.

Agricultural effluent includes the domestic sewage from farms, which is frequently discharged directly to streams because of the impracticability of connecting isolated farms to the sewerage systems. Similarly, the drainage from fields and farmland is not usually subjected to treatment, and, as a result, the synthetic compounds found in pesticides and fertilisers contaminate water resources. Particular dangers ensue when organochlorine pesticides such as aldrin and DDT are used, whilst toxic arsenical compounds are used in the control of foot rot. When nitrogenous fertilisers are applied to the land most of the nitrate is leached into rivers and boreholes, and it has been suggested by the Institution of Water Engineers (1970) that borehole water in southern England, previously regarded as amongst the safest in the country, may be dangerous to infants as a drinking-supply because of nitrate accumulation. The waste from pea vining and silage is also objectionable, and Klein (1962) cites the case of seepage from silos which may be over 200 times as strong as domestic sewage.

(*d*) *Extractive Industry*. The principal type of effluent associated with mining and quarrying is inert suspended matter. It usually occurs in the form of china clay or coal slurry, or in washings from sand quarries. This sort of physical pollution can cause fish mortality by asphyxiation from clogged gills. The drainage from deep mines is often extremely acidic, with a high proportion of ferrous compounds which take some of the dissolved oxygen out of the stream.

(*e*) *Cooling Water*. Another form of physical pollution comes from the discharge of cooling water. The release of heated effluents from industrial premises and electricity generating stations is the major source of thermal pollution in rivers and estuaries. Although the discharges may be of relatively good quality in other respects, the reduced solubility of oxygen at higher temperatures causes de-oxygenation. In some rivers the oxygen content may be negligible in summer as shown by the figures in table 11 recorded for the river Tees estuary over a period of four years (Central Advisory Water Committee 1949). In terms of indirect effects many toxic agents, such

TABLE 11

MINIMUM CONCENTRATION OF DISSOLVED OXYGEN (% OF SATURATION) IN TEES ESTUARY

Water temperature		
°C	*°F*	*Dissolved oxygen*
0–7	32–45	76
7–10	45–50	66
10–13	50–55	55
13–16	55–61	46
16–19	61–66	31
19–21	66–70	10

as potassium cyanide, become even more lethal with a rise in temperature. Thermal pollution may also have direct consequences for aquatic life, since fish die if their thermal environment rises beyond a certain threshold. The critical temperature depends on a number of factors, but it has been found that trout are unable to survive in water at 25°C (77°F) whilst pike die at 30°C (86°F).

The Extent of Pollution

The most recent information on the extent of water pollution in Britain is contained in a report by the Department of the Environment (1971). This report relates to a survey undertaken in England and Wales in 1970, and a comparison with a similar but unpublished government survey in 1958 permits some assessment of pollution trends. Although both surveys covered all rivers and streams with a dry weather flow of at least 0·05 m^3/s (1 mgd), the results are not strictly comparable since the earlier investigation was less detailed and the total lengths of river included in each survey are not identical, as shown in table 12.

TABLE 12

EXTENT OF WATER POLLUTION IN ENGLAND AND WALES 1958 AND 1970

Location	*Class*	*Description*	*1958* Length (Km)	*1958* % Total	*1970* Length (Km)	*1970* % Total
Rivers (non-tidal)	1	Unpolluted	23 510	73	27 370	76
	2	Doubtful	4 613	15	5 297	15
	3	Poor	2 059	6	1 724	5
	4	Grossly polluted	2 057	6	1 533	4
Canals	1	Unpolluted	1 449	58	1 127	45
	2	Doubtful	612	25	968	39
	3	Poor	209	9	219	9
	4	Grossly polluted	193	8	166	7
Tidal Rivers and Estuaries	1	Unpolluted	1 159	41	1 388	48
	2	Doubtful	934	33	675	23
	3	Poor	402	14	485	17
	4	Grossly polluted	354	12	336	12

In terms of length of watercourse most pollution necessarily occurs in non-tidal rivers, but it can be seen that the condition of canals and tidal rivers is proportionately worse so that in 1970 over 75 per cent of non-tidal rivers were free from pollution compared with 45 per cent for canals and 48 per cent for tidal rivers and estuaries.

As far as pollution trends are concerned, it is possible to compare the total lengths within the grossly polluted category because the same criteria did apply in both 1958 and 1970 and for non-tidal rivers it can be seen that there has been a reduction in Class 4 of over 520 km or about 25 per cent. This net improvement of gross river pollution has been achieved despite the increasing effluent discharge to rivers and the greater amount of water abstraction from them and may be attributed to the steadily rising expenditure on sewage and trade effluent treatment during the post-war years. At 1970 prices this expenditure increased from £14·6 million in 1948/9 to £112·8 million in 1968/9. In general the improvement has occurred over short stretches of a large number of rivers but special mention should be made of the progress over longer lengths of the rivers Bure, Yare, Gipping and Orwell in East Anglia, and in parts of the Severn drainage basin. On the other hand the overall situation remains essentially similar. The evidence available points to a slower rate of improvement in canals and tidal rivers and many large non-tidal rivers in the main industrial areas of south-east Lancashire, south Yorkshire, Tyneside, Teesside and the west Midlands will remain highly polluted for some time to come.

The real extent of pollution is, in fact, partly concealed by the nature of the survey by the Department of the Environment (1971) since river length rather than volume of discharge was selected as the basic criterion. Thus, a high proportion of the unpolluted rivers are relatively small headwater streams with flows not much in excess of the 0·05 m^3/s (1 mgd) threshold, and these are given as much weight as the more heavily polluted lower reaches of the large river systems. This deficiency was made apparent when all Class 1 and 2 stretches of non-tidal river were considered as potential sources for future public water supplies, and it was found that over 73 per cent of such stretches were unsuitable for this purpose. No less than 56 per cent of the total lengths of rivers in Class 1 and 2 were unsuitable because of insufficient quantity and this was easily the most important reason in both Classes. In Class 1 rivers the conflicting interests of other users was a further major difficulty whilst excess of ammonia was a common secondary factor in Class 2 waters.

Most pollution can be traced to deficiencies in our system of sewage disposal which, although the most comprehensive in the world, is also out-dated and inadequate in certain respects. Many areas are served by a combined sewer network which carries rain-water together with household sewage and industrial effluent to the local works for treatment. After a rain-storm the washings from streets and roofs may be many times the volume of the waste alone and beyond the capacity of the treatment works. In this situation relief weirs operate to divert the excess discharge directly to the nearest watercourse, and this so-called storm sewage is a major cause of intermittent pollution as shown by Southgate (1969). Occasional pollution may also arise from industrial sources as a result of the accidental spillage of toxic substances and according to Ashby (1971) there is some evidence that oil pollution, for example, has increased in densely populated areas over the last few years. Nevertheless, the problem of continuing pollution is due largely to the poor quality of many treated effluents, and in 1965, the waste discharged from almost 60 per cent of all sewage works failed to meet the Royal Commission standards laid down at the beginning of this century (Working Party on Sewage Disposal 1970). In turn this fact is due to the overloading of the entire sewage disposal system which has not been expanded and modernised at a sufficient rate to keep pace with the increased consumption of water during recent decades.

The variety and complexity of river pollution in Britain ensures that the typically polluted stream does not exist. Some rivers, especially in Scotland, remain largely untouched, whilst others become contaminated almost from their source. In general, however, pollution does increase progressively downstream as agricultural waste and effluent from small rural sewage works gives way to massive inputs of urban and industrial waste from towns and cities in the lower reaches. The extent of pollution clearly influences the use of river water and may create potential hazards. Thus the trend towards water supply abstraction from lowland rivers means that the proportion of effluent in the river water taken for domestic supplies will increase. It has been estimated by Law (1966) that in a supply taken from the river Ouse, the average content of sewage effluent will grow from 13 per cent in 1965 to 28 per cent in 1981, whilst immediately upstream of the Metropolitan Water Board's largest intake on the river Lee, the average dilution of treated sewage effluent by river water is already down to 3·5:1 and the ratio is often as low as 1:1 during summer flow conditions (Central Advisory Water Committee 1971). Toxic discharges in industrial areas have serious implications, and in one study of eight industrial effluents reported by Lloyd and Jordan (1963), it was found that no less than seven were toxic. Altogether 85 per cent of the toxicity was attributed to only five substances – ammonia, phenol, cyanide, zinc and copper – which are known to be of importance in fish mortality. Pollution of this nature clearly limits the recreational potential of a river and may also be a danger to public health.

Frequently the worst pollution is found in river estuaries which have a smaller capacity for absorbing effluent than might be expected in view of the large dilution they appear to offer. During hot, dry weather no dissolved oxygen may be present and hydrogen sulphide, formed by the bacterial reduction of sulphate, may be liberated from central estuarine areas. A major reason for this type of pollution is the slow interchange of water within deep estuaries. In the case of the lower Thames, material is retained in the estuary for about a month and is, therefore, largely oxidised there before dispersal out to sea. Much attention has recently been devoted to the Thames Estuary as shown by Southgate (1969) so that pollution is now reduced below that existing in other estuaries near large conurbations such as the Mersey, Tees and Tyne. By far the greater part of this pollution comes from untreated sewage effluent. Approximately 500 untreated discharges are absorbed into the Tees Estuary, whilst only 5 per cent of the sewage from Tyneside is now treated (Working Party on Sewage Disposal 1970). The progressive decline of these estuaries has destroyed salmon fisheries and created health hazards both from sewage deposits on bathing beaches near the estuary mouths and from the contamination of shell fisheries. In the most grossly polluted areas riverside amenity has been damaged.

The Control of Pollution

Once it is accepted that rivers remain the only practical method of disposing of our liquid waste, it follows that the primary aim must be to restrict the conflict which arises with other aspects of water resource utilisation. In order to accomplish this, there must be some awareness of the desirable standards below which water quality should not fall.

It is extremely difficult to define standards of water quality in relation to pollution which are applicable on a national scale. In addition to natural variations in water quality, and the need to look at standards in relation to the specific use which is proposed for the water, pollution standards also require an appraisal of the quality of both effluent and diluting water plus a knowledge of the volumetric ratio between them. In the last resort, pollution can only be restricted either by raising the standard of effluents or increasing the amount of dilution available in our rivers. In some areas, a combination of these approaches may be necessary. An improvement in effluent standards depends on adequate financial investment in treatment works, whilst the deteriorating ratio between effluent and dilution water makes expenditure on river regulating structures equally necessary. For example, it has been estimated by Lester (1967*a*) that, between 1912 and 1960, water use and effluent discharge increased by 300 per cent thereby reducing the water available for dilution in rivers by more than one-third. Viewed in this light, net abstractions may be seen as a form of indirect pollution (Mercer 1967). Water quality standards must be sufficiently flexible to cater for the dynamic nature of pollution, whilst the introduction of new pollutants may create difficult problems of treatment and quality assessment almost overnight. Obvious examples which may be cited here include synthetic detergents, toxic agricultural chemicals and even radioactive substances.

While there can probably be no totally satisfactory definition of a minimally polluted, healthy river, most inland waters may be measured against several yardsticks of water quality which, together, provide a reliable guide to overall conditions. These parameters include tests for specific pollutants such as ammonia concentration, which is usually linked to the proportion of sewage effluent, but the two most widely employed measures are the biochemical oxygen demand and the ability of the river to support fish life.

In view of the importance of organic pollution in our rivers, it follows that a measure of the resulting depletion of dissolved oxygen content will be of general use in the assessment of pollution. This was recognised by the Royal Commission on Sewage Disposal, which sat at the beginning of the present century, and, in their

Eighth Report published in 1912, they recommended a test to determine the biochemical oxygen demand (BOD) of an effluent (Royal Commission on Sewage Disposal 1912). This test was believed to be the most reliable chemical index of the state of purity of a stream and, with minor modifications, it has remained as one of the most widely applied parameters in Britain. As originally proposed, the test involved the measurement of the oxygen demand of a sample of liquid after a 5-day incubation period at the standard temperature of 65°F. This temperature was considered to represent average thermal conditions during summer in British streams, but, to bring the test into line with international practice, incubation now takes place at 20°C. The Royal Commission recommended that the BOD of effluents should not exceed 20 mg/l, and went on to use the BOD criterion as a basis for stream classification using sample analyses taken from above and below major effluent outfalls. The classification was as follows:

Stream Condition	*5-day BOD (mg/l)*
Very clean	1
Clean	2
Fairly clean	3
Doubtful	5
Bad	10

The Royal Commission stated that rivers with a BOD of less than 4 mg/l were generally free from pollution. It was then suggested that, assuming all sewage effluents were treated so that their BOD was restricted to less than 20 mg/l and the suspended solids content remained below 30 mg/l, the general stream BOD could be kept below 4 mg/l if the dilution by clean water (no more than 2 mg/l BOD) was at least 8 to 1. In circumstances where this dilution ratio was not available, more stringent effluent standards would be needed to maintain the river in a satisfactory condition.

Although the BOD test and other chemical analyses, such as direct dissolved oxygen concentration, can provide the most precise laboratory measurements of river pollution, the first field evidence often comes from fish mortalities. Fish are sensitive indicators of river quality since they respond, not only to dissolved oxygen concentration, but also to other polluting agents, including suspended solids and toxic substances. Clearly some difficulties arise from the fact that different species show marked variations in their tolerance of particular pollutants, but a river which is unable to support a thriving fishery is most unlikely to be of much use for domestic use or as a source for any industrial purposes.

The River Trent – a Case Study

In order to provide some specific illustration of the variation in water quality throughout a river system in response to the effluent load and the capability of the river for self-purification, a case study of the river Trent will be relevant. The Trent is a suitable example to take because with a total catchment area of over 10 360 km^2 (4000 sq miles) and a population of five to six million people, it is one of the largest and most intensively utilised British rivers. The Trent and its tributaries exhibit almost the complete range of water quality found in Britain, but the Trent itself is somewhat unusual in that, as a result of self-purification and downstream dilution, the general trend is towards increasing cleanliness towards the mouth.

The degree of water utilisation in the Trent basin is illustrated in table 13 which lists the abstraction licences in force within the River Authority area. It can be seen that in 1969 there was a gross abstraction requirement of almost 6 400 000 $\times$ 10^3 m^3 (1 408 000 $\times$ 10^6 gal), of which 93 per cent was obtained from surface sources.

Although the demand for cooling water is the largest gross requirement, the high re-use factor involved in cooling and power production probably makes public water supply the greatest abstraction load on the system. There is a total of nineteen water undertakings within the area, of which no less than sixteen have supply sources within the Trent basin (Trent River Authority 1970). The major water supply development has involved the surface sources of the rivers Derwent and Dove, which flow south from the Derbyshire Peak District, although considerable use has been made of groundwater from the Bunter sandstone. The Derwent is the most important source and currently supplies about 3·6 m^3/s (68 mgd) to three separate undertakings, whilst some 1·1 m^3/s (20 mgd) is taken from the Dove. There are plans to increase the supply from both these rivers using regulating reservoirs. The Trent itself is not used for drinking supplies, but a co-operative scheme between the Trent and Lincolnshire River Authorities envisages the transfer of Trent water to the river Ancholme in order to meet industrial demands on South Humberside.

The river Trent flows through part of the productive East Midlands coalfield and this fact, in conjunction with the relative facility with which electricity may be transmitted over the country from this central position, has led to a concentration of thermal power-stations on the middle and lower reaches of the river. In fact, cooling water

TABLE 13

ABSTRACTION LICENCES IN FORCE IN THE TRENT RIVER AUTHORITY AREA ON 31 MARCH 1969

After Trent River Authority (1970)

Purpose	*Surface Sources* No.	*Surface Sources* Licensed Quantities, 000s of cubic metres per annum	*Ground Sources* No.	*Ground Sources* Licensed Quantities, 000s of cubic metres per annum
Public water supply	55	479 859	95	269 353
Industry	215	27 464	271	39 922
Cooling water	98	80 286	41	8469
Cooling water (CEGB)	24	4 201 309	4	1313
Industry and industrial cooling	103	309 245	174	62 483
Agriculture other than spray irrigation	33	536	1562	3463
Spray irrigation	484	8614	113	1531
Power production	36	806 145	—	—
Private water supply	36	1032	73	1531
Sand and gravel washing	22	12 154	53	33 548
Miscellaneous	—	—	2	9682
Total	1106	5 926 644	2388	431 295

NOTE: Of the quantities shown against the purpose 'Public water supply', 217 353 thousand cubic metres from surface sources and 8355 thousand cubic metres from groundwater sources are in respect of 'Stepped' licences where special conditions forbid the abstraction of water until future years.

comprises about 70 per cent of all abstractive uses and is taken mostly by the Central Electricity Generating Board (CEGB), although other industrial cooling is significant. As in other areas, there is considerable re-use, and the gross demand is declining due to the change-over from direct cooling methods to the use of cooling towers with internal circulatory systems. Nevertheless, the *evaporated* demand is rising steadily. Already it has been estimated by Lester

(1967*b*) that the mean maximum temperature of the lower Trent is artificially raised by about 4°C (8°F) due to thermal pollution.

There is also a large non-abstractive use of the Trent. The Trent itself is navigable for over 150 km (93 miles) from the Humber to just downstream of Trent Bridge, Nottingham, whilst according to Marsh (1963) the lowest 80 km (50 miles) constitutes the longest stretch of natural navigable river in Britain. Other rivers in the basin, notably the Soar, form important navigable waterways in addition to the canal network. The Trent also provides an important recreational function for the Midlands. Apart from pleasure boating on numerous waterways, angling is the major leisure activity. Trout and grayling are obtained from many of the Derbyshire rivers such as the Derwent, Dove and Wye as well as from most of the water supply reservoirs, whilst coarse fishing is widely available on the other rivers and canals.

It follows that the intensive use of the Trent for abstractive and *in situ* requirements will lead to heavy utilisation for effluent disposal. There are particular problems caused, for example, by the discharge of high chloride concentrations in mine water from collieries in the upper Trent, Anker, Erewash and Idle valleys, but over 90 per cent of the pollution entering the Trent basin comes from local authority sewage works (Lester 1967*a*). Excluding works with a dry weather flow of less than 6·8 m^3/d (1500 gal/day), there are 636 sewage treatment works operated by 103 local authorities, with a further 128 works maintained by private institutions. In addition, excluding water used solely for cooling, trade effluent discharges in excess of 6·8 m^3/d (1500 gal/day) are introduced at a total of 435 points. Most of the pollution enters the Trent above Nottingham, and it is estimated that the total effluent discharge averages 20 m^3/s (382 mgd) which is made up of 16·4 m^3/s (312 mgd) of sewage flows and 3·6 m^3/s (70 mgd) of industrial waste. Most of the sewage effluent is of an unsatisfactory standard and is discharged from outdated and over-loaded treatment works.

To place this pollution load in some general context, the 20 m^3/s of effluent discharge may be compared with the mean annual runoff of 84 m^3/s (1600 mgd) computed for the entire Trent basin by Nixon (1967). Thus, even under average flow conditions, about one-quarter of the Trent's discharge is effluent. In the summer months natural runoff falls to a July mean of only 39 m^3/s (750 mgd). Effluent is then more than half the total flow and rises to a significantly higher proportion during really dry spells in summer.

The spatial variation of water quality is shown in figure 8.2 which is a diagrammatic map of river quality based on the mean content of ammoniacal nitrogen in mg/l between 1965 and 1967. The classification is based on ammoniacal nitrogen concentration because, with the dominance of domestic sewage pollution in the Trent, this has been found to be the most reliable pollution index, but average BOD values for selected sampling points are also included on the map.

Although the Trent rises in a moorland area, it is soon contaminated in its course through the Potteries. Large inputs of sewage and industrial effluent from Stoke cause gross pollution of the upper Trent and the Fowlea Brook, the latter having a mean ammoniacal nitrogen content of 11·6 and a BOD of 66. As a result of dilution from the rivers Sow and Blithe, some self-purification takes place before the confluence with the Tame. However, the river Tame is one of the most polluted stretches of inland water in Britain, and is in a thoroughly unsatisfactory state throughout its length of 74 km (46 miles). It receives the effluents from Birmingham and most of the Black Country, which total about 0·79 m^3/s (15 mgd) in dry weather. The main problem is caused by inadequate domestic sewerage systems in the area, but there are also highly toxic effluents from metal finishing and other industries. Despite the fact that the river is free-flowing, the Tame is effectively anaerobic during summer. The BOD figures show evidence of some improvement downstream, but, even at the confluence with the Trent, the average river quality fails to meet the Royal Commission standards for treated effluent discharges.

The flow of the Tame is slightly greater than the Trent at their confluence, and the main river therefore suffers considerable pollution from the Tame. Downstream to Burton, the Trent is unable to support fish life, but after the entry of the river Dove a fishery is maintained for the next 129 km (80 miles) down to Gainsborough. The middle reaches of the Trent are still of poor quality, owing to sewage disposal from large cities such as Nottingham, whilst surges of storm sewage may enter the river from the Tame, but dilution from cleaner rivers prevents further deterioration. For example, the Dove is of excellent quality when it joins the Trent, and, although the Derwent deteriorates below Derby, this river also remains satisfactory. The Soar and Erewash tributaries introduce some further

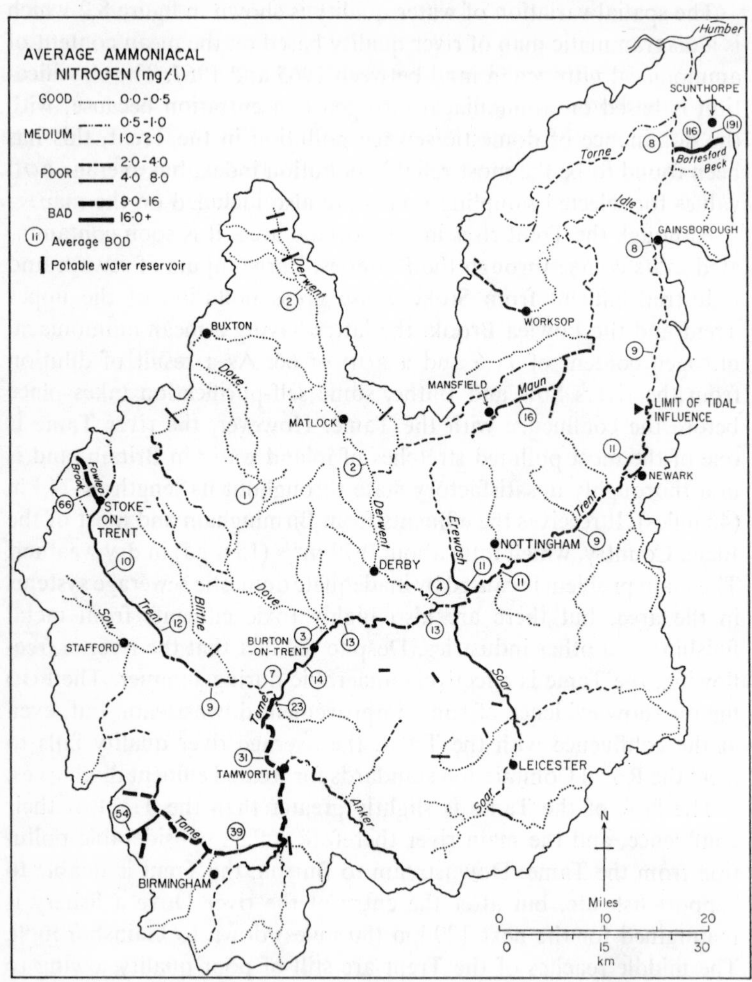

Figure 8.2 The variation in water quality over the river Trent drainage basin 1965–67. After Trent River Authority (1970).

pollution, caused by sewage from Leicester and trade effluents respectively, but their discharge is insufficient to influence the average quality of the main river. Below the tidal limit the Trent improves from poor to medium quality water. In this section too the tributaries have little influence. Even the Bottesford Beck, which enters from the Scunthorpe area with startling BOD levels between 116 and 191 – about six times the strength of a desirable effluent – is absorbed and dissipated to the Humber estuary with apparently only localised effects.

9 Problems and Policies

Water availability in Britain is a regional rather than a national problem, and difficulties arise from the maldistribution of supply and demand rather than from a basic inadequacy of resources. Further storage and a more efficient distribution of water are the obvious twin solutions, but most areas offer alternative means whereby these aims may be achieved. Consequently, future water resource development is controversial, not only in terms of making the best possible use of the resource itself, but also because of the impact on questions of land use and regional economy. This final chapter seeks to consider some of these issues in the light of present evidence.

THE GENERAL PROBLEM

The climate of Britain, with its regular, low-intensity precipitation, places the country in a favourable resource situation as shown in table 14. Only England has an average rainfall below the world mean

TABLE 14

MEAN ANNUAL GROSS YIELD OF RESOURCES

Water Potential	*England*	*Wales*	*Scotland*	*N. Ireland*	*U.K.*
Mean rainfall (mm) 1916–50	831	1356	1420	1079	1079
Gross yield (m^3/s)	1578	568	2630	252	5028

of 991 mm (39 in.), whilst Scotland and Wales are especially well off. Assuming a mean annual evaporation loss of 432 mm (17 in.) the *gross yield* represents the amount of water held in the soil, lakes, rivers and aquifers during an average year. Actual evaporation, therefore, accounts for only some 40 per cent of precipitation over Britain, and only slightly more than half over England.

The corresponding gross demand over England and Wales is shown in table 15, which summarises the licensed abstractions in force on 30 September 1969. Comparable information is not, of course, available for Scotland and Northern Ireland. Although the total abstraction amounts to more than half the gross yield available

TABLE 15

LICENSED ABSTRACTIONS IN ENGLAND AND WALES IN 1969
(000s of cubic metres)
After Water Resources Board (1970*a*)

Use	*Surface water*	%	*Ground water*	%	*Total* %
Public and private water supply	5 195 603	13·07	2 714 485	6·86	19·93
Cooling (CEGB)	22 060 484	55·50	16 826	0·04	55·54
Other industrial cooling	2 537 363	6·38	197 926	0·50	6·88
Other industrial use	3 916 961	9·85	872 274	2·19	12·04
Spray irrigation	116 391	0·29	38 551	0·10	0·39
Other agricultural use	11 460	0·03	124 645	0·31	0·34
Miscellaneous	1 840 043	4·63	98 037	0·25	4·88
Total	35 678 305	89·75	4 062 744	10·25	100

Total licences 48 848 *Total abstractions* 39 741 049

in England and Wales, over 60 per cent is delivered to industry for cooling purposes, thus leading to a large amount of re-use. The licensed abstractions quoted are also the maximum permitted withdrawals rather than the actual amounts taken and, together with the re-use factor, this means that probably less than 20 per cent of the total abstractive demand is actually consumed. Thus, the present demand is little more than 189 m^3/s (3600 mgd), which is only about 10 per cent of the gross yield.

It is clearly impossible to make a precise estimate of supply and demand, and, whilst the gross abstractive demand presents an over-pessimistic picture, the gross yield, which would theoretically allow 4000 l. (900 gal) daily per head of the present population of England and Wales, provides an unrealistically generous estimate of the available resources. There are already significant variations in the comparative regional development of resources. It was estimated by the Central Advisory Water Committee (1959) that in 1965 the developed resources would amount to as little as 2 per cent of the gross yield in Devon and Cornwall, but up to 36 per cent in Essex and 40 per cent in the Thames and London area. Even such regional estimates are too optimistic. Little of the theoretical 60 per cent of the gross resources apparently available around London could be economically brought into supply because of depressed water-tables, pollution and other complications arising from over-exploitation. Furthermore, no account is taken of the detailed local distribution of water within these regions, or of the existing storage in relation to dry weather conditions. Indeed, it is the omission of dry years from the above estimates which perhaps does most to conceal the real problem. Drought, coupled with the rising demand for water, places a different interpretation on the situation. In a dry year the total quantity of water potentially available in the rivers and aquifers of England and Wales is equivalent to a daily mean flow of only 840 m^3/s (16 000 mgd) and, if the demand rises to the projected figure of 526 m^3/s (10 000 mgd) by AD 2000, then two-thirds of the yield will be required according to Calvert (1967).

Bearing in mind the needs of effluent disposal, it appears that, by the end of the century, we could be approaching the total usable dry weather flow of our rivers. Already such demands are exceeded in certain areas, and it is only the successive re-use of water which makes the situation tolerable. On the Yorkshire Calder, for example, it has been shown by the Water Resources Board (1970*a*) that abstraction licences amount to a volume which is between 20 and 30 times the natural dry weather flow of the river and, as on the Mersey and Weaver river system, total abstractions exceed the mean natural discharge of the river. This intensity of use is characteristic of several heavily industrialised areas, and there are instances where industrial demand from one site exceeds the dry weather flow so that, in effect, at certain times the entire river is diverted through a single factory. Similar problems exist with regard to peak irrigation demand in some agricultural areas. As early as 1960 it was recognised that if the potential demand for spray irrigation was met it would produce virtually zero flow in the rivers of the Great Ouse basin during a dry summer (Ministry of Housing and Local Government 1960).

Although some parts of the country are well supplied with water, deficiencies exist, at least intermittently, in other areas. The core of this problem is found in south-east England which suffers from the greatest concentration of population in the region of lowest rainfall, together with isolation from areas to the North and West where surplus resources exist. The relative situation was summarised by Pugh (1963) who estimated that by 1990, after the demands on the public undertakings had been satisfied, the surplus reserves in south-east England would total only 1068 l. (235 gal) per head daily, compared with 11 820 l. (2600 gal) in Northern Ireland and 33 049 l. (7270 gal) in Scotland. There is a need, therefore, for new supplies and more efficient conservation throughout the country to ensure the optimum use of resources.

NEW RESOURCES

Limitation of Demand

It has already been seen that the increasing demand for water causes concern with regard to the availability of future supplies. There is general acceptance that both overall and *per capita* needs will continue to increase, but it is possible that the rate of increase may be slowed down by the introduction of further controls on use. If successful, this would lead indirectly to the creation of additional resources.

It has often been argued that, because piped supplies are almost universally available in Britain, there is the general feeling that resources are limitless. Whatever the truth of this, there is no doubt that water is cheap and, despite our enormous consumption, existing supplies absorb only 1 per cent of the total national consumer expenditure according to Silver (1969). Generally, water supply costs for manufacturing industry in the United Kingdom compare favourably with the outlay necessary elsewhere in Europe where a broad economic gradient can be recognised between the low-cost Alpine and Scandinavian countries and the high-cost regions of the European lowlands. Thus, a recent study of water-use in the non-ferrous metals industry by Savage (1971) has shown that, in terms of the average cost of water supplies obtained from all sources, Britain was ranked fifth out of the eleven countries taking part in the survey. As a result, it is sometimes suggested that the time has now come for a more economic approach to water, as befits the growing scarcity of a valuable resource, through a pricing policy. On the other hand, the official attitude of the Water Resources Board is that sufficient water can be made available for demands well into the next century with little increase in price to the consumer. Higher charges are, therefore, resisted by the Board on the grounds that they are unnecessary and would also need to be substantial in order to curb demand effectively.

The argument for increasing charges to an 'economic' level is most usually applied to the domestic supplies delivered by the public undertakings. The thesis has been well summarised by Rees (1969) who states that the fixed rateable charge for water is a relic from the days when people had to be encouraged to use water, and that there is no justification for basing future resource planning simply on an extrapolation of current trends. She argues that, during critical droughts, water economies have to be enforced by administrative controls – such as restrictions on non-essential uses like garden hoses – whilst a more rational allocation could be achieved by financial methods if domestic supplies were metered.

Domestic metering is common in other advanced countries. There is no real evidence from such countries that the system jeopardises public health, and there is little doubt that metering in Britain would cause some reduction in demand, particularly for the less essential uses. The main problem is to determine the precise effect of metering and, with the recent absorption of the Malvern undertaking, which originally metered domestic supplies to conserve a small spring source, there is little opportunity for comparative testing. However, the introduction of domestic meters would only influence a limited proportion of water use since, even with the exclusion of the requirements of the Central Electricity Generating Board (CEGB), nearly 70 per cent of all water used is already metered. Thus, taking the optimistic assumption that universal metering would depress domestic consumption by 20 per cent, the overall saving, again excluding the CEGB, would be only 6 per cent (Goode 1969). With a current rate of demand increase of about 2·5 per cent per year, this would postpone the development of a new water source by no more than three years, which is an insignificant breathing space in relation to long-term trends. Even with metering, it seems inevitable that rising living standards will create increased *per capita* demands, and in the United States, for example, where domestic metering is widely practised, the consumption per head is more than double that in Britain.

The practical task of changing to a wholly metered system would be formidable. Sharp (1967) has estimated that a complete change-over by the end of the century would necessitate putting over 600 000 new and existing houses on a metered system, whilst the cost of installation and maintenance would be very high. Nevertheless, the development of new materials may eventually make metering cheaper in relation to water costs, whilst as living standards rise people should be prepared to pay more for their supply. At some point in the future, therefore, domestic metering may become a feasible proposition.

Other suggestions for reducing domestic consumption have included a dual-flushing w.c. system. This would involve the substitution of an optional flush of either 4·5 or 9 l. (1 or 2 gal) to replace the present 9 l. (2 gal) flush. This would have an even more limited impact on demand since it would involve only the domestic water used for sanitation purposes, although it has been claimed that the economy might be between 12 and 25 per cent of all domestic use (Risbridger 1963).

A factor which affects all public consumption, both domestic and industrial, is the waste of water which occurs as leakage throughout the distribution network. Some leakage is inevitable, but it has been estimated that by AD 2000 waste in distribution will amount to more than 15 per cent of *per capita* domestic demand. Despite current efforts, it is likely that more waste prevention could be achieved by the water undertakings. However, if domestic metering were to be introduced, the undertakings would then presumably equate their annual revenue with annual consumption rather than with overall costs as at present. Therefore, as long as wastage occurred on the consumers' side of the meter, and was chargeable, there would be even less incentive for efficient waste detection than exists now.

As far as industrial water itself is concerned, this is already paid for by measure and, despite the fact that water is a cheap raw material, there is no evidence of excessive industrial wastage in Britain. It is, of course, true that economies could result from the re-cycling of water within industrial premises either for the same purpose or for other uses, but this is a complex issue on which generalisation is impossible. In some cases there is little doubt that industrialists are taking advantage of cheap water supplies and not bothering to re-cycle. On the other hand, while increased costs may force the industrialist to re-use water, the resultant effluent may be of such poor quality that it either requires extensive treatment or is even impossible to treat. In general, the greatest social and economic benefits are likely to come from an improvement of effluent standards from both industry and sewage works so that better quality river water can sustain successive re-use of the diluted effluents by downstream interests.

Multi-purpose River Regulation

Since it appears unlikely that demand will be restricted by price controls in the foreseeable future, it follows that additional resources must be developed. Owing to the dominant use of surface sources compared with groundwater, river regulation will almost certainly be the most important method of supply augmentation. In addition to providing the major source of supplies in north and west Britain, river regulation can help to remedy deficiencies in the east and south where river systems such as the Severn, Thames, Great Ouse and Trent are suitably orientated to facilitate a west–east transfer of water.

Although deliberate river regulation is a relatively new technique, many British rivers are already man-made systems which are indirectly controlled by artificial storage and use. The main regulation arises from the existing direct-supply reservoirs, which not only smooth streamflow in the headwaters, but also improve flow regularity in the lower reaches through the continuous discharge of sewage and trade effluents from towns. For example, the public supply storage in the Thames basin provides a reliable discharge which is between three and four times the natural dry weather flow of the river (Water Resources Board 1970*a*). In turn, this supports the largest direct abstraction for public supply on any British river, since the Metropolitan Water Board depends for most of its supplies on the Thames, as does Oxford Corporation upstream. In 1965 the Metropolitan Water Board took from the Thames an amount of water equivalent to 18 per cent of the total flow during that year at the abstraction point, whilst in the drought years of 1921–22 and 1934–35 it has been shown by Skeat (1969) that the withdrawals amounted to 26·9 per cent and 24·3 per cent respectively of the annual discharge. Public supplies from the Thames, as well as from many rivers in the South-east, including the Great Ouse and the Essex rivers, thus depend more and more on the successful re-use of effluents discharged upstream.

The principal advantage of river regulation is that the benefits of the headwater storage are spread throughout the river system. With increasing pressure on our resources, these schemes provide for the development of large regional sources so that the water caters for the widest variety of needs. This is achieved partly because headwater regulation provides the maximum opportunity for successive re-use down the entire river course, but also because the total yield is a function of the unreservoired catchment and its discharge, as well as of the reservoired area. Unlike direct-supply reservoirs, with their continuous compensation discharge, the releases from regulating reservoirs may be confined to periods of low natural streamflow. At all other times both the abstractive and non-abstractive requirements are maintained by the runoff from the larger unreservoired catchment so that, theoretically, all the storage may be usefully employed. The overall object is to maintain river discharge above some prescribed minimum level and, although the reservoir releases may be varied to suit downstream needs, in some cases even greater flexibility can be achieved by means of a pumped storage reservoir downstream. This can balance supplies against demand much more precisely than the releases from the main headwater storage above, since there is an inevitable time-lag between discharge from the upstream reservoir and increased flow in the river near the abstraction points.

An illustration of the comprehensive benefits obtained from river regulation can be given by the Clywedog reservoir scheme in the upper Severn basin. The river Severn has regional and even national importance. Apart from being one of the largest British rivers, its middle course takes it along the western edge of the West Midlands within some 32 km (20 miles) of Birmingham. In addition, it may eventually be necessary to pump water from the Severn near Gloucester over the Cotswolds into the upper Thames near Cirencester. By this means, water could be successively re-used from the Severn headwaters to the Thames estuary.

The Clywedog reservoir is the first regulation project on the Severn and came into full operation on 1 April 1968 as detailed by Fordham *et al.* (1970). Its origins date back to the early 1950s when the water supply possibilities of the Severn were investigated by both the South Staffordshire Waterworks Company and Birmingham Corporation. At this time the source was larger than either undertaking required and, in any case, the then Severn River Board was not prepared to sanction any abstractions without storage. Eventually, however, a group of potential abstractors presented a Bill to Parliament in November 1962. The resulting Act, which provided for the formation of the Clywedog Reservoir Joint Authority, was passed in 1963 and, although it pre-dated the Water Resources Act of that year, much of the spirit of comprehensive conservation was incorporated into the scheme.

The chief function of the scheme is river regulation. The reservoir, which has a capacity of 50×10^6 m^3 ($11\,000 \times 10^6$ gal) provides a minimum discharge of 0·2 m^3/s (4 mgd) immediately downstream of the dam and a minimum flow of 17 m^3/s (323 mgd) on the Severn at Bewdley. Since the mean flow is 62 m^3/s, the guaranteed regulation amounts to 27 per cent of the mean discharge at Bewdley. These regulated flows are utilised by no less than twelve abstracting authorities, whilst the total abstractive yield of the scheme is about 8·9 m^3/s (170 mgd).

In its natural state the Severn has the flooding regime typical of upland rivers. For many years the river has been a flood hazard downstream as far as Shrewsbury, but particularly to Newtown and Welshpool. Flood alleviation clauses were incorporated into the Act, and the Reservoir Authority has a duty to retain flood storage capacity during the winter months. Prescribed maximum water-levels in the reservoir range from 3·6 m (12 ft) below capacity on 1 November up to full capacity on 1 May, from when the reservoir is expected to improve summer flows. Even before the scheme was completed some flood reduction was achieved, as in January 1968 when a rainfall of 70 mm (2·75 in.) was experienced with 305 mm (12 in.) of snow lying on the hills (Anonymous 1968*a*), whilst it is thought that the reservoir will lower the height of a major flood at Newtown by approximately 0·6 m (2 ft).

Water discharged from the reservoir is used to generate electricity, and the power from the turbines is fed into the national grid. Recreation and amenity have been provided for by landscaping, together with picnic areas and car parks. The Clywedog Sailing Club now has about 300 members and about 100 boats are regularly sailed on the reservoir. Angling, mainly for trout, has taken place since the summer of 1968.

Although such river regulation schemes provide clear benefits, there are certain disadvantages, both in the operation of the reservoirs and the effect of the projects on the community as a whole. In some ways, rivers are less suitable for transporting water for long distances than pipelines which are under more complete control, respond more rapidly to changing abstractive demands and are not subject to pollution like the river water which, for public supply purposes, will require treatment near the centres of demand. Similarly, flood reduction can only be a partial measure. The Clywedog reservoir controls a catchment of 57 km² (22 sq miles) which comprises only 13 per cent of the Severn catchment down to Newtown, and severe flooding could still result from the unregulated tributaries especially after a localised thunderstorm.

At the present time there is a lack of knowledge concerning the optimum operation of regulating reservoirs. In order to provide more information, the Water Resources Board has organised a large research programme described by Collinge (1967) to investigate the workings of the Dee project. The work is being undertaken by a variety of organisations, and an important priority involves a more precise estimation of the yield of the reservoirs so that operational wastage may be reduced. In order to optimise operation, it will be necessary to have better prediction of riverflows, and attempts are being made to improve hydrological forecasting both for routine releases and for flood control.

Although regulating reservoirs provide an efficient and relatively cheap method of developing surface resources, they sometimes arouse opposition from the general public. The objections which may be raised take several forms and often come from different sections of the community. With the increased emphasis on access and leisure activities, regulating reservoirs are more acceptable to recreational interests than direct-supply projects, but certain schemes may create opposition on a regional or even a national scale. This seems to happen most frequently when environmental or landscape amenity is threatened, especially in the National Parks or the Areas of Outstanding Natural Beauty. The Peak District and the Lake District have both been placed under severe pressure with regard to water supply development, and a notable case of successful organised opposition occurred in 1961 when Manchester Corporation's proposals to build a reservoir in Bannisdale were rejected by the House of Lords. Although the preservation of general amenity is perhaps the most usual platform of opposition, some proposals may lead to more specific criticisms. For example, there was considerable scientific opposition, mainly from botanists, when plans for the construction of a regulating reservoir at Cow Green in Upper Teesdale were made public. Here the objectors were anxious to safeguard the habitat of some rare Arctic–Alpine flora, and the scheme was sanctioned only after prolonged enquiries had taken place.

At a more local level, protests are invariably made about the dislocating effects of new reservoirs. The resident community, not unnaturally, complains when houses and land are flooded, and much opposition stems from the belief that such schemes are engineered solely for the benefit of water consumers many miles away. In Wales the strength of this local feeling is greatly increased by national sentiment, and several schemes, both existing and projected, have been the target of direct militant action.

Whilst it must be admitted that reservoir projects are promoted in the uplands largely for the benefit of the lowlands, it is also true that some advantages do pass to the local community. Modern schemes usually make provision for the improvement of local water supplies and the Montgomeryshire Water Board, for example, is one of the abstractors benefitting from the Clywedog reservoir. The development of recreation and tourism may well bring some economic return to the locality, whilst flood reduction, improvements to fisheries and general river amenity resulting from guaranteed discharges are all side-benefits enjoyed by the local area. These benefits may be of little interest to the hill-farmer who is badly hit by the flooding of his best quality land in the valley bottom, and there is a case for making better compensation provision when this occurs. On the other hand, the hill land taken out of agricultural use will be significantly less productive than the farmland which would be required by siting the reservoir further downstream, and, in national terms at least, the agricultural losses caused by impounding are probably more than compensated by the increased production resulting from the use of the stored water for irrigation purposes.

Groundwater Regulation

Compared with some surface storage schemes, the advantages of further groundwater development appear impressive. There is virtually no disturbance of amenity or land-use interests, and groundwater exploitation is usually cheaper than the development of an equivalent yield from surface sources because of the small-scale of the headworks involved. The natural availability of storage underground is considerably larger than that of surface reserves. Furthermore, the major aquifers are in south and south-east England where the greatest regional water deficiencies exist and where sites for surface reservoirs, even if they can be found, are most expensive. Surface storage in the lowlands implies shallow reservoirs of large area and, apart from the potential land-use conflicts, these reservoirs suffer relatively high evaporation losses against which underground resources are completely protected.

The existing utilisation of groundwater confirms that it is in southern England where these resources will continue to make the most contribution. At the present time, even when the surface-orientated demands of the CEGB are excluded, groundwater accounts for no more than 25 per cent of the total licensed abstractions in England and Wales. The largest single use, accounting for 60 per cent of all groundwater, is public water supply, while industrial use takes a further 20 per cent. Most of the remainder is mine drainage. Not surprisingly, there are large regional variations in the importance of groundwater, which supplies about 40 per cent of the statutory undertakings demands in England and Wales, but only about 10 per cent of the public need in Scotland and Northern Ireland. Similarly, in the Northumbrian River Authority area, groundwater comprises only 2 per cent of all abstractions, whilst it totals 44 and 59 per cent in the Lincolnshire and the Avon and Dorset areas respectively according to Ineson (1970).

In the past, the exploitation of groundwater has been less controlled than that of surface sources. Many schemes have been developed without consideration of wider issues, and this uncoordinated activity has led to persistent over-pumping in a number of areas. The chalk beneath London has been over-developed for at least 150 years with a resulting fall in restwater levels of up to 91 m (300 ft) in places as confirmed by the Water Resources Board (1967). Near many coastal and estuarine areas a fall in water-table has caused saline intrusion. Thus, the Permo-Triassic aquifer underlying industrial south Lancashire has been over-pumped on a regional scale during the last sixty years, and it has been estimated by Bow *et al.* (1969) that present abstractions may exceed the annual replenishment by 10 per cent. Local restwater levels are now more than 30m

(100 ft) below sea level, and there is evidence that saline waters are reaching the aquifer from both the Mersey estuary and the Cheshire salt-field.

Such problems can only be solved by appraisals of groundwater resources on a regional scale and in the context of the complete hydrological cycle. It has already been seen that, in the major groundwater provinces, aquifers may provide 80 per cent or more of the annual river discharge, and it will be clear that groundwater abstraction in such areas is bound to produce a depletion of riverflow at some time in the year. It would be unfortunate if this depletion should occur during the summer months, for it is by sustaining dry weather flows in summer that groundwater storage exercises its most important hydrological function of reducing the ratio between winter and summer discharges. Compared with relatively impermeable catchments in the North and West, rivers draining the main groundwater areas experience considerable natural flow regulation, but the overall discharge on many of these rivers is small in relation to demand, so that a further reduction in the seasonal flow ratio is required.

Groundwater can be envisaged as a major storage element which has potential for seasonal manipulation in the same way as artificial surface storage. The basic aim of contemporary groundwater development must be to maximise on this storage by increasing the groundwater component of riverflow even further during the summer and early autumn when rivers are low, and by restricting unnecessary aquifer seepage in winter when surface runoff is sufficient to maintain acceptable river discharges. This aim can be achieved by deliberately over-pumping the aquifer in summer as shown in figure 9.1. When river discharge reaches a prescribed minimum flow, the river may be augmented by groundwater pumped from the aquifer any time during June to November (Ineson 1970). This abstraction will depress the water-table and, by creating an artificial drawdown, will obtain a greater yield from the aquifer than would have been supported by the relatively low amplitude of natural groundwater fluctuation. When pumping ceases in November, the excess rainfall of the winter six months from December to May will be largely taken up in the natural replenishment of the aquifer and less groundwater will emerge wastefully from springs and other sources during the winter period. Thus, the temporary seasonal over-development of the aquifer may be used to increase the available riverflow during summer without any long-term artificial depression of the water-table.

It is likely that several large groundwater management schemes will employ these general principles. The Thames Conservancy has

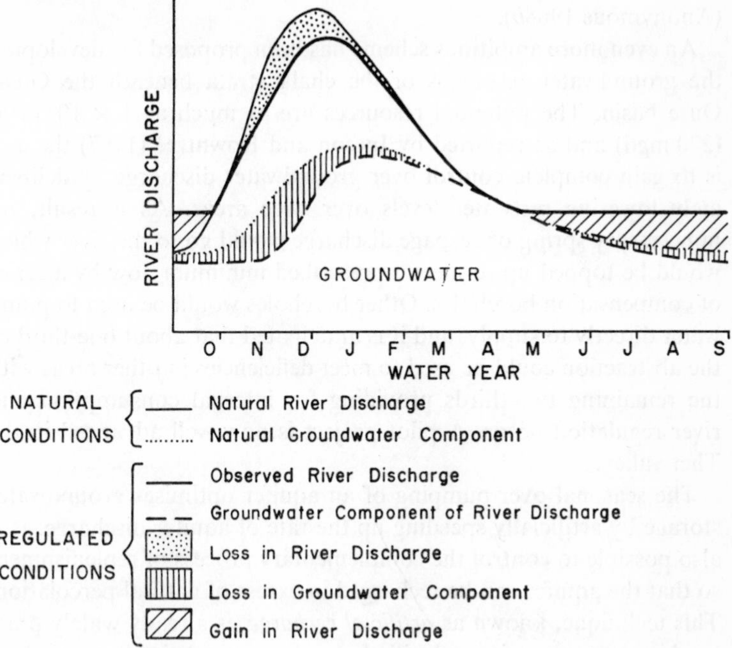

Figure 9.1 A diagrammatic representation of river regulation based on controlled groundwater development. After Ineson (1970).

proposed a project to augment the flow of the Thames and its tributaries by up to 14 m^3/s (270 mgd) by pumping from 248 boreholes in the chalk and Jurassic limestones (Anonymous 1967). The scheme, which was first announced in October 1965, is designed to meet the need for the additional 1·7 m^3/s (33 mgd) estimated to be required by water undertakings and industrial users in the lower Thames basin by 1971. The probable cost of the scheme has been reckoned at only about one-tenth of the outlay for surface reservoirs of the same capacity which would, in any case, necessitate flooding 80 km^2 (31 sq miles) of the Thames Valley. A pilot investigation has been conducted in the lower Lambourn valley, a tributary of the river Kennet, with a view to testing the proposals from a hydro-geological viewpoint. Pumping tests have shown that the aquifer should yield the expected quantities of water, and it is anticipated that drilling on the main boreholes for the scheme will start in the early 1970s (Anonymous 1968*b*).

An even more ambitious scheme has been proposed for developing the groundwater resources of the chalk strata beneath the Great Ouse basin. The potential resources are as much as 1×10^6 m^3/d (220 mgd) and as reported by Ineson and Rowntree (1967) the aim is to gain complete control over groundwater discharge by deliberately lowering restwater levels over wide areas. As a result, no unnecessary spring or seepage discharge would go to the river which would be topped up to meet a prescribed minimum flow by a series of compensation boreholes. Other boreholes would be used to pump water directly to supply, and it is anticipated that about one-third of the abstraction could be used to meet deficiencies in other areas with the remaining two-thirds providing for internal consumption and river regulation needs. A pilot project is now well advanced in the Thet valley.

The seasonal over-pumping of an aquifer optimises groundwater storage by artificially speeding up the rate of aquifer discharge. It is also possible to control the complementary process of replenishment so that the aquifer can be recharged in excess of natural percolation. This technique, known as *artificial recharge*, is already widely practised in some countries and will play an increasingly important role in groundwater regulation in Britain. Normally boreholes are used solely for water abstraction, but they can also be employed to inject surplus riverflows to the aquifer. This can produce a number of benefits including higher abstractive yields, the reduction of peak flood flows and the improvement of the chemical and biological quality of the resulting water compared with the injected raw river water.

It has been suggested by Taylor (1964) that artificial replenishment may partly overcome some of the problems due to over-development in the London Basin, whilst it may also be used to control saline infiltration. A line of recharge wells located between the coast and the aquifer undergoing development could be employed to raise local groundwater levels and thus restrict the inland progression of the saline waters. This type of recharge, using surface water, has been proposed by Downing and Williams (1969) in order to facilitate further abstractions from the Lincolnshire limestone.

One of the main problems associated with artificial recharge is that, if it is undertaken during winter when surplus supplies are most likely to be available, it may only steepen the hydraulic gradient towards the river and simply result in an increased rate of groundwater discharge. Thus, the advantages of storage are minimal if the water almost immediately reappears as riverflow. In order to accentuate the lag between recharge and the subsequent seepage to rivers, it may be necessary to inject the water as far away from the river as possible, either on the interfluves or in dry valleys. Such a system could involve high running costs if water has to be pumped uphill a long way to a suitable injection point.

Estuary Barrages

Just as river regulation provides for a more total development of surface resources than direct-supply reservoirs, so the maximum surface storage for any catchment area may be achieved at the lowest practical impounding point on the river. The possibility of such complete utilisation is now under investigation in the form of proposed coastal barrage schemes for several British rivers. These proposals seek to introduce an entirely new element into our water technology, and the novelty of the scheme, together with the broad implications for communications, agricultures, industrial development, recreation and land reclamation on a regional scale, has necessitated preliminary feasibility studies embracing both the engineering and wider cost/benefit aspects.

Barrage schemes are potentially capable of yielding very large additional water supplies without inundating any more land, and such proposals have an immediate appeal to the anti-reservoir lobby. The creation of large freshwater lakes and the reclamation of certain estuarine land areas could also provide new opportunities for recreational and economic development respectively, whilst the barrage summit could be utilised as a road link between the opposite shores of the estuary. Equally, however, the introduction of a coastal barrier may well result in important disadvantages. For example, the cost of treated water from a barrage scheme would be appreciably higher to the consumer than water supplied from a conventional source. Part of this cost is due to the distribution expenses, probably involving pumping, of delivering water from sea level. A more important element is treatment costs and the maintenance of adequate quality standards, since a barrage system depends essentially on the collection and eventual return to supply of the liquid wastes from the entire catchment area. At the present time, little practical experience of such a vast re-circulating system is available. In addition the physical presence of a barrage could have adverse economic and ecological consequences by restricting navigation and fish migration respectively. Changes in tidal processes and the movement of coastal sediments may well alter coastal conditions some distance away, whilst a disturbance of groundwater levels and land drainage is also likely to result.

The proposals for a barrage across Morecambe Bay, which were put forward in the early 1960s as a means of providing additional water supplies to the Manchester conurbation without further reservoir construction in the Lake District, illustrate something of the overall complexity of these schemes. The original plan outlined by the Water Resources Board (1966*a*) envisaged a single barrage right across the Bay which would yield a supply of some 26 m^3/s (500 mgd) or about four times the present consumption of the Manchester undertaking. This water would be obtained from an enclosed freshwater lake 77 km^2 (30 sq miles) in extent, which would also provide a considerable recreational asset for industrial south Lancashire. It was further estimated that 60 km^2 (15 000 acres) of polder land could be reclaimed for agricultural or industrial development, whilst the construction of a dual two-lane highway across the barrage would provide a direct road link between the Furness peninsula and the M6 motorway. However, it now appears that smaller, twin barriers across the Kent and Leven estuaries may be preferable, with the fresh water contained in a separate pumped storage reservoir located above high water-level out in Morecambe Bay. Although such an alternative scheme would be capable of providing an equivalent yield at approximately the same overall cost, there would be a strong intermediate financial advantage in that the construction of the barrages and the storage reservoir could be phased in with the rise in water consumption over a period of years. On the other hand, the benefits of a transport link may not be as clear-cut as in the case of a complete barrage. Amenity objections could be aroused by the storage reservoir, whilst any of the proposed schemes could alter the resort function of Morecambe itself and adversely influence the commercial shrimp fishing industry in the Bay.

A complete feasibility report on the Morecambe Bay barrage is not expected before 1972, and the investigation of other projects on the Dee, Solway and Wash is rather less advanced. Each scheme offers slightly different advantages. For example, the Dee project is based at least as much on improved communications across the estuary between North Wales and Merseyside, plus the associated industrial development on reclaimed land, as on the potential increment to water resources, whilst the proposals for a Wash barrage rest much more directly on the growing water shortage which is expected in south-east England. It is clear that complex decisions are necessary before any scheme can gain final approval. All the projects under consideration are likely to have some regional significance, and a decision on the basis of water resources alone cannot be given until it is seen how a particular barrage either compares with, or may be integrated with, alternative water storage in conventional inland reservoirs.

Desalination

Ultimately, desalination appears to be an attractive solution to water deficiencies for an advanced, technological community living in a group of islands everywhere within 160 km (100 miles) of the coast. In theory, desalination offers an almost unlimited and constant supply of fresh water, quite independent of weather conditions, without flooding any more land areas. Unlike barrage storage, this method of resource supplementation is already operational in Britain and according to the Water Resources Board (1969) over 100 industrial plants have been constructed to supply relatively small quantities of high quality boiler-feed water to electricity power-stations. Nevertheless, the only plants serving the public supply system are in the Channel Islands. On Guernsey a plant of 0·03 m^3/s (0·5 mgd) output has been constructed mainly to safeguard the island's tomato production during dry weather, whilst a much larger plant of 0·08 m^3/s (1·5 mgd) capacity on Jersey is designed to meet peak public demands, especially in summer, when holiday visitors impose a strain on resources.

Successful desalination depends on reducing the natural concentration of dissolved salts in sea-water from about 35 000 mg/l to less than 500 mg/l for most public supply purposes, down to as little as 50 mg/l for certain industrial uses. Technically, desalination is possible by a variety of processes such as distillation, electro-dialysis, freezing and reverse osmosis (Kronberger 1967), but in each case the resulting fresh water is markedly more expensive than water obtained by more traditional British methods. The main reason for this is the large input of heat energy which is required for conversion, and also the expensive nature of the conversion equipment involved.

The most common method of desalination is by distillation, whereby sea-water is boiled and the salt-free steam then condensed to produce fresh water. It is now possible for manufacturers to build distillation units up to an output of 0·5 m^3/s (10 mgd), but the cost of fresh water from a single-purpose plant was estimated by the Water Resources Board (1969) at between 35p and 40p per 4500 l. (1000 gal). Further costs must be added to this to cover distribution to the consumer. Since conventional water resource development is expected to yield further supplies at a cost of not more than 15p per 4500 l. (1000 gal) throughout the present century, it will be apparent that desalination is not, at present, economically competitive with inland storage reservoirs. Some economies can be achieved if the distillation plant is linked to electricity production, either at thermal or nuclear power-stations. Even so, and still excluding delivery costs to the service reservoirs, the production costs are estimated by the Water Resources Board at no less than 24p per 4500 l. (1000 gal), which remains about 60 per cent more than for impounding schemes.

For basic economic reasons, desalination appears unlikely to have widespread application in Britain over the foreseeable future. However, recent research has indicated that the secondary refrigerant freezing process has become more competitive with distillation costs, and it is now considered that in certain of the most deficient areas such water could be the cheapest means of supplementing conventional supplies. Plants capable of producing up to 0·26 m^3/s (5 mgd) may eventually prove to be economic although smaller pilot schemes will undoubtedly appear first. More developments may well occur to meet both industrial demands and peak holiday needs at seaside resorts, but there are further problems even for these specialised uses. Thus, desalination plants require good quality sea-water for the most efficient operation, and the water available in many industrial estuaries is likely to be too corrosive for present-day equipment. Desalination equipment is also housed in quite large, industrial-type structures, and the erection of such plants along the coast, particularly near to seaside resorts, might lead to amenity objections on the scale of inland reservoir protests.

CONCLUSION

It now remains necessary to place the existing and possible future water resource developments in the context of regional strategies for the country as a whole.

Scotland. Scotland has the most favourable water resource endowment of any British region and, even in a dry year, over 1050 m^3/s (20 000 mgd) could potentially be made available from upland impounding schemes alone according to Campbell (1961). Since the total demand is unlikely to exceed 3 or 4 per cent of this volume in the forseeable future, the exploitable surplus is very large. Recent legislation has remedied much of the unco-ordinated nature of the Scottish water supply industry described by Little (1961), and there are still reserves capable of development near to the major demand zone of the Central Lowlands. Occasionally it is suggested that water transfer by pipeline from Scotland could ease shortages south of the border, but the physical difficulties and expenditure involved have so far prevented any really concrete proposals.

Wales. The position in Wales is rather different from that in Scotland because surplus reserves are not only smaller, but are also more heavily committed, both to demands within the Principality as well as in England. The exploitable water surplus in Wales has been placed somewhere between 12 and 42 m^3/s (235 and 800 mgd) by the Welsh Advisory Water Committee (1961) depending on the actual programme of inland reservoir development. At the present time, demands are outstripping authorised resources most rapidly in the area of industrial South Wales served by the West Glamorgan Water Board. These demands are likely to be met by further storage provision in the Usk basin, and an appreciable surplus in mid-Wales will still be available for potential export to England via the river systems of the Severn, Wye and Dee. Approximately half of the water already developed from Welsh sources for public supply is ultimately destined for use in England, and, once internal requirements have been

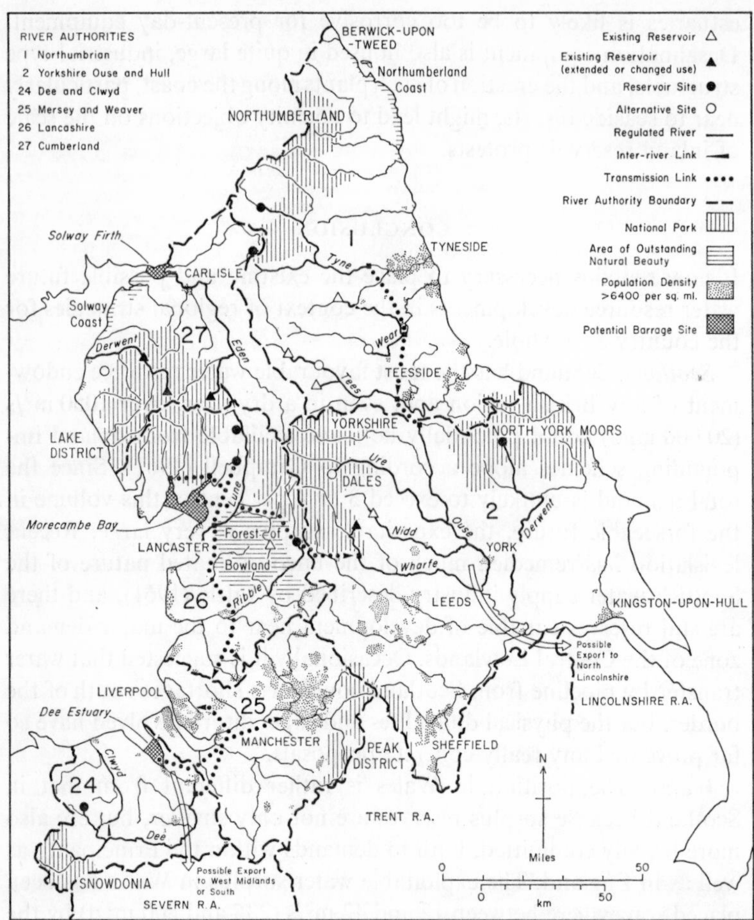

Figure 9.2 Some choices and conflicts in the further development of water resources in the north of England. After Water Resources Board (1970*b*).

guaranteed, there appears to be no good reason why this proportion should not be increased in the future.

North of England. Like Wales, the north of England is characterised by an overall surplus of resources over demand, but it has a larger number of zones where supplementary resources will be necessary in a few years time. A recent report from the Water

Resources Board (1970*b*) indicates that, in the six northern River Authority areas shown in figure 9.2, the total deficiency of authorised resources compared with demand is likely to reach 16 m^3/s (310 mgd) in 1981 and 51 m^3/s (965 mgd) by the end of the century. Most of this deficiency will be created by extra demands on the public supply sector, which has a relatively large trade component because of the industrial nature of much of the region. In turn, this results in a high *per capita* consumption and, in 1967, the demand on the public undertakings averaged 281 l. (62 gal) per person per day compared with 254 l. (56 gal) per head daily in south-east England. Nevertheless, it is estimated that a further 118 m^3/s (2250 mgd) could be provided by river regulation alone, without allowing anything for re-use, whilst the total potential resources of the region, including barrage schemes across Morecambe Bay, the Dee estuary and the Solway Firth amount to over 158 m^3/s (3000 mgd), or more than three times the projected need up to AD 2001 as estimated by the Water Resources Board (1970*b*).

The real problem in northern England is to select the most appropriate of several alternative water resource strategies, bearing in mind the need for urgent and flexible planning coupled with an awareness of the sensitivity of public opinion on certain possible solutions. Figure 9.2 illustrates, for example, the wide distribution of National Parks and Areas of Outstanding Natural Beauty within the region where any reservoir project is likely to arouse some opposition. These designated areas pose a difficult problem for the water resource planner because they include many districts with high potential water yields. Thus, whilst the six National Parks which lie wholly or partly within the region occupy only 18 per cent of its total area, they contain no less than one-third of the average runoff from northern England.

The pattern of water resource development at the turn of the century will depend on decisions taken within the next few years. Some of these decisions are necessary now in order to meet existing deficiencies, but broader policies must wait until the feasibility of the west coast barrage schemes has been determined. Up to 1981, however, shortages are almost certain to be met by inland storage. Deficiencies in north-east England, notably on Teesside, are likely to be satisfied by regulation of the river Tyne and the transfer of water southwards by means of a Tyne-Tees aqueduct. Further

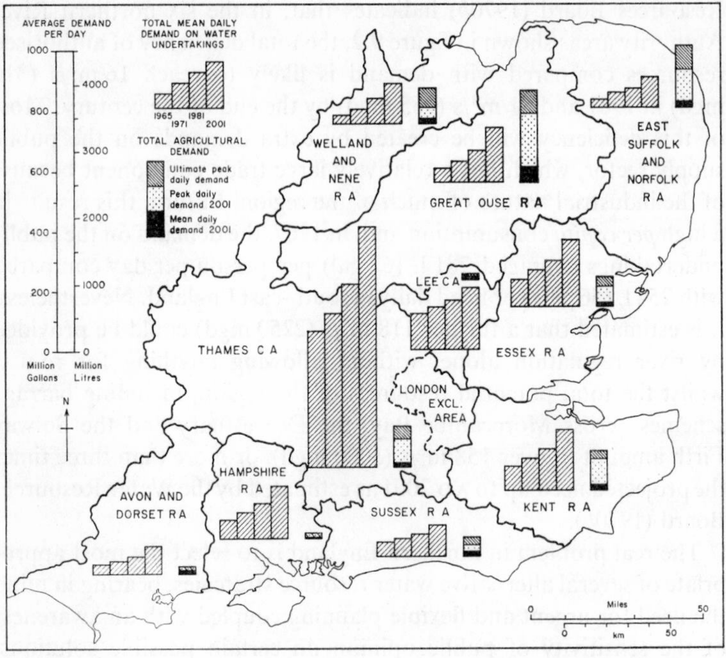

Figure 9.3 Existing and estimated future demands for water in south-east England. Based on Water Resources Board (1966*b*).

regional transfer would be possible by linking this aqueduct to the Yorkshire Ouse river system. By this means, water from Northumbria could be used to supply south Yorkshire and the anticipated urban growth on Humberside.

On the west coast the major demand centres are in south Lancashire and on Merseyside. Unfortunately, the river systems on this side of the Pennines do not favour a direct north–south transfer, and such water distribution is currently achieved by the aqueducts linking Manchester Corporation to its sources in the Lake District. Additional resources could be provided by new regulating reservoirs in the Lancashire Pennines for the Manchester area, whilst further storage on the river Dee could be used on Merseyside. Alternatively, more water could be tapped from the Lake District.

By the end of this century, increments could also be added from at least one of the potential barrage schemes. Most of this water would be utilised on the west of the Pennines, but development of either the Morecambe Bay or Solway barrages could provide for water transfer eastwards to top up the Yorkshire rivers or the Tyne respectively.

South-east England. This area has the most urgent water problems in the country and was the subject of the Water Resources Board's first regional report in 1966 (Water Resources Board 1966*b*). The report considered demands and resources up to the year 2001 in the ten River Authority areas, plus the London Excluded Area, shown in figure 9.3. At the time of the report, the region contained a population of some nineteen million people. The public undertakings supplied just over 53 m^3/s (1000 mgd), and the total amount of water taken into use, including cooling water for power-stations and water for irrigation, averaged some 92 m^3/s (1750 mgd). It can be seen from figure 9.3 that the largest demand is for public supplies in the Thames Conservancy area. The mean daily agricultural demand is relatively low throughout the region, but in the Great Ouse and East Suffolk and Norfolk River Authority areas the peak daily agricultural demand at the end of the century is expected to be greater than the average demand on the water undertakings.

All areas in the South-east will experience increases in demand, and it is anticipated that an overall water deficiency of 58 m^3/s (1100 mgd) will exist by the year 2001. As shown in table 16 and

TABLE 16

ESTIMATED GROWTH OF WATER DEFICIENCIES IN S.E. ENGLAND (m^3/s)

	1971	1981	2001
Total deficiencies	5	21	58
Deficiencies in central area	4	14	34

figure 9.4, most of this shortage will occur in the central area stretching from Northampton through the London basin to the Essex coast. This area will become increasingly dependent on supplies imported from outside the zone, and certain possible sources for development, including the exploitation of chalk aquifers, the transfer of surface

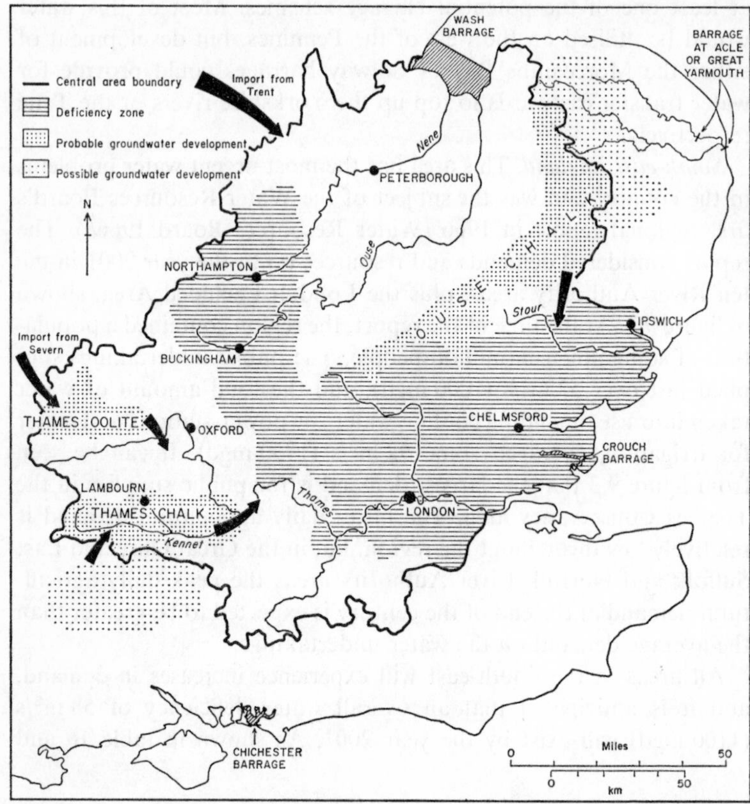

Figure 9.4 The central deficiency zone showing sources capable of potential development. After Water Resources Board (1966*b*).

resources from the Trent or the Severn catchments and estuarial barrage construction (notably across the Wash), are shown in figure 9.4.

The most economical and generally acceptable strategy would appear to be based on the regulation of the groundwater resources of the Thames and Great Ouse areas as outlined earlier in this chapter. The detailed allocation of resources from such schemes, including the re-use of effluent, is likely to follow the pattern shown in figure 9.5A. However, the deficiency in the central zone by the end of the century is almost directly comparable with the estimated yield for a Wash

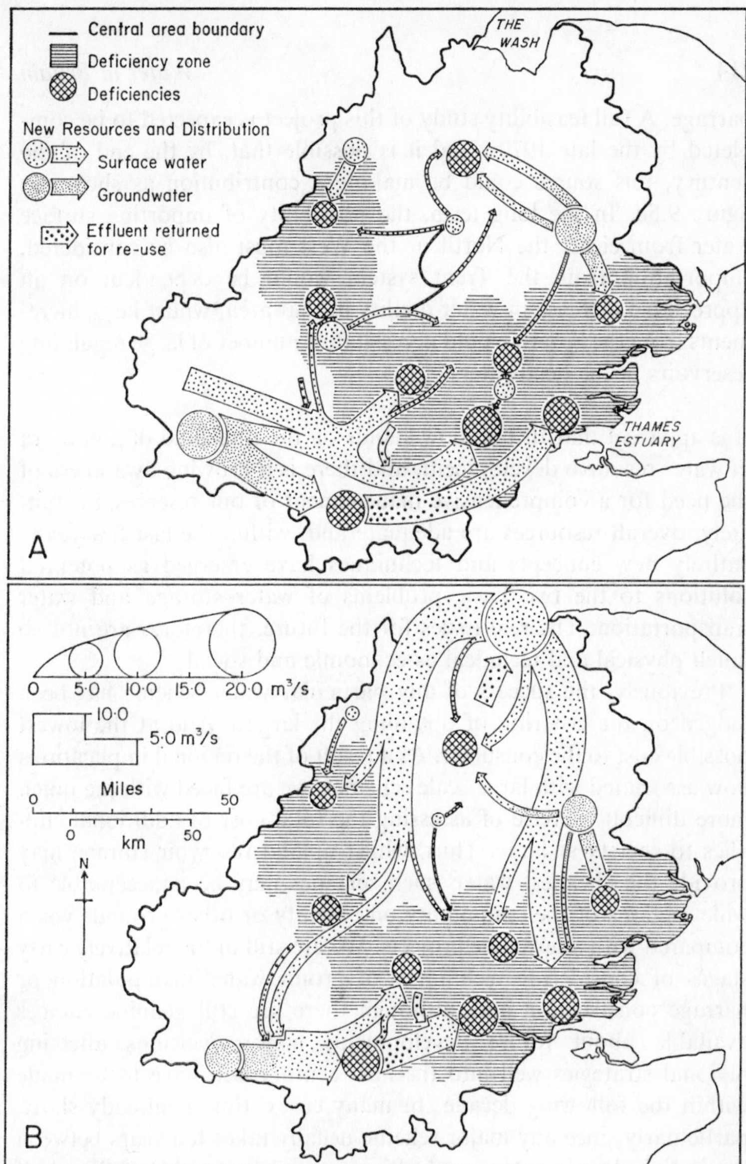

Figure 9.5 Two possible solutions to the water deficiency in south-east England in the year 2001.

A—Pattern based on groundwater development and import from the west.

B—Pattern based on a Wash barrage and groundwater development.

After Water Resources Board (1966*b*).

barrage. A full feasibility study of this project is expected to be completed by the late 1970s, and it is possible that, by the end of the century, this source could be making a contribution as shown in figure 9.5B. In the long term, the possibility of importing surface water from either the North or the West must also be considered. Importation from the Trent system would be dependent on an appreciable increase in water quality in that area, whilst large increments from the Severn would necessitate a number of large regulating reservoirs in the headwaters.

It is apparent that Britain now stands on the threshold of a new era in water resource development, and there is a growing awareness of the need for a comprehensive management of our reserves. Fortunately, overall resources are adequate and, within the last few years, entirely new concepts and techniques have emerged as potential solutions to the two basic problems of water storage and water transportation. The real issues for the future, therefore, are not so much physical and technical as economic and social.

Previously, the success of any particular water scheme has been judged on the criterion of obtaining the largest yield at the lowest possible cost to the consumer. As a result of the regional implications now associated with large-scale schemes, we are faced with the much more difficult exercise of assessing the total cost of additional supplies to society at large. Thus, whilst upland reservoir storage may provide the cheapest water, such schemes may be unacceptable to wide sections of the community on amenity or other grounds when compared with alternative projects. We are still in the relatively early stages of considering techniques of groundwater manipulation or barrage construction and, although there are still genuine choices available about future development, major decisions affecting regional strategies well into the next century will have to be made within the following decade. In many cases, time is already short, particularly since any major scheme usually takes ten years between the initial planning stage and ultimate completion. More than half of this time is normally spent on feasibility investigations and enquiries into the potential amenity impact of the project.

In addition to the option between conventional and more novel water resource development, there is the allied issue of water quality. Once again, this can only be resolved by economic and social choice.

On the one hand, it is perfectly possible to improve water quality through better effluent standards and greater dilution in rivers, but it is not yet clear that the nation is prepared to meet the financial implications of cleaner rivers. Some reduction in pollution will certainly be necessary in order to provide for a greater degree of re-use of water in the future as forecast by Southgate (1969) and many others, and there is no doubt that the reclamation of polluted water can be highly successful. Thus, a recent report by Ashby (1971) has quoted evidence showing that, whilst in 1957–8 no fish were able to survive in the lower Thames between Richmond and Gravesend, some forty-two species were observed a decade later as a result of river improvement, together with the re-establishment of fish migration through the polluted estuary.

The passing of the Water Resources Act in 1963 laid the foundations for much solid progress in the field of water conservation and a number of early assessments, such as those of Goode (1965) and Speight (1966), tended to regard this legislation as a lasting solution to the existing problems. More recently, however, a growing body of opinion has emerged which advocates further rationalisation of the water resources administration in this country, and The Institution of Water Engineers (1970), the Working Party on Sewage Disposal (1970), and the Water Resources Board (1971) have all stated the need for more centralisation.

Briefly, the difficulties arise from two main sources. Firstly, the increasing necessity for large integrated schemes of regional water resource development means that progress could be achieved more easily with less fragmentation of interests. For example, it has been estimated that by the year 2000 perhaps 25 per cent of all public water supplies will be transferred across existing River Authority boundaries, whilst in certain cases – such as that of the Mersey and Weaver River Authority – as much as 70 per cent of the supplies may originate outside the area. Further difficulties sometimes occur as a result of misunderstandings about the division of responsibilities between the River Authorities and the statutory water undertakings when new supplies are to be developed. The second, and more important problem, relates to the growing significance of water quality, and it is now clear that planning for water use must be matched by similar planning for the disposal of effluent after use. So far, sewage disposal has been left to local government, and there are about 1400 sewage treatment authorities in England and Wales. These authorities are responsible for 5000 treatment works, under 20 per cent of which serve populations over 10 000 according to the Working Party on Sewage Disposal (1970). Many of these authorities are too small for efficient operation and are incapable of planning for future requirements.

The Central Advisory Water Committee (1971) reviewed the broad problem of future water resource management in England and Wales and isolated the four critical functions of water supply, sewage disposal, river management and planning/co-ordination to be dealt with. The Committee recognised the need for a new organisational framework based on a small number of Regional Water Authorities, responsible for the overall water policies within their areas, coupled with a substantial reduction in the number of separate units operating in the fields of water supply and sewage disposal. No specific solution was recommended, but a number of alternative schemes was put forward including a scheme of ten multi-purpose Regional Water Authorities which would carry out all four functions over the whole country. On the other hand, an entirely different proposal was for a reform dependent on single-purpose bodies comprising ten Regional Water Authorities, charged with planning and co-ordination, together with twenty-nine River Authorities, fifty bodies responsible for water supply and fifty bodies responsible for sewage disposal.

The Government accepted the case for legislative change and opted for radical reform involving the total integration of water services within large, all-purpose units (Department of the Environment 1971). At the time of writing, the Government envisage the creation of not more than ten multi-purpose Regional Water Authorities (including one for Wales) based as far as possible on natural watersheds and existing River Authority boundaries. The new Regional Water Authorities will assume responsibility for the water conservation, water quality control, navigation and recreation functions of the present River Authorities together with the water supply and sewage disposal duties currently performed by the local authorities. They will take over responsibility for canals and river navigation from the British Waterways Board, which is to be disbanded, and will also replace the existing joint water boards and joint sewerage boards. However, it is possible that the thirty-one statutory water companies, which supply over 20 per cent of the total water delivered by statutory water undertakers, may continue as supply agents of the Regional Water Authorities. It is expected that the proposed new structure will come into operation on 1 April 1974, at the same time as the reformed local government areas, and it is to be hoped that the legislative recognition of the fundamental unity of hydrology, water resource development and pollution control will provide an efficient administrative basis for the solution of our water problems in the coming years.

Guide to Further Reading

This short list of books is not intended to be fully comprehensive, but aims to assist the reader in finding his way to a number of recent works, neither cited in the text nor specifically restricted to Britain, which contain abundant references to more specialised systematic fields.

BRUCE, J. P., and CLARK, R. H. (1966). *Introduction to Hydrometeorology*, Pergamon, Oxford.

CHILDS, E. C. (1969). *Introduction to the Physical Basis of Soil Water Phenomena*, Wiley, Chichester and New York.

DAVIES, D. (1967). *Fresh Water*, Aldus Books, London.

DE WIEST, R. J. M. (1965). *Geohydrology*, Wiley, New York.

OVERMAN, M. (1968). *Water*, Aldus Books, London.

PENMAN, H. L. (1963). *Vegetation and Hydrology*, Commonwealth Agricultural Bureaux, Farnham Royal.

RAIKES, R. (1967). *Water, Weather and Prehistory*, Baker, London.

TODD, D. K. (1959). *Groundwater Hydrology*, Wiley, New York.

TWEEDIE, A. D. (1966). *Water and the World*, Nelson, Melbourne.

WIESNER, C. J. (1970). *Hydrometeorology*, Chapman and Hall, London.

WISLER, C. O., and BRATER, E. F. (1959). *Hydrology*, Wiley, New York.

References

1. *The Global Context*

BARRY, R. G. (1969). The world hydrological cycle, *Water, Earth and Man*, (ed. R. J. Chorley), Methuen, London.

BENTON, G. S., BLACKBURN, R. T., and SNEAD, V. O. (1950). The role of the atmosphere in the hydrologic cycle. *Trans. Am. geophys. Un.*, **31**, 61–73.

CHORLEY, R. J., and KATES, R. W. (1969). Introduction, in *Water, Earth and Man*, (ed. R. J. Chorley), Methuen, London.

ISAAC, P. C. G. (1965). Water, waste and wealth. An inaugural lecture, University of Newcastle-on-Tyne.

LEOPOLD, L. B., and DAVIS, K. S. (1966). *Water*, Life Science Library, New York.

MAUNDER, W. J. (1970). *The Value of the Weather*, Methuen, London.

NACE, R. L. (1960). *Water Management, Agriculture and Groundwater Supplies*, U.S. Geol. Survey, Circular 415.

——— (1969). World water inventory and control, in *Water, Earth and Man*, (ed. R. J. Chorley), Methuen, London.

ROWNTREE, N. A. F. (1968). The problem of future water supplies. *Wat. & Wat. Engng.*, **72,** 505–10.

SELLERS, W. D. (1965). *Physical Climatology*, University of Chicago Press, Chicago.

SHAW, E. M. (1962). An analysis of the origins of precipitation in northern England, 1956–60. *Q. Jl. R. met. Soc.*, **88,** 539–47.

U.S. GEOLOGICAL SURVEY (1967). *Water for Peace*, USGS, Washington.

VALLENTINE, H. R. (1967). *Water in the Service of Man*, Penguin, Harmondsworth.

WALTON, W. C. (1970). *The World of Water*, Weidenfeld and Nicolson, London.

2. *Historical Background*

BATEMAN, J. F. (1846). Observations on the relation which the fall of rain bears to the water flowing from the ground. *Mem. Proc. Manchr. lit. phil. Soc. 2nd Series,* **7,** 157–90.

BEARDMORE, N. (1850). *Manual of Hydrology*, Waterlow, London.

BINNIE, A. R. (1892). On mean or average rainfall and the fluctuations to which it is subject. *Proc. Instn. civ. Engrs.*, **109,** 89–172.

BISWAS, A. K. (1970). *History of Hydrology*, North-Holland Publishing Co., Amsterdam–London.

CENTRAL ADVISORY WATER COMMITTEE (1959*a*). *Sub-Committee on the Growing Demand for Water*, HMSO, London.

——— (1959*b*). *Sub-Committee on Information on Water Resources*, HMSO, London.

——— (1960). *Sub-Committee on the Growing Demand for Water*, HMSO, London.

——— (1962). *Sub-Committee on the Growing Demand for Water*, HMSO, London.

CRUICKSHANK, A. B. (1965). Water-resource development in the Campsies of Scotland. *Geogrl. Rev.*, **55**, 241–64.

DALTON, J. (1802*a*). Experiments and observations to determine whether the quantity of rain and dew is equal to the quantity of water carried off by the rivers and raised by evaporation; with an enquiry into the origin of springs. *Mem. Proc. Manchr. lit. phil. Soc.*, **5**, 346–72.

——— (1802*b*). Experimental essays on the constitution of mixed gases; on the force of steam or vapour from waters and other liquids in different temperatures, both in a Torricellian vacuum and in air; on evaporation; and on the expansion of gases by heat. *Mem. Proc. Manchr. lit. phl. Soc.*, **5**, 535–602.

DOBSON, D. (1777). Observations on the annual evaporation at Liverpool in Lancashire, and on evaporation considered as a test of the dryness of the atmosphere. *Phil. Trans. R. Soc.* (*Lond.*), **67**, 244–59.

HALLEY, E. (1687). An estimate of the quantity of vapour raised out of the sea by the warmth of the sun: derived from an experiment shown before the Royal Society, London, at one of their late meetings. *Phil. Trans. R. Soc.* (*Lond.*), **16**, No. 189, 366–70.

——— (1691). An account of the circulation of the watery vapours of the sea and the cause of springs. *Phil. Trans. R. Soc.* (*Lond.*), **16**, No. 192, 468–73.

HEBERDEN, W. (1769). Of the different quantities of rain, which appear to fall at different heights, over the same spot of ground. *Phil. Trans. R. Soc.* (*Lond.*), **59**, 359–62.

H.M. GOVERNMENT (1962). *Water Conservation, England and Wales*, Cmnd 1693, HMSO, London.

HUDLESTON, F. (1933). A summary of seven years' experiments with rain-gauge shields in exposed positions, 1926–32, at Hutton John, Penrith. *Br. Rainf. 1933*, 274–81.

JEVONS, W. S. (1861). On the deficiency of rain in an elevated raingauge as caused by wind. *Lond. Edinb. Dubl. Phil. Mag*. **22**, 421–33.

KEEN, B. A. (1931). *The Physical Properties of the Soil*, Longmans, London.

KLEIN, L. (1962). *River Pollution;* **Vol. 2,** *Causes and Effects*, Butterworths, London.

LLOYD, J. G. (1968). River Authorities and their work. *J. Instn. Wat. Engrs.*, **22**, 343–402.

MANNING, R. (1891). On the flow of water in open channels and pipes. *Trans. Instn. civ. Engrs. (Ireland)*, **20,** 161–207.

MILLER, J. F. (1849). On the meteorology of the Lake District of Cumberland and Westmorland; including the results of experiments on the fall of rain at various heights above the earth's surface, up to 3166 feet above the mean sea level. *Phil. Trans. R. Soc. (Lond.)*, Parts **1** and **2,** 73–89 and 319–29.

PATERSON, M. M. (1896). *Compensation Discharge in the Rivers and Streams of the West Riding*, Spon, London.

PENMAN, H. L. (1948). Natural evaporation from open water, bare soil and grass. *Proc. R. Soc. (Lond.) Series A*, **193,** 120–45.

——— (1950). The water balance of the Stour catchment area. *J. Instn. Wat. Engrs.*, **4,** 457–69.

RISBRIDGER, C. A. (1963). Compensation water, re-use of water and waste prevention. *Conservation of Water Resources*, Institution of Civil Engineers, London, 97–106.

RODDA, J. C. (1963). Eighteenth Century evaporation experiments. *Weather*, **18,** 264–69.

SCHOFIELD, R. K. (1935). The pF of the water in the soil. *Trans. 3rd Internat. Cong. Soil Sci.*, **2,** 37–48.

SHEPPARD, T. (1917). William Smith: his maps and memoirs. *Proc. Yorks. geol. Soc.*, **19,** 75–253.

STRAHAN, A. *et al.* (1909). Report of progress in the investigation of rivers. *Geogrl. J.*, **34,** 622–50.

SYMONS, G. J. (1889). On the amount of evaporation. *Br. Rainf. 1889*, 18–42.

THOMSON, D. H. (1921). Hydrological conditions in the chalk at Compton, W. Sussex. *Trans. Instn. Wat. Engrs.*, **26,** 228–61.

——— (1938). A 100 years record of rainfall and water-levels in the chalk at Chilgrove, West Sussex. *Trans. Instn. Wat. Engrs.*, **43,** 154–96.

THORNTHWAITE, C. W. (1948). An approach toward a rational classification of climate. *Geogrl. Rev.*, **38,** 55–94.

TOPLIS, F. *et al.* (1878). National water supply – suggestions for dividing England and Wales into watershed districts. *J. Soc. Arts*, **27,** 696–804.

TOWNELEY, R. (1694). Observations on the quantity of rain falling monthly for several years successively. *Phil. Trans. R. Soc. (Lond.)*, **18,** 51–58.

WATER POWER RESOURCES COMMITTEE (1920). *Second Interim Report, Cmnd 776*, Board of Trade, London.

3. *Hydrological Networks and Data*

BLEASDALE, A. (1961). Rainfall records and maps: Conference on surface water resources and the drought of 1959. *J. Instn. Wat. Engrs.*, **15,** 153–58.

BLEASDALE, A. *et al.* (1963). Study and assessment of water resources, *Conservation of Water Resources*, Institution of Civil Engineers, London, pp. 121–36.

BOULTON, A. G. (1967*a*). The measurement of flow, in *River Management*, (ed. P. C. G. Isaac), Maclaren and Sons, London.

——— (1967*b*). Surface water survey and modernisation: Informal discussion of the Hydrological Group. *Proc. Instn. Civ. Engrs.*, **36**, 909–13.

GILMAN, C. S. (1964). Rainfall, in *Handbook of Applied Hydrology*, (ed. V. T. Chow), McGraw-Hill, New York.

GRAY, D. A. (1964*a*). Groundwater conditions of the chalk of the Grimsby area, Lincolnshire. *Water Supply Papers of the Geological Survey*, Research Report No. 1. DSIR, London.

——— (1964*b*). Instrumentation in groundwater studies. *Wat. & Wat. Engng.*, **68**, 185–88.

HAND, D. W. (1968). An electrically-weighed lysimeter for measuring evaporation rates. *Agric. Met.*, **38**, 269–82.

HARRISON, A. J. M. (1965). Some problems concerning flow measurement in steep rivers. *J. Instn. Wat. Engrs.*, **19**, 469–77.

HARRISON, A. J. M. and OWEN, M. W. (1967). A new type of structure for flow measurement in steep streams. *Proc. Instn. Civ. Engrs.*, **36**, 273–96.

HOLLAND, D. J. (1967). Evaporation, *Br. Rainf. 1961*, HMSO, London, 3–34.

INESON, J. (1966). Groundwater: principles of network design, *Int. Ass. Sci. Hydrol.* Pub. No. 68 (Quebec), pp. 476–83.

INESON, J., and DOWNING, R. A. (1964). The groundwater component of river discharge and its relationship to hydrogeology. *J. Instn. Wat. Engrs.*, **18**, 519–41.

LAPWORTH, H. (1965). Evaporation from a reservoir near London. *J. Instn. Wat. Engrs.*, **19**, 163–81.

MAIDENS, A. L. (1965). New Meteorological Office raingauges. *Met. Mag.*, **94**, 142–44.

METEOROLOGICAL OFFICE (1956). *Handbook of Meteorological Instruments.* Part 1, HMSO, London.

——— (1968). The Directorate of Services – Special Topic: Hydrometeorology. *Annual Report of the Meteorological Office 1967*, HMSO, London, pp. 1–16.

PENMAN, H. L. (1948). Natural evaporation from open water, bare soil and grass. *Proc. R. Soc. (Lond.) Series A.*, **193**, 120–45.

ROBINSON, A. C., and RODDA, J. C. (1969). Rain, wind and the aerodynamic characteristics of raingauges. *Met. Mag.*, **98**, 113–20.

RODDA, J. C. (1970). On more realistic rainfall measurements and their significance for agriculture, in *The Role of Water in Agriculture*, (ed. J. A. Taylor), Pergamon, Oxford.

SHARP, R. G. (1970). *The hydrometric data system of the Water Resources Board*, Paper presented to Instn. Civ. Engrs., Scottish Hydrological Group, Glasgow, 23 January, 9 pp. (duplicated typescript).

SMITH, K. (1966). Percolation, groundwater discharge and stream flow in the Nidd Valley. *J. Instn. Wat. Engrs.*, **20**, 459–71.

STRANGEWAYS, I. C., and MCCULLOCH, J. S. G. (1965). A low-priced automatic hydrometeorological station. *Bull. Int. Ass. Sci. Hydrol.*, **4,** 57–62.

THORNTHWAITE, C. W. (1948). An approach toward a rational classification of climate. *Geogrl. Rev.*, **38,** 55–94.

WATER RESOURCES BOARD (1971). *Seventh Annual Report – Year Ending 30th September, 1970*, HMSO, London.

WILSON, J. K. C. (1965). Measurement of surface water flows: Informal discussion of the Hydrological Group. *Proc. Instn. Civ. Engrs.*, **31,** 322–24.

4. An Outline of British Hydrology

BALCHIN, W. G. V. (1964). Hydrology, in *The British Isles: A Systematic Geography*, (eds. J. Wreford Watson and J. B. Sissons), Nelson, London.

BLEASDALE, A. (1963). The distribution of exceptionally heavy daily falls of rain in the United Kingdom, 1863 to 1960. *J. Instn. Wat. Engrs.*, **17,** 45–55.

BLEASDALE, A. *et al.* (1963). Study and assessment of water resources. *Conservation of Water Resources*, Institution of Civil Engineers, London, pp. 121–36.

BUCHAN, S. (1963). Geology in relation to groundwater. *J. Instn. Wat. Engrs.*, **17,** 153–64.

GLASSPOOLE, J. (1924). Fluctuations of annual rainfall: three driest consecutive years. *Trans. Instn. Wat. Engrs.*, **29,** 83–101.

——— (1949). Seasonal weather sequences over England and Wales. *Met. Mag.*, **78,** 193–98.

GRAY, D. A. (1964). Groundwater conditions of the chalk of the Grimsby area, Lincolnshire. *Water Supply Papers of the Geological Survey*, Research Report No. 1, DSIR, London.

GRAY, D. A. *et al.* (1969). The groundwater hydrology of the Yorkshire Ouse river basin. *Water Supply Papers of the Institute of Geological Sciences*, Hydrogeological Report No. 4, NERC, London.

GREEN, F. H. W. (1964). A map of annual average potential water deficit in the British Isles. *J. appl. Ecol.*, **1,** 151–58.

——— (1970). Some isopleth maps based on lysimeter observations in the British Isles in 1965, 1966 and 1967. *J. Hydrol.*, **10,** 127–40.

GREGORY, S. (1957). Annual rainfall probability maps of the British Isles *Q. Jl. R. met. Soc.*, **83,** 543–49.

GRINDLEY, J. (1960). Calculated soil moisture deficits in the dry summer of 1959 and forecast dates of first appreciable runoff. *Int. Ass. Sci. Hydrol.*, Pub. No. 51 (Helsinki), 109–20.

——— (1967). The estimation of soil moisture deficits, *Met. Mag.*, **96,** 97–108.

HOLLAND, D. J. (1967). Evaporation, *Br. Rainf, 1961*, HMSO, London, pp. 3–34.

INESON, J. (1962*a*). Some aspects of groundwater hydrology and hydrogeology. *Wat. and Wat. Engng.*, **66,** 333–38.

INESON, J. (1962*b*). A hydrogeological study of the permeability of the chalk. *J. Instn. Wat. Engrs.*, **16,** 449–63.

——— (1966). Groundwater: principles of network design. *Int. Ass. Sci. Hydrol.*, Pub. No. 68 (Quebec), 476–83.

INESON, J., and DOWNING, R. A. (1965). Some hydrogeological factors in permeable catchment studies. *J. Instn. Wat. Engrs.*, **19,** 59–80.

LACY, R. E. (1951). Observations with a directional raingauge. *Q. Jl. R. met. Soc.*, **77,** 283–92.

LAMB, H. H. (1964). *The English Climate*, English Universities Press, London.

LAW, F. (1957). Measurement of rainfall, interception and evaporation losses in a plantation of Sitka spruce trees. *Int. Ass. Sci. Hydrol.* (Toronto), 397–411.

LLOYD, D. (1963). Contribution to discussion of C. H. Dobbie and P. O. Wolf, The Lynmouth flood of August 1952. *Proc. Instn. civ. Engrs.*, **2,** 522–88.

LOVELOCK, P. E. R. *et al.* (1967). Groundwater levels in England during 1963. *Water-Supply Papers of the Geological Survey*, Research Report No. 3, NERC, London.

MACDONALD, A. T., and KENYON, W. J. (1961). Runoff of chalk streams. *Proc. Instn. civ. Engrs.*, **19,** 23–38.

MINISTRY OF AGRICULTURE, FISHERIES AND FOOD (1962). *Irrigation*, Bulletin No. 138, HMSO, London.

PARDÉ, M. (1955). *Fleuves et Rivières*, Armand Colin, Paris.

PEGG, R. K., and WARD, R. C. (1971). What happens to the rain? *Weather*, **26,** 88–97.

PENMAN, H. L. (1949). The dependence of transpiration on weather and soil conditions. *J. Soil Sci.*, **1,** 74–89.

——— (1950). The water balance of the Stour catchment area. *J. Instn. Wat. Engrs.*, **4,** 457–69.

REYNOLDS, G. (1969). Rainfall, runoff and evaporation on a catchment in West Scotland. *Weather*, **24,** 90–98.

RISBRIDGER, C. A., and GODFREY, W. H. (1954). Rainfall, runoff and storage: Elan and Claerwen gathering grounds. *Proc. Instn. Civ. Engrs.*, **3,** 345–88.

RODDA, J. C. (1967). A country-wide study of intense rainfall for the United Kingdom. *J. Hydrol.*, **5,** 58–69.

SMITH, K. (1964). A long-period assessment of the Penman and Thornthwaite potential evapotranspiration formulae. *J. Hydrol.*, **2,** 277–90.

——— (1971). Some features of snowmelt recession in the upper Tees basin. *Wat. and Wat. Engng.*, **75,** 345–46.

THORNTHWAITE, C. W. (1948). An approach toward a rational classification of climate. *Geogrl. Rev.*, **38,** 55–94.

WALTERS, R. C. S. (1936). *The Nation's Water Supply*, Nicholson and Watson, London.

WARD, R. C. (1967). *Principles of Hydrology*, McGraw-Hill, London.

WARD, R. C. (1968). Some runoff characteristics of British rivers. *J. Hydrol.*, **6**, 358–72.

5. Floods and Droughts

ANDREWS, F. M. (1962). Some aspects of the hydrology of the Thames basin. *Proc. Instn. civ. Engrs.*, **21**, 55–90.

ATKINSON, B. W. (1968). A preliminary examination of the possible effect of London's urban area on the distribution of thunder rainfall 1951–60. *Trans. Inst. Br. Geogr.*, **44**, 97–118.

——— (1969). A further examination of the urban maximum of thunder rainfall in London 1951–60. *Trans. Inst. Br. Geogr.*, **48**, 97–119.

BARRETT, E. C. (1964). Local variations in rainfall trends in the Manchester region. *Trans. Inst. Br. Geogr.*, **35**, 55–71.

BLEASDALE, A., and DOUGLAS, C. K. M. (1952). Storm over Exmoor on August 15, 1952. *Met. Mag.*, **81**, 353–67.

BOOTH, R. E. (1961). Rainfall in England and Wales during the five months July to November 1960, with special reference to southern England. *Met. Mag.*, **90**, 93–101.

BRIERLEY, J. (1964). Flooding in the Exe Valley 1960. *Proc. Instn. civ. Engrs.*, **28**, 151–70.

BROOKS, C. E. P. and GLASSPOOLE, J. (1928). *British Floods and Droughts*, Benn, London.

CONWAY, V. M., and MILLAR, A. (1960). The hydrology of some small peat-covered catchments in the northern Pennines. *J. Instn. Wat. Engrs.*, **14**, 415–24.

DOBBIE, C. H., and WOLF, P. O. (1953). The Lynmouth flood of August 1952. *Proc. Instn. Civ. Engrs.*, **2**, 522–88.

DOUGLAS, C. K. M. (1953). Gale of January 31, 1953. *Met. Mag.*, **82**, 97–100.

EDMONDS, D. T., PAINTER, R. B., and ASHLEY, G. D. (1970). A semi-quantitative hydrological classification of soils in north-east England. *J. Soil Sci.*, **21**, 256–64.

GLASSPOOLE, J., and ROWSELL, H. (1947). Absolute droughts and partial droughts over the British Isles 1906–40. *Met. Mag.*, **76**, 201–205.

——— (1950). Absolute drought of August 1947. *Met. Mag.*, **79**, 260–62.

HANWELL, J. D., and NEWSON, M. D. (1970). The Great Storms and Floods of July 1968 on Mendip. *Wessex Cave Club, Occasional Publications*, Series 1, No. 2, Pangbourne.

HARDING, D. M., and PORTER, E. A. (1969). Flood loss information and economic aspects of flood plain occupance: Introductory note for Informal Discussion of Hydrological Group. *Instn. of Civil Engineers, November 1969*, (duplicated typescript).

HARRISON, A. J. M. (1961). The 1960 Exmouth Floods. *The Surveyor*, **120**, 127–32.

HARVEY, A. M. (1971). Seasonal flood behaviour in a clay catchment. *J. Hydrol.*, **12,** 129–44.

HOLLIS, G. E. (1970). The estimation of the hydrologic impact of urbanisation: an example of the use of digital simulation in hydrology. *Occasional Papers in Geography*, No. 5 University College, London.

HOWE, G. M., SLAYMAKER, H. O., and HARDING, D. M. (1967). Some aspects of the flood hydrology of the upper catchments of the Severn and Wye. *Trans. Inst. Br. Geogr.*, **41,** 33–58.

INSTITUTE OF HYDROLOGY (1969). *Record of Research, 1968*, NERC London.

INSTITUTION OF CIVIL ENGINEERS (1967). *Flood studies for the United Kingdom.* Report of the Committee on Floods in the UK, Institution of Civil Engineers, London.

NIXON, M. (1959). A study of the bank-full discharges of rivers in England and Wales. *Proc. Instn. civ. Engrs.*, **12,** 157–74.

——— (1963). Flood regulation and river training in England and Wales. *Conservation of Water Resources*, Institution of Civil Engineers, London, pp. 137–50.

PARRY, M. (1956). An urban rainstorm in the Reading area. *Weather*, **11,** 41–48.

REYNOLDS, E. R. C. (1967). The hydrological cycle as affected by vegetation differences. *J. Instn. Wat. Engrs.*, **21,** 322–30.

RODDA, J. C. (1970). Rainfall excesses in the United Kingdom. *Trans. Inst. Br. Geogr.*, **49,** 49–60.

SKEAT, W. O. (ed.) (1961). *Manual of British Water Engineering Practice*, (3rd edn), Heffer, Cambridge.

STEERS, J. A. (1953). The east coast floods January 31–February 1, 1953. *Geogrl. J.*, **119,** 280–95.

STUBBS, P. (1971). Is London still changing it? *New Scientist*, **50,** No. 754, p. 552.

SURFACE WATER SURVEY (1960). Dry weather flows. *Surface Water Survey*, Tech. Note 10, London.

SUTCLIFFE, J. V. (1964). Hydrological forecasting in Britain. *Methods of Hydrological Forecasting for the Utilisation of Water Resources*, U.N. Water Resources Series, **27,** 162–64.

WALLING, D. E., and GREGORY, K. J. (1970). The measurement of the effects of building construction on drainage basin dynamics. *J. Hydrol.*, **11,** 129–44.

WILSON, E. M. (1969). *Engineering Hydrology*, Macmillan, London.

WOLF, P. O. (1952). Forecast and records of floods in Glen Cannich in 1947. *J. Instn. Wat. Engrs.*, **6,** 298–324.

——— (1966). Comparison of methods of flood estimation in *River Flood Hydrology*, The Institution of Civil Engineers, London.

WRIGHT, C. E. (1970). Catchment characteristics influencing low flows. *Wat. and Wat. Engng.*, **74,** 468–71.

6. Public Water Supply

ANONYMOUS (1966). Grafham Water and associated works of the Great Ouse Water Authority. *Wat. & Wat. Engng.*, **70,** 321–41.

——— (1967). The Afon Alaw scheme of the Anglesey County Council Water Department. *Wat. & Wat. Engng.*, **71,** 3–14.

——— (1971). *Loch Lomond Water Supply*, Central Scotland Water Development Board.

AYLWIN, E., and WARD, R. C. (1969). *Development and Utilisation of Water Supplies in the East Riding of Yorkshire*, Occasional Papers in Geography, No. 10. University of Hull.

BALCHIN, W. G. V. (1958). A water use survey. *Geogrl. J.*, **124,** 476–93.

BALDWIN, A. B. (1961). *The Yorkshire River Derwent Scheme*, Waterworks Office, Sheffield.

BRADFORD CORPORATION WATER DEPARTMENT (1955). *Centenary Handbook 1855–1955*, Waterworks Office, Bradford.

——— (1957). *Annual Report of the Water Committee 1957*, Waterworks Engineer's Office, Bradford.

DARBY, H. C. (1967). The recreational and amenity use of water. *J. Instn. Wat. Engrs.*, **21,** 225–31.

EVANS, R. J. (1950). *The Victorian Age 1815–1914*, Arnold, London.

GREGORY, S. (1958*a*). Conurbation water supplies in Great Britain. *J. Tn. Plann. Inst., Lond.*, Sept.–Oct., 250–54.

——— (1958*b*). The contribution of the uplands to the public water supply of England and Wales. *Trans. Inst. Br. Geogr.*, **25,** 153–65.

——— (1969). Water resources and regional economic development in England and Wales. *Tijdschr. econ. soc. Geogr.*, Mar.–Apr., 122–31.

LOCKYER, A. G. (1957). A study of water supply in Derbyshire. *E. Midld. Geogr.*, **8,** 32–44.

MINISTRY OF HEALTH (1949). *Interim Report of the Committee on Causes of Increase in the Consumption of Water*, HMSO, London.

MINISTRY OF HOUSING AND LOCAL GOVERNMENT (1956). *Re-grouping of Water Undertakings*, Circular No. 52/56, HMSO, London.

PRICKETT, C. N. (1963). Use of water in agriculture. *Conservation of Water Resources*, Institution of Civil Engineers, London, pp. 15–29.

RISBRIDGER, C. A. (1963). Compensation water, re-use of water and waste prevention. *Conservation of Water Resources*, Institution of Civil Engineers, London, pp. 97–106.

ROWNTREE, N. A. F. (1963). River control and the development of surface-water resources in England and Wales. *Conservation of Water Resources*, Institution of Civil Engineers, London, pp. 155–59.

SHARP, R. G. (1967). Estimation of future demands on water resources in Britain. *J. Instn. Wat. Engrs.*, **21,** 232–49.

SHEFFIELD CITY WATER COMMITTEE (1961). *The Water Supply of Sheffield*, Waterworks Office, Sheffield.

SKEAT, W. O. (ed.) (1961). *Manual of British Water Engineering Practice*, (3rd edn), Heffer, Cambridge.

SMITH, K. (1966). *The Water Resources of Nidderdale*, Research Papers in Geography, No. 4. University of Liverpool.

——— (1967). The availability of water on Teesside. *J. Br. Wat. Wks. Ass.*, **49,** 481–89.

STERN, W. M. (1955). Water supply in Britain: the development of a public service. *J. Br. Watwks. Ass.*, **37,** 14–21.

WILKINSON, D., and SQUIRE, N. (eds.) (1970). *Water Engineer's Handbook 1970*, Fuel and Metallurgical Journals Ltd., London.

7. The Non-domestic Demand for Water

AITKEN, P. L. (1963). Hydro-electric power generation, *Conservation of Water Resources,* Institution of Civil Engineers, London, pp. 34–42.

AYLWIN, E., and WARD, R. C. (1969). *Development and Utilisation of Water Supplies in the East Riding of Yorkshire*, Occasional Papers in Geography, No. 10, University of Hull.

BALCHIN, W. G. V. (1958). A water-use survey. *Geogrl. J.*, **124,** 476–93.

BAXTER, G. (1961). River utilisation and the preservation of migratory fish life. *Proc. Instn. civil Engrs.*, **18,** 225–44.

——— (1963). Preservation of fish life, amenities and facilities for recreation, *Conservation of Water Resources.* Institution of Civil Engineers, London, pp. 59–65.

BODDINGTON, T. J. (1967). River management in relation to river flow, (and discussion), in *River Management*, (ed. P. C. G. Isaac), Maclaren and Sons, London.

BRAYSHAW, J. D. (1967). The effects of river discharge on inland fisheries, in *River Management*, (ed. P. C. G. Isaac), Maclaren and Sons, London.

BRITISH WATERWAYS BOARD (1964). *The Future of the Waterways,* Interim Report of the Board, HMSO, London.

CALVERT, N. H. (1967). The conservation and use of water resources in the U.K., with particular reference to the Water Resources Act 1963. *J. Instn. Wat. Engrs.*, **21,** 203–209.

CLARK, D., and ENGLAND, G. (1963). Thermal power generation, *Conservation of Water Resources*, Institution of Civil Engineers, London, pp. 43–51.

COOPER, J. A., and SMITH, L. G. (1960). The utilisation and conservation of water in the chemical industry. *Proc. Instn. civ. Engrs.*, **17,** 1–14.

DARBY, H. C. (1967). The recreational and amenity use of water. *J. Instn. Wat. Engrs.*, **21,** 225–31.

GIBSON, J. R. (1958). The paper industry of north-west England: Part 2 – Influence of water-supply and effluent disposal on location. *Paper Mkr., Lond.*, Oct., 64–6.

GRIFFITHS, E. R. (1954). Farm water supplies in the mid-Cheshire area. *J. Instn. Wat. Engrs.*, **8,** 373–410.

HOPTHROW, H. E. (1963). Utilisation of water in industry. *Conservation of Water Resources*, Institution of Civil Engineers, London, pp. 30–33.

INSTITUTION OF WATER ENGINEERS (1963). Report on the recreational use of waterworks. *J. Instn. Wat. Engrs.*, **17**, 71–92.

KAVANAGH, N. J. (1968). The economics of the recreational uses of rivers and reservoirs. *Wat. & Wat. Engng.*, **72**, 401–408.

LEA, C. (1967). Water use in industry. *J. Instn. Wat. Engrs.*, **21**, 216–21.

MARSH, C. M. (1963). Use of water for navigation, *Conservation of Water Resources*, Institution of Civil Engineers, London, pp. 52–58.

MINISTRY OF AGRICULTURE AND FISHERIES (1954). *The Calculation of Irrigation Need*, Tech. Bull. No. 4, HMSO, London.

MINISTRY OF AGRICULTURE, FISHERIES AND FOOD (1962). *Irrigation*, Bulletin No. 138, HMSO, London (3rd edn).

MORE, R. J. M. (1964). *A geographical analysis of irrigation use in S.E. England, with particular reference to the Great Ouse Valley*, unpublished Ph.D. thesis, University of Liverpool.

NATURAL RESOURCES (TECHNICAL) COMMITTEE (1962). *Irrigation in Great Britain*, HMSO, London.

O'RIORDAN, T. (1970). Spray irrigation and the Water Resources Act 1963. *Trans. Inst. Br. Geogr.*, **49**, 33–47.

PENMAN, H. L. (1967). Water use in agriculture. *J. Instn. Wat. Engrs.*, **21**, 222–24.

PRICKETT, C. N. (1963). Use of water in agriculture, *Conservation of Water Resources*, Institution of Civil Engineers, London, pp. 15–29.

——— (1970). Current trends in the use of water for agriculture, in *The Role of Water in Agriculture*, Pergamon, Oxford.

REES, J. A. (1969). *Industrial Demand for Water: A Study of south-east England*, Weidenfeld and Nicolson, London.

SAXTON, K. J. H. (1969). The recreational use of Grafham Water. *J. Instn. Wat. Engrs.*, **23**, 425–32.

SMITH, K. (1970). Water resource management and the needs of agriculture, in *The Role of Water in Agriculture*, Pergamon, Oxford.

SPEIGHT, G. E., and DAVIS, C. M. (1970). Review of water-supplies and effluent disposal, *Management of Water in the Iron and Steel Industry*, The Iron and Steel Institute, London, pp. 1–6.

WATER RESOURCES BOARD (1966). *Water Supplies in south-east England*, HMSO, London.

8. *Effluent Disposal and Pollution Control*

ASHBY, E. (Chairman) (1971). *Royal Commission on Environmental Pollution: First Report*, HMSO, London.

BRIGGS, R., MELBOURNE, K. V., and EDEN, G. E. (1967). The monitoring of water quality, in *River Management*, (ed. P. C. G. Isaac), Maclaren and Sons, London.

CENTRAL ADVISORY WATER COMMITTEE (1949). *Prevention of River Pollution*, HMSO, London.

——— (1971). *The Future Management of Water in England and Wales*, HMSO, London.

DEPARTMENT OF THE ENVIRONMENT (1971). *Report of a River Pollution Survey of England and Wales, 1970*, Vol. 1, HMSO, London.

HOUGHTON, G. U. (1967). River water quality criteria in relation to waterworks requirements, in *River Management*, (ed. P. C. G. Isaac), Maclaren and Sons, London.

INSTITUTION OF WATER ENGINEERS (1970). *Evidence submitted by the Institution of Water Engineers to the Central Advisory Water Committee*, Published at the Offices of the Institution, London.

KLEIN, L. (1962). *River pollution:* Vol. 2, *Causes and Effects*, Butterworth, London.

LAW, K. K. (Discussion on HOATHER, R. C.) (1966). Chemical characteristics of river waters. *Proc. Soc. Wat. Treat. Exam.*, **15**, 43–49.

LESTER, W. F. (1967*a*). Management of river water quality, in *River Management*, (ed. P. C. G. Isaac), Maclaren and Sons, London.

——— (1967*b*). Pollution in the river Trent and its tributaries, and related problems of regeneration. *J. Instn. Wat. Engrs.*, **21,** 261–74.

LLOYD, R., and JORDAN, D. H. M. (1963). Predicted and observed toxicities of several sewage effluents to rainbow trout. *J. Inst. Sew. Purif.*, **2,** 167–73.

LOVETT, M. (1957). River pollution: general and chemical effects, in *The Treatment of Trade-waste waters and Prevention of River Pollution*, (ed. P. C. G. Isaac), Newcastle-on-Tyne.

MARSH, C. M. (1963). Use of water for navigation, *Conservation of Water Resources*, Institution of Civil Engineers, London, pp. 52–58.

MERCER, D. (1967). The effects of abstractions and discharges on river water quality, in *River Management*, (ed. P. C. G. Isaac), Maclaren and Sons, London.

NIXON, M. (1967). Planning of water resources in the Trent River Authority area. *J. Instn. Wat. Engrs.*, **21**, 291–96.

ROYAL COMMISSION ON SEWAGE DISPOSAL (1912). *Standards and Tests for Sewage and Sewage Effluents Discharging into Rivers and Streams*, Eighth Report, **1,** HMSO, London.

SOUTHGATE, B. A. (1969). *Water: Pollution and Conservation*, Thunderbird Enterprises Ltd., London.

TEBBUTT, T. H. Y. (1971). *Principles of Water Quality Control*, Pergamon, Oxford.

TOWNEND, C. B., and LOVETT, M. (1963). Prevention of pollution: sewage and effluent disposal, *Conservation of Water Resources*, Institution of Civil Engineers, London, pp. 89–96.

TRENT RIVER AUTHORITY (1970). *Annual Report for year ended 31 March 1969*, Head Office, Nottingham.

WATER RESOURCES BOARD (1968). *The Surface Water Year Book of Great Britain 1964–65*, HMSO, London.

WORKING PARTY ON SEWAGE DISPOSAL (1970). *Taken for Granted*, Ministry of Housing and Local Government, HMSO, London.

9. Problems and Policies

ANONYMOUS (1967). Thames Conservancy river flow augmentation scheme. *Wat. & Wat. Engng.*, Vol. 71, pp. 100–102.

——— (1968*a*). The Clywedog reservoir. *Wat. & Wat. Engng.*, **72,** 323–26.

——— (1968*b*). Thames Conservancy river flow augmentation scheme. *Wat. & Wat. Engng.*, **72,** 141–44.

ASHBY, E. (Chairman) (1971). *Royal Commission on Environmental Pollution, First Report*, HMSO, London.

BOW, C. J., HOWELL, F. T., PAYNE, C. J., and THOMPSON, P. J. (1969). The lowering of the water-table in the Permo-Triassic rocks of south Lancashire. *Wat. & Wat. Engng.*, **73,** 461–63.

CALVERT, N. H. (1967). The conservation and use of water resources in the United Kingdom, with particular reference to the Water Resources Act 1963. *J. Instn. Wat. Engrs.*, **21,** 203–209.

CAMPBELL, R. M. (1961). The pattern of existing water use. *Wat. & Wat. Engng.*, **65,** 24–28.

CENTRAL ADVISORY WATER COMMITTEE (1959). *Sub-Committee on the Growing Demand for Water, First Report*, HMSO, London.

——— (1971). *The Future Management of Water in England and Wales*, HMSO, London.

COLLINGE, V. K. (1967). Research on river management, in *River Management*, (ed. P. C. G. Isaac), Maclaren and Sons, London.

DEPARTMENT OF THE ENVIRONMENT (1971). *Reorganisation of Water and Sewage Services: Government Proposals and Arrangements for Consultation*. Circular 92/71, HMSO, London.

DOWNING, R. A., and WILLIAMS, B. P. J. (1969). The groundwater hydrology of the Lincolnshire Limestone with special reference to the groundwater resources. *Water Resources Board, Pub. No. 9*, HMSO, London.

FORDHAM, A. E., COCHRANE, N. J., KRETSCHMER, J. M., and BAXTER, R. S. (1970). The Clywedog reservoir project. *J. Instn. Wat. Engrs.*, **24,** 17–48.

GOODE, W. (1965). Water resources in England and Wales. *National Provincial Bank Review*, **71,** 9–17.

——— (1969). Planning water resources: Paper presented to Conference of the Council for the Preservation of Rural England, 25–27 September 1969. *Wat. & Wat. Engng.*, **73,** 415–18.

INESON, J. (1970). Development of groundwater resources in England and Wales. *J. Instn. Wat. Engrs.*, **24,** 155–77.

INESON, J., and ROWNTREE, N. A. F. (1967). Conservation projects and planning. *J. Instn. Wat. Engrs.*, **21,** 275–90.

INSTITUTION OF WATER ENGINEERS (1970). *Evidence Submitted by the Institution of Water Engineers to the Central Advisory Water Committee*, Published at the Offices of the Institution, London.

KRONBERGER, H. (1967). Desalination developments in the U.K. *J. Instn. Wat. Engrs.*, **21,** 297–304.

LITTLE, G. (1961). Scotland's water resources. *Wat. & Wat. Engng.*, **65,** 53–56.

MINISTRY OF HOUSING AND LOCAL GOVERNMENT (1960). *River Great Ouse Basin: Hydrological Survey*, HMSO, London.

PUGH, N. J. (1963). Water supply, *Conservation of Water Resources*, Institution of Civil Engineers, London, pp. 8–14.

REES, J. A. (1969). *Industrial Demand for Water: A Study of south-east England*, Weidenfeld and Nicolson, London.

RISBRIDGER, C. A. (1963). Compensation water, re-use of water and waste prevention, *Conservation of Water Resources*, Institution of Civil Engineers, London, pp. 97–106.

SAVAGE, R. (1971). Water conservation in the non-ferrous metal industry. *Wat. & Wat. Engng.*, **75,** 19–23.

SHARP, R. G. (1967). Estimation of future demands on water resources in Britain. *J. Instn. Wat. Engrs.*, **21,** 232–49.

SILVER, R. S. (1969). The possibilities of desalination as a contribution to the solution of water supply problems: Paper presented to Conference of the Council for the Preservation of Rural England, 25–27 September 1969. *Wat. & Wat. Engng.*, **73,** 418–19.

SKEAT, W. O. (ed.) (1969). *Manual of British Water Engineering Practice*, Vol. 2, *Engineering Practice* (4th edn), Heffer, Cambridge.

SOUTHGATE, B. A. (1969). *Water: Pollution and Conservation*, Thunderbird Enterprises Ltd., London.

SPEIGHT, H. (1966). Britain's water resources, *Tn. Ctry. Plann.*, June, pp. 314–22.

TAYLOR, L. E. (1964). The problem of groundwater recharge, with special reference to the London basin. *J. Instn. Wat. Engrs.*, **18,** 247–54.

WATER RESOURCES BOARD (1966*a*). *Morecambe Bay Barrage*, Desk Study: Report of Consultants, HMSO, London.

——— (1966*b*). *Water Supplies in south-east England*, HMSO, London.

——— (1967). *Third Annual Report, Year ending 30 September 1966*, HMSO, London.

——— (1969). *Report on Desalination for England and Wales*, HMSO, London.

——— (1970*a*). *Sixth Annual Report, Year ending 30 September 1969*, HMSO, London.

——— (1970*b*). *Water Resources in the North*, HMSO, London.

——— (1971). *Seventh Annual Report, Year ending 30 September 1970*, HMSO, London.

WELSH ADVISORY WATER COMMITTEE (1961). *Report on the Water Resources of Wales*, HMSO, London.

WORKING PARTY ON SEWAGE DISPOSAL (1970). *Taken for Granted*, Ministry of Housing and Local Government, HMSO, London.

Name Index

Subject Index